Our Virtual World: The Transformation of Work, Play and Life via Technology

Laku Chidambaram
University of Oklahoma, USA

Ilze Zigurs
University at Colorado at Boulder, USA

 IDEA GROUP PUBLISHING
Hershey USA • London UK

Acquisition Editor: Mehdi Khosrowpour
Managing Editor: Jan Travers
Development Editor: Michele Rossi
Copy Editor: Elizabeth Arneson
Typesetter: Tamara Gillis
Cover Design: Deb Andre
Printed at: Sheridan Books

Published in the United States of America by
        Idea Group Publishing
        1331 E. Chocolate Avenue
        Hershey PA 17033-1117
        Tel: 717-533-8845
        Fax: 717-533-8661
        E-mail: jtravers@idea-group.com
        Web site: http://www.idea-group.com

and in the United Kingdom by
        Idea Group Publishing
        3 Henrietta Street
        Covent Garden
        London WC2E 8LU
        Tel: 171-240 0856
        Fax: 171-379 0609
        Web site: http://www.eurospan.co.uk

Library of Congress Cataloging-in-Publication Data

Our virtual world : the transformation of work, play, and life via technology / [edited by]
Laku Chidambaram, Ilze Zigurs.
        p. cm.
  Includes index.
  ISBN 1-878289-92-6 (paper)
    1. Information society. 2. Information technology--Social aspects. 3. Internet--Social
aspects. I. Chidambaram, Lakshmanan, 1963- II. Zigurs, Ilze, 1948-

HM851 .O97 2000
303.48'33--dc21   00-053914

British Cataloguing in Publication Data
A Cataloguing in Publication record for this book is available from the British Library.

Our Virtual World: The Transformation of Work, Play and Life via Technology

Table of Contents

WORK IN THE VIRTUAL WORLD

PLAY IN THE VIRTUAL WORLD

LIFE IN THE VIRTUAL WORLD

DEDICATION

To all the A's in my life ... there is nothing virtual about your love!

> Laku Chidambaram
> Norman, Oklahoma

To my mother, Anna Zigurs, who recently asked me what this "dot.com" fuss was all about, providing me the challenge of explaining our virtual world in Latvian. To the memory of my father, Janis Zigurs. And to Michael Beck, with whom life is great every day.

> Ilze Zigurs
> Boulder, Colorado

September, 2000

PREFACE

A recent commercial for wireless telephone service depicts a family having dinner together, making phone calls to one another at the table as well as to a child upstairs in his room. We expect that some people react to that commercial with enthusiasm, praising the increased ease with which family members can communicate. Others, however, are likely to be horrified at the intrusion of technology into the personal space of what is an increasingly rare family gathering. That dilemma is at the heart of *Our Virtual World*. Is technology a friend or foe? How can we make sure it is more friendly and useful than it is intrusive and even frightening? One thing we do know: the increasing virtualization of everyday interaction—whether at work, play, or life—is something that we all must face, and an awareness of the tradeoffs is the first step to managing them.

Many people wonder and worry about our virtual world. What will technology bring? How has it already changed our lives? What has it done and what will it do to our children? What will the workplace look like even a few short years from now? Will human interaction be completely replaced by computers? These are only a few of the questions that are on people's minds, and these questions reflect the topics that are explored in this book.

We began this project because we were intrigued by the magnitude and breadth of change that technology was bringing every day, in so many ways and to so many places. We wanted to explore those changes, in straightforward language and in a format that anyone could read, understand and enjoy. Our goal and rallying cry for this book was that it be "eminently readable." We believe that we and our colleagues have met that goal and hope that our readers agree.

The diversity of authorship in the book's chapters ensures that many different points of view are presented about the important questions surrounding work, play and life in our virtual world. Our authors come from a variety of disciplines and places, as can be seen from their biographical sketches and from the chapters themselves. Some chapters describe studies that the authors have conducted on an aspect of our virtual world while other chapters are based on their ongoing experiences in the virtual world. Regardless of methodology, all of the chapters are written in a straightforward, easily readable style that is jargon-free and accessible to all.

We see many different audiences for the book. Casual readers will find provocative ideas to think about and apply to their own worlds, giving them a broader sense of what they might expect from technology. Students and teachers can use the book for courses in business, social sciences, and the humanities, concentrating on whatever perspective is appropriate for them. Policy makers will find issues that need their care and attention, as the virtual world increasingly challenges our traditional ways of dealing with one another. We hope that all our readers enjoy the diversity of viewpoints and the depth of analysis presented in these chapters.

We are grateful to our families, friends, and colleagues for their support and help with this book. We first developed the idea for this book while both of us were visiting professors at Agder College in Kristiansand, Norway, in the fall of 1996. There is nothing like spending a winter near the Arctic circle to stimulate your thinking! However, the cold outside was offset by the warmth inside offered by the excellent and cordial faculty at the EDB Institute. The welcoming and stimulating environment there created a good beginning for our book. Tusen takk! We also thank our colleagues and students at our respective universities for stimulating conversations about technology and all its impacts.

The authors who contributed their ideas and time in writing the chapters for this book were a genuinely delightful group of people. We thank them sincerely for their insightful ideas and their willingness to work with us on the vision we had for the book. As with most people, our chapter authors had many other things to attend to while working on the book, but they were both gracious and responsive to our schedule.

Our appreciation also goes to the folks at Idea Group Publishing—Jan Travers, Mehdi Khosrowpour and Michele Rossi—who encouraged us along the way, nudged us when we flagged and patted us when we delivered.

Finally, we thank our families and dedicate this book to them.

> Laku Chidambaram
> Ilze Zigurs
>
> September, 2000

Chapter 1

Introduction

Laku Chidambaram
University of Oklahoma, USA

Ilze Zigurs
University of Colorado at Boulder, USA

Since the dawn of civilization, new technologies—from the plow to the locomotive to the computer—have transformed human lives. These changes have often been for the better, but occasionally also for the worse. No matter what the consequence, these changes have always been irrevocable and pervasive. Today's new technologies, from the well-connected computer to the digital communication infrastructure, are no exception. They are dramatically changing the way we work, play and live. This book explores how these real changes have helped create our virtual world. It also examines the impact of these changes on individuals, organizations and society.

FOCUS AND CONTRIBUTIONS

The central theme of the book is the interplay of the ubiquity of the virtual environment (in which we work, play and live) and our evolving interactions in this changed context. Time-honored interaction techniques—such as looking a person in the eye or judging an adversary based on the strength of the handshake—are not relevant in the virtual world. New rules are at work. We make purchases without looking at the products (much less the salesperson), we meet people without ever seeing them and we even fall in love with people we have never met. What are the unexpected consequences of such interactions? Will we gain time or lose our privacy? Will our private and public institutions prosper or perish? Will society advance to new levels as proponents claim or will people lose their humanity as detractors suggest?

These are just a few questions that this book addresses.

Specifically, this book is designed to make the following four contributions:

- Address the challenges of events and technologies that are fundamentally changing how we work, play and live,
- Provoke an informed debate about how we should deal with such changes,
- Serve as a source of information about the individual, organizational, and social implications of new technologies, and
- Assist policy makers, researchers, academicians and analysts involved in the design, implementation, evaluation and use of communication and computing technologies.

CATALYSTS AND CONSEQUENCES

Fueling the emergence of our virtual world are dramatic advances in information technology, coupled with our insatiable appetite for faster, cheaper and more efficient ways to work and play. Other catalysts for change include the convergence of communication and computing technologies, the mega-mergers of giant firms in these industries, the exponential growth of the Internet, the decline in hardware costs, and the emergence of a technology-savvy populace. The symptoms of change are everywhere:

- In 1994, computers outsold TV sets for the first time in U.S. history.
- In 1999, the venerable Sears Catalog, the last bastion of the paper-based mail-order catalogs, went virtual.
- A year later, bestselling author Stephen King "published" a book online, scaring traditional publishers and delighting his fans.
- The word "Napsterization" was added to our lexicon signifying the fact that music is now traded freely on the Web—again, to the delight of users and the chagrin of traditional retail chains and recording artists.
- Current estimates are that at least 5 million desktop video cameras are sold annually in the U.S. These cameras have been put to a wide variety of uses: from enabling corporate conferences to showing babies being delivered to peeking at voyeur-cams.
- Professions are getting virtual makeovers: Teachers are teaching courses online, doctors are diagnosing ailments from thousands of miles away, and architects are redesigning houses without ever stepping inside them.
- Special interest groups meet in cyberspace via listservs, chat rooms, and newsgroups. These encounters range from productive to pleasant to perilous.

- Teens and children move through cyberspace—at times in unsupervised environments—participating in play and work with peers and others who are continents away.

FRAMEWORK

As we might expect with such rapid and radical changes, unresolved questions remain. As technology permeates every aspect of our work, play and life, will our virtual world become more real than our traditional world? If so, what are the implications for individuals, organizations, and society? This book addresses these and related issues. As Figure 1 shows, the book is organized along two dimensions: (1) the three levels at which impacts may occur—Individual, Organizational, and Societal; and (2) the three areas being impacted—Work, Play, and Life. Each combination of level and area of

Figure 1: Dimensions of Transformation in Our Virtual World

AREAS OF TRANSFORMATION

		WORK	PLAY	LIFE
L E V E L O F T R A N S F O R M A T I O N	**INDIV-IDUAL**	*Chapter 3:* Am I Doing What's Expected? New Member Socialization in Virtual Groups	*Chapter 7:* Online Poker and the Individuals Who Play It	*Chapter 10:* Citizens & Spokesmen: Politics and Personal Expression on the Web
		Chapter 4: How are You Going to Keep Them in the Classroom After They've Seen MTV? On-line Education in a Virtual World		*Chapter 11:* The Virtual Community: Building on Social Structure, Relations and Trust to Achieve Value
	ORGANIZ-ATIONAL	*Chapter 5:* Meeting Current Challenges for Virtually Collocated Teams: Participation, Culture & Integration	*Chapter 8:* Online Recreation & Play in Organizational Life: The Internet as Virtual Contested Terrain	*Chapter 12:* Sloan 2001: A Virtual Odyssey
	SOCIETAL	*Chapter 6:* Succeeding in the Virtual World: How Relationships Add Value on the Web	*Chapter 9:* Play's the Thing ... on the Web!	*Chapter 13:* The Search for a New Identity: Post-Organ Transplant Recipients and the Internet

impact is addressed by separate chapters in the book. In addition, Chapter 2, "Going Virtual: The Driving Forces and Arrangements," cuts across the dimensions in Figure 1 and provides an overall discussion of the issues that are addressed in more depth in the later chapters. A brief summary of the chapters follows.

OVERVIEW OF THE CHAPTERS

In Chapter 2 (Going Virtual: The Driving Forces and Arrangements), Igbaria, Shayo, Olfman and Gray discuss how the profound gains in information technology (IT) innovations over the past five decades form the basis for the emergence of today's virtual society. In the virtual society, people create and sell goods and services using communication and computer technologies with minimal physical contact. This chapter examines the driving forces — including global economics and politics, enlightened and diversified populations, and innovative technologies — powering the virtual society and the specific arrangements — including telework, computer supported cooperative work, virtual corporations, online communities, and virtual society— used in it. Although the authors view IT as its own driving force, it is also seen as the constant in the virtual society. IT is both the enabler and shaper of all the driving forces including itself. The authors discuss how the virtual society will result in changes, both in how people behave and in the technology they use.

The rest of the book is divided into three sections (corresponding to the framework described earlier): working, playing and living in the virtual world. The chapters that comprise these sections are summarized below.

WORK IN THE VIRTUAL WORLD

This section includes four chapters that deal with work in the virtual world. Chapters 3 and 4 deal with this issue from an individual perspective, while Chapter 5 deals with it from an organizational perspective and Chapter 6 deals with it from a societal perspective.

In Chapter 3 (Am I Doing What's Expected? New Member Socialization in Virtual Groups), Galvin and Ahuja examine how virtual groups are beginning to present new questions and challenges for managers. For example, without access to co-located team members to help make sense of the work environment—including the task environment and the social environment—can technology adequately facilitate socialization of newcomers into a virtual workplace? If so, what are the mechanisms that might make it easier for newcomers to become effective potential contributors? Some answers to these questions are presented. Interestingly, we find that key differences do exist in the patterns of communication between established members and newcomers in the group. Details and implications of these differences are presented in the chapter.

In Chapter 4 (How Are You Going Keep Them in the Classroom After They've Seen MTV? Online Education in a Virtual World), Niederman and Rollier describe how the education landscape is changing and is likely to change. An underlying theme in this chapter deals with the development of new structures and new processes, along with how well students can learn and be taught in this changing landscape. The chapter also explores different online learning approaches and the costs of the various approaches along with the future of the virtual university. Important issues related to who is responsible for education in the virtual world and how these responsibilities are changing are also addressed in this chapter.

In Chapter 5 (Meeting Current Challenges for Virtually Collocated Teams: Participation, Culture, and Integration), Mark discusses the experiences of virtual teams at Boeing. Numerous challenges face geographically distributed teams that are expected to perform as physically collocated teams: to provide deliverables, meet project schedules, and to generate feasible and even innovative problem solutions—all from a distance. Limitations of technology and distance make it difficult for geographically distributed teams to develop the necessary social processes in order to function as a "well-formed" team. In this chapter, Mark discusses three challenges for these teams: 1) achieving a high standard of participation, which affects impressions, interaction patterns, and trust; 2) developing an appropriate culture, for motivation and cooperation; and 3) integrating the remote team suitably into members' local working spheres.

In Chapter 6 (Succeeding in the Virtual World: How Relationships Add Value on the Web), Gant argues that the social forces influencing the development of the structure of the World Wide Web are the same forces that influence organizations to create inter-organizational relationships off-line. She uses examples from a field study to examine the relationship between inter-organizational links off-line and on the World Wide Web.

PLAY IN THE VIRTUAL WORLD

This section includes three chapters that deal with play in the virtual world. Chapter 7 deals with this issue from an individual perspective, while Chapter 8 deals with it from an organizational perspective and Chapter 9 deals with it from a societal perspective.

In Chapter 7 (Online Poker and the Individuals Who Play It), Venkataraman examines the game of poker played using Internet Relay Chat (IRC) technology, a precursor to modern day chat rooms. This game is perhaps the most popular among the large offering of casino-style card games available on the Internet. The chapter discusses the infrastructure needed to support multiple players from different locations playing over a sustained period of time. It also discusses how individual players perceive online games compared to live poker games, their commitment to the game and challenges in pursuing the game in a virtual environment. Also, as a basis of comparison, experiences with another virtual alternative—e-mail based poker—are discussed. One interesting theme in the chapter deals with critical success factors underlying the continued success of IRC-based poker.

In Chapter 8 (Online Recreation and Play in Organizational Life: The Internet as Virtual Contested Terrain), Oravec explores how online recreation and play are becoming new "contested terrains" in organizations as employees and managers seek to understand and control them, often at cross-purposes. This chapter analyzes emerging forms of online recreation and play in the workplace and addresses how their benefits and drawbacks are being defined. It discusses how online work and play are often becoming seamlessly melded and sometimes confused. The chapter argues that the issues will ultimately be moot: work and play, the productive and the personal will be nearly indistinguishable as computing becomes more enjoyable to use and everyday tasks can be accompanied with some levity, either instilled from our human or our cybernetic online companions.

In Chapter 9 (Play's the Thing … on the Web!), Chidambaram and Zigurs discuss the social implications of virtual leisure. The impacts of virtual leisure appear to span the two ends of a spectrum: from unwanted social influences to desirable social outcomes. A goal for society would be to promote the latter and reduce the former. However, no clear or easy answers exist for this and related dilemmas, but the issues they raise have been and continue to be examined via public discourse. This chapter presents four scenarios that describe various types of virtual leisure and their impacts on society. Some overarching themes and implications for society are drawn from these scenarios.

LIFE IN THE VIRTUAL WORLD

This section includes four chapters that deal with life in the virtual world. Chapters 10 and 11 deal with this issue from an individual perspective, while Chapter 12 deals with it from an organizational perspective and Chapter 13 deals with it from a societal perspective.

In Chapter 10 (Citizens and Spokesmen: Politics and Personal Expression on the Web), Petersen presents a unique and often overlooked view of the Internet. The Net is popularly represented as a tool by which the lone activist can defeat institutions, if not governments. News media and the popular press frequently reinforce the notion that horizontal networks will revitalize political debate and democracy across the world. Petersen argues that the hype of individuals becoming empowered or citizens being moved to action via the Internet has so far not been realized. She contends that the Internet has not drastically changed the way we interact with political institutions, nor has it changed voting habits, nor is there compelling evidence of major switches in patterns of information consumption for the mass of the voting public. This chapter suggests that with few exceptions, the Internet actually reinforces dominant institutions, existing messages and the political status quo.

In Chapter 11 (The Virtual Community: Building on Social Structure, Relations and Trust to Achieve Value), Gattiker, Perlusz, Bohmann and Sørensen examine how Internet technologies offer the opportunity to create virtual communities. The authors view a virtual community as representing a communal experience whereby people may not necessarily know each other very well or meet in person very frequently, if ever. Instead, communication is conducted using electronic networks. This chapter tries to advance our understanding of virtual communities by examining the experiences of a group of European professionals interested in Internet security who meet online on a regular basis. The authors discuss various issues related to virtual communities including similarities and differences between social and virtual communities and how efforts in a virtual community can and should be undertaken to motivate its members.

In Chapter 12 (Sloan 2001: A Virtual Odyssey), Orlikowski, Yates and Fonstad chronicle the shared online experiences of incoming students to MIT's MBA program prior to their arrival on campus. The authors analyze a technology-enabled transformation that radiated outward from a change in work practices for one clearly defined organizational group — admitted MBA students linked via the Internet — to a change in life for a much larger group of people. It is a particularly interesting example of how unanticipated opportunities and unintended consequences unfold as communities adopt and improvise with technology to facilitate virtual ways of organizing and communicating.

In Chapter 13 (The Search for a New Identity: Post-Organ Transplant Recipients and the Internet), Koufaris describes the use of a small part of the Internet—newsgroups —by a specific social group—transplant recipients. His observations primarily deal with organ transplant recipients and their use of this newsgroup to define a new identity for themselves after the disorienting lifesaving procedure of having a foreign organ grafted onto their bodies. Using an "anthropological" method of observation, by being a virtually unobserved observer, he examined the interactions of the newsgroup members without interrupting their natural patterns of communications. The lessons he learned and shares in this chapter are truly indicative of the power and potential of this new medium.

Chapter 2

Going Virtual: The Driving Forces and Arrangements

Magid Igbaria
Claremont Graduate University, USA & Tel Aviv University, Israel

Conrad Shayo
California State University, San Bernardino, USA

Lorne Olfman and Paul Gray
Claremont Graduate University, USA

" Microprocessor and computer technologies, contrary to current fashionable opinion, are not new forces recently unleashed upon an unprepared society, but merely the latest installment in the continuing development of the Control Revolution." James Beniger (1986, p. vii).

INTRODUCTION

During the last decade, the adjective "virtual" has become a common place descriptor of social forms where people do not have to live, meet or work face to face in order to create goods and services or maintain significant social relationships. There are specialized literatures about new social forms, such as virtual corporations, virtual organizations, virtual communities, virtual libraries, and virtual classrooms, as well as related practices such as telecommuting, computer-supported cooperative work (CSCW), tele-education, teleconferencing, tele-medicine, tele-marketing, and tele-democracy. There is general agreement in the literature that the profound impact of information technology (IT)[1] and its rapid adoption by individuals, groups, organizations, and communities has given rise to the proliferation of "virtual societies." While computer networks figure frequently as enablers and shapers of "virtual societies," other kinds of communication technologies, including paper mail, telephone and fax, also play roles in linking people and groups. Some of the literature celebrates the flexibility and enhanced possibilities of these new forms of "virtual social life." But there are also important critical empirical studies of specific virtual social forms that examine the possible losses.

In this chapter we examine the driving forces behind the growth of virtual societies and discuss existing arrangements and practices at the individual, group, organization, and community levels. We also examine the implications of how people will live and work in societies where these arrangements and practices are widespread and mixed with face-to-face relationships. Our discussion follows the model of virtual society presented in Figure 1. Figure 1 describes an evolutionary model conceptualizing an entire hierarchy for studying the virtual society and summarizes both the driving forces and arrangements that are critical components of this proposed framework. Specifically, this chapter is organized as follows: We first discuss the driving forces which include global economics, policies and politics, enlightened

Figure 1. A Framework for the Virtual Society

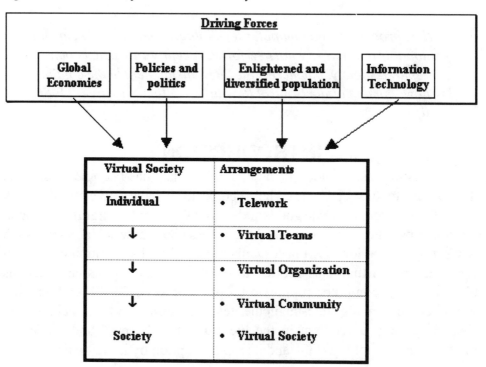

population, and information technology; second we describe existing arrangements and practices at the individual, group, organization, and community levels. Finally, we examine the dilemmas and implications of the virtual society on peoples' lives and work.

DRIVING FORCES

The virtual society transcends towns, states, countries, and continents, and represents an evolutionary as opposed to a revolutionary movement. Although information technology (IT) is the main enabling force of the virtual society, other components are also at work, namely, economic, political, cultural, and social forces (Agres, Edberg and Igbaria, 1998). This section discusses these macro forces at a more finite level — identifying the forces that are moving us to a virtual society. As shown in the framework presented in Figure 1, the finite level forces include: global economies, policies and politics, enlightened and diversified population, as well as information technology. These forces continue to create the necessary conditions for the eventual growth of the virtual society. Current virtual workplace arrangements and practices of "virtuality" include: telework (at the individual level), virtual teams (at the group level), virtual corporations (at the organizational level), and virtual communities (at the community level). Other arrangements and practices continue to evolve. Once a critical mass of these virtual activities and practices permeates all levels of society, the outcome will be the virtual society. Following Beniger's (1986) thesis that we are currently in the information society,[2] we argue that the seeds of the virtual society already exist in the womb of the information society and we are already seeing some results. The economic, social, political and technological forces unleashed by the information society are inevitably leading us to the virtual society.

Global Economies

During the last five decades, the world has witnessed an unprecedented expansion of business into global markets. These gains build upon the economic spiral set forth by the agricultural and industrial revolutions (Beniger, 1986). The GDP of the world is now $30 trillion— an increase of 84% since the end of the second world war. The ascendance of economic liberalism in the last decade characterized by deregulation, the collapse of the Eastern block, privatization, free markets, lower tariffs; and the move toward more democratic and egalitarian systems in industrializing nations have opened new opportunities for trade and investment. According to David (1997), current trends toward reduction of income inequalities between nations have increased effective demand for goods and services and made it beneficial for transnational and multinational corporations to increase direct foreign investment in developing and industrializing countries. He predicts that global trade and investment activities will grow at US $ 6 trillion per year for the next twenty years, and the world's GDP could grow by $50 trillion in the next 50 years.

Some firms are already distributing value chain activities throughout the world. Globalization has become an important emerging business mandate relevant to most individuals and businesses. Firms are realizing the need to think globally and are concerned about business beyond their domestic marketplace. Local and global competition is forcing firms to identify opportunities for growth and increased market share for their products and services. Firms routinely move an important piece of work, such as a proposal or design idea across time zones and countries so they can work on them literally around the clock. Borders are becoming transparent for trade as global money becomes more of a reality and regional trading blocs such as NAFTA, the European Union (EU) and the Association of South East Asian Nations (ASEAN) move forward.

Moreover, new investment in IT infrastructure by both national governments and multinational corporations has enabled businesses with diverse shapes and forms of organization and control to operate in multiple countries. Global businesses can link directly to their customers, suppliers, and partners around the world. For example Nike Inc. has distributed its value chain activities of inbound logistics, operations, and outbound logistics to a network of suppliers and business partners while focusing on product design, marketing and sales service. Product designers in the USA are linked with contractors in Asia through sophisticated IT networks and CAD/CAM systems. Computerized control and coordination systems monitor each value chain activity. This capability makes it possible to set prices, balance supply and demand and control the physical distribution of sneakers through designated retail outlets all over the world. Other organizations such as General Motors, Toyota, and Kodak have similar global arrangements.

The global efforts to standardize economic operations by enhancing free trade policies, creating robust telecommunications infrastructures, changing the nature of payment and money, upgrading global monetary standards and policies, and adopting a common language for conducting business are moving us to the virtual workplace and eventually, a virtual society.

Policies and Politics

The world's trading partners have differing views of government's role in IT implementation (Mowery, 1995). Governments, businesses, and users have concerns about ownership, access, and distribution of information. Governments play a major role in emphasizing the importance of telecommunications to national and business infrastructures by building and maintaining national backbones and helping to provide gateways to other nations. While a few governments still treat IT policy as part of the national science policy, most governments have realized the need to treat science policy and IT policy as two separate entities (Metcalfe, 1995). Singapore, for example, initiated and established the first formal IT policy in 1980. It was expanded in 1986 to include communication infrastructure as a key element of the new national IT strategy. The National Computer Board in Singapore in 1992 announced the IT2000 Plan to extend the role of IT beyond its domestic needs to embrace the rapidly developing Asia-Pacific region. Some European countries already view the free flow of information as a way to improve their economies and are instituting policies that demonstrate clearly their commitment toward creating a global marketplace. For example, the Danish government is aggressively pushing the country toward a virtual workplace. It has developed a technical blueprint for achieving this goal including a plan to have 75% of the households equipped with personal computers and modems by the year 2000. The US National Information Infrastructure Initiative wants every school to have access to the Internet. Although this attitude toward a virtual community is not yet commonplace worldwide, some countries' political commitment to building virtual communities is noteworthy because government is taking the responsibility to create the foundation for change.

Enlightened and Diversified Population

According to projections reported in Workplace 2000 (Johnston & Packer, 1987), the United States workforce is becoming increasingly diverse. Johnston and Packer (1987) projected that by the year 2000, approximately 47 percent of the workforce will be women and 61 percent of all women of working age will be employed. Women are also expected to make up about three-fifths of the new entrants into the labor force in this decade. Mai-Dalton (1992) also projected that by the year 2000, African Americans will comprise 12 percent of the U.S. workforce, Asians 4 percent, Hispanics 10 percent, and women 48 percent. It is also projected that by the year 2050, one-half of the U.S. population will consist of African Americans, Asians, Hispanics, and Native Americans (Fernandez, 1991). Further, the nature of jobs will also change, with professional, technological, and sales jobs becoming the fastest growing sector (U.S. Bureau of Census, 1992).

On the global level, of the $30 trillion GDP of the world, 20% is produced by the USA. Seventy-six percent (76%) of the world's GDP is concentrated in North America, Japan, and Western Europe. This means 14% of the world population produces and consumes 76% of the world's wealth. However, it is projected that in the next 20 years, global income inequalities will be reduced dramatically and emergent developing and industrializing nations will create and consume more than 50% of the world's wealth (David, 1997). At the heart of this development is the ability of the various populations of the world to engage in global production and operations that employ information, communication, and transportation technologies.

Use of these technologies requires individual computer and information literacy skills. Computer skills include knowledge of what computers can do and cannot do, an understanding of computer jargon and buzzwords, programming and typing skills. Information literacy includes knowledge of what information is needed to make specific decisions, when and who needs what information, when computers should or should not be used to get information, sources for various types of needed information, and how to validate and secure information. Countries whose people are computer and information literate will have a temporary edge in performing virtual work. However, this edge will disappear as older workers leave the workforce and a young group of computer and information literates takes over.

People need exposure to IT at a young age so that they are able to build effectively on their learning and are able to adapt to change. School curricula are starting to offer computer classes in the elementary grades to expose children during their formative years to the ways they can use information to enrich their futures. A new generation of computer and information literates will have the requisite skills to interact in a virtual workplace.

The evolution of a virtual society is dependent on having people understand, accept, and implement the consequences of the new virtual society culture. The growth of the virtual society will help both dual-career parents and single-parent families to balance child care needs and family responsibilities and commitments. Work can be completed frequently from home, under specific conditions, for a designated number of days during normal business hours. People can be entertained at a distant location without regard to physical location.

There is therefore a need to increase the computer competency and information literacy of all potential players in the global virtual society. This should be the responsibility of national governments, global businesses, and individuals. All stakeholders should also accept an altered social norm. This new social form is biased toward people who have good computer skills, are information literate, are willing to accept changes in work processes, and are able to address and reconcile social and physiological impacts. Workers will also have to accept the idea that the job security offered by corporations is a thing of the past.

Information Technology

The interest and growth in the virtual society has been further spurred by advances in information technology. Increased demand for goods and services on a national and global scale has increased the need for faster and reliable information processing and telecommunication technologies. As noted by Beniger (1986),

"... [information] technology appears autonomously to beget [information] technology and, ... innovations in matter and energy processing create the need for further innovation in information processing and communication" (p. 434).

Advances in telecommunication and network technology and the reduction in hardware and software costs have been equal to the challenge. Interorganizational information systems (IOS) allow computer networks to process data and share information across organizational boundaries (Applegate, McFarlan, and McKenney, 1996). IOSs are being used to expand organizational relationships by decoupling value chain activities while maintaining a controlled and coordinated environment. The Nike Inc. example given earlier on is a case in point. IT allows each organization linked by an IOS to concentrate on its core competence. Nike Inc. decided to concentrate in product design, sales and marketing, and service as its core competence. The outcome is a virtual organization that has the global advantages of economies of scale and scope but the responsiveness of a small local company.

Technology by itself does not ensure the coming of the virtual society. Rather, it is an enabler and shaper. Digital technology has made it possible to convert characters, sounds, pictures, and motions into a computer language. Codification of data, including text and numbers as well as multimedia digitalization, allows us to be less time- and location-dependent. The emergence of multimedia standards, and the shift to distributed computing and inter-networking are providing the raw power for digital convergence. A cornucopia of supporting technologies have emerged, including the Inter/Intra/Extranet, electronic mail, groupware, videoconferencing, workflow, data management, data warehousing, and improved networking capabilities.

In the 1990s, the Internet moved from supporting only science and research to becoming an integral tool for commerce. The Internet is at the forefront of the global growth of these enablers. The growth of the Internet has been astounding. The growth rate in the number of Internet hosts is exponential. For example, in 1995, 148 out of 185 (86%) United Nations members had Internet service, compared to 46% in 1991 (Chon, 1996). In June 1996, approximately 400,000 businesses worldwide had domain addresses (InterNic, 1996). It is estimated that more than 60 percent of US companies have invested in some form of Internet-related infrastructure and that 25 percent have Internet-related pilot projects underway.

Interactive communications are required if business is to be conducted virtually on the Internet (or its successors). Electronic mail is the foundation for such communication and is available at relatively modest cost, but the simple sending of text messages is not enough. Multimedia applications are coming to increase the gains of groupware, video conferencing, data management, and data warehousing in the virtual world. Improved networking infrastructures will underlie the higher bandwidth, security, and reliability that enable this technology.

Internet electronic commerce is replacing traditional electronic commerce, which relied on value-added and private messaging networks—both of which were relatively expensive and provided limited connectivity. Traditional electronic commerce tools, such as electronic data interchange (EDI), fax, symbol technology, bar coding, inter-enterprise messaging, and file transfer technologies, are being augmented, and, in some cases replaced by the Internet (Pyle, 1996). Internet technologies (networks, computers, software, etc.) continue to increase in capability and functionality. The new technology holds many possibilities for virtual societies. It enables individuals, groups, communities, organizations and societies, among others, to exchange information, do business, participate in newsgroup discussion, and publish information electronically. The new technology enables innovative ways of communicating and doing business. It is an important element of creating the virtual society.

The new advances in IT are also shaping the evolution of the virtual society. The current manifestations of the virtual society which include telework, virtual teams, virtual corporations, virtual libraries, virtual museums, and tele-medicine are possible because the potential benefits seem to outweigh the costs. As these current practices become entrenched, they will be accepted as standard practice— and hence shape the future evolution of the virtual society. Future advances in distributed networks, distributed databases, bandwidth, storage, and network security will continue to influence the evolution of the virtual society.

EXISTING ARRANGEMENTS AND PRACTICES

In this section, we cover four different arrangements and practices in the virtual society, including telework, virtual teams, virtual organizations, and virtual communities.

Telework

The Telecommute America '97 (TCA'97) survey results indicated that more than 11 million Americans (about 10% of the workforce) performed telework at home, a 30% increase from those who performed telework at home in 1995 (Ullrich, 1997). The average teleworker was 40.2 years old and earned an average annual income of US $ 51,000. Sixty (60%) were married and 46% had children present at home.

Telework originated with the idea that work could be moved to where the workers are rather than moving the workers to the work. People can work in a variety of locations (e.g., home, neighborhood office, at a client location) and participate in the work of the organization.

Teleworking has grown due to the demands of three constituencies: employees, organizations and society. First, substantial changes to the family structure have made employees demand more flexible work arrangements. For example, traditional families with a working husband and a stay-at-home wife are down to 10% of American families (Schepp, 1990). The growth of dual-career households, i.e., those with preschool age children, those with older children, and those with a dependent spouse or parent, may increase the work-family conflict resulting from trying to perform multiple roles such as worker, spouse and parent. Telecommuting provides a flexible work arrangement by allowing employees to eliminate time-consuming and unproductive tasks, such as commuting to the workplace. Telecommuting also provides more flexibility on when and where work is completed.

Attitudinal changes have also contributed to the demand for more flexible work options. The selfishness and materialism that characterized the 1980s have given way to greater concern for personal and family time (Wright, 1993). Employees seek to live in pleasant surroundings, participate in leisure activities, and have time for family. They are more concerned about the quality of life, and they seek work arrangements that allow them to meet their desires. Thus, the telework arrangements may make it easier for individuals to achieve a better balance between their work and personal lives.

Second, due to demographic changes, organizations need to make accommodations to attract and retain employees. The next generation of workers will be much smaller than the current workforce. As older workers, who are experienced and trained, retire, the smaller pool of younger workers will cause a shortage of needed employees. Flexible work options will be required to recruit and retain quality employees.

Pressures toward cost reduction and productivity improvement are also pushing organizations to adopt teleworking programs. Teleworkers are more productive and have better home lives once they start working at least part-time from home. Further, the fixed costs of teleworking are lower than the costs associated with conventional offices.

Societal demands for environmental awareness are the third factor contributing to the demand for flexible work. Teleworking helps organizations deal with the regulatory requirements of the Clean Air Act and the Americans With Disabilities Act. The Clean Air Act requires large companies to reduce the number of automobiles commuting to work on a daily basis. Allowing employees to work at home helps organizations to comply with this legislation. The Americans With Disabilities Act requires organizations to make reasonable accommodations for disabled employees to perform their jobs. Allowing physically challenged individuals to telework allows organizations to comply with this legislation as well. Flexible work also provides an organization with a contingency plan to cope with disasters. Recent weather problems and other disasters, such as the Northridge earthquake in California and the blizzard of 1996, which paralyzed the U.S. East Coast, all but required employers to consider alternate work arrangements.

As public concern for the environment continues to increase, both individuals and organizations are attempting to make more environmentally conscious decisions. Teleworking reduces the number of people commuting to work, thereby contributing to lower traffic congestion and less pollution.

On balance, companies appear to use productivity improvements and cost reductions for justifying telecommuting more than they use regulation or disaster-prevention as a rationale. Companies also cite that new advances in computer technology are making IT managers able to remotely support the teleworker and troubleshoot computers and other technology at the teleworker's home office (Ullrich, 1997). Greater productivity is obtained by the employer through: zero tardiness, less time taken due to illness or family crisis, improved recruiting due to larger labor pool, lower attrition rates, and lower subsidies provided to cover transport, parking, or catering. The employee benefits through: lower work interruptions, avoidance of travel difficulties, increased personal safety, ability to cope with family matters, and reduced child and/or elder care. The society or community pays less taxes and gains better health through: reduced vehicle service costs for roads, reduced road maintenance and gas emissions, and less need to build and maintain alternative modes of transport (Ullrich, 1997).

Virtual Teams

Virtual teams are defined as groups that work on a specific high-level task or goal, but the team members do not have to be co-located in space, nor do their meetings have to be restricted to specific times. Two factors appear to have guided organizations to adopt virtual teams. First, the change in organization structure away from traditional hierarchies was predicated on the need to bring together cross-functional expertise to solve problems. Moreover, organizations recognized that they could acquire specific kinds of expertise, which was too costly to maintain locally, by going outside the organizational boundaries. Second, advances in networking, computer and communications technologies led to the development of methods that could support meetings across time and space (see Information Technology section under Driving Forces above).

A team is also known as a work group. In terms of socio-technical systems terminology, groups can be seen as having both technical and social systems components. The technical system defines the work process and task accomplishment goals that derive from that process. The social system defines the group process and the quality of work life goals that are required to make the group function effectively. In order to achieve all of these goals, groups/teams have certain requirements. Table 1, derived from Mandviwalla and Olfman (1994), outlines these requirements in terms of their technical and social system components.

Teams carry out multiple sub-tasks in order to accomplish their overall goal, and they perform these sub-tasks using a variety of work methods. The sub-tasks are typically embedded in many layers of complexity, but for illustrative purposes, we look at a high-level set of sub-tasks that lead to the final goal of a team. For example, take a team charged with developing a new product. It must do market research, create design alternatives, do market

Table 1: Group/Team Requirements

Technical System	Social System
Multiple group tasks	Development of the group
Multiple work methods	Interchangeable interaction methods
	Permeable group boundaries
	Adjustable group context
	Multiple behavioral characteristics

testing, and so forth. Each of these high-level sub-tasks requires different work methods including survey design, data collection and analysis, engineering, etc.

Throughout the work process, teams must maintain their social functions. They develop over time as members learn to work together. This requires that teams be able to communicate in a variety of ways. They must be able to share documents, as well as to use written, spoken, and visual approaches to communication. Throughout the team's life, various members may join or leave due to needs for specific expertise or other behavioral factors (e.g., someone decides to take a new job). Moreover, team members must be supported so that they can easily fit into the group tasks, and the group must be able to manage its process given the needs of the various members plus the goals set for the team.

The complexity of group work as outlined in the above-stated requirements is further complicated by the concept of virtuality. Varying the time and space dimensions of the team process adds additional levels of complexity to the concept of the group (or team).

Concepts of Time and Place

A simple framework for understanding the concept of virtual teams is provided by Johansen (1988; see Figure 2). Johansen, borrowing from the work of DeSanctis and Gallupe (1987), outlines two dimensions for considering time and place. Time refers to the synchronicity of a meeting and can be either synchronous (takes place at the same time for all participants) or asynchronous (takes place independent of time). Place refers to the physical location of the meeting and can be either in the same place (everyone in one room) or in different places (team members spread across two or more rooms). Different places can be along one hallway, on different floors of the same buildings, in different buildings in the same metropolis, or in different spaces across the global landscape (e.g., in a car, on a airplane, in another country, etc.).

Synchronous/Co-located meetings are the most traditional for groups,

Figure 2: Concepts of Time and Place

	Same Time	**Different Times**
Same Place	Synchronous/Co-located	Asynchronous/Co-Located
Different Places	Synchronous/Separated	Asynchronous/Separated

and are usually referred to as face-to-face meetings. Everyone must be in the same room during the same time period in order to carry out the team meeting. Alternatively, by relaxing one or both of the "same" constraints, a variety of other possibilities present themselves.

Synchronous/Separated meetings include participants who are located in more than one setting (typically in different venues). All participants' actions and/or words are seen and/or heard as they occur. Of course, if the meeting locations are in different time zones, participants are not meeting at the same clock times.

Asynchronous/Co-located meetings imply that the participants work in one venue, but they contribute to a common task and associated group process by using a single repository that is physically restricted from "outside" access. Asynchronous/Separated meetings extend the above concept to allow communications to be made at any time, and to and from a variety of locations.

Most likely, a virtual team will use some or all of the above methods to conduct their business. They may begin with a synchronous meeting (possibly face to face). Later, the focus may be on asynchronous communications as sub-tasks are being accomplished. At certain milestones, synchronous communications may be utilized to ensure the highest levels of exchanges between participants.

Virtual Team Technologies

Virtual teams began to be a reality with the advent of teleconferencing, which enabled groups to communicate synchronously in separate locations via audio. However, these groups had to have copies of mutual paper documents available at the outset of a meeting (or had to depend on fax to transfer documents across locations "on the fly"), and there was a reduction in potential information via the voice-only medium, which was further muffled through a speakerphone arrangement. Videoconferencing potentially added another level of richness to such meetings, but the high costs and poor quality of transmissions reduced the demand for this technology. As with all technology, time has improved transmission quality, but costs are still relatively high.

By the late 1970s, the idea that groups could meet through the computer was being realized (Hiltz and Turoff, 1978). Computer conferences aimed to exploit the potential for asynchronous/separated meetings by providing a structured forum through which to exchange messages. In essence, this structure remains one of the key methods for facilitating asynchronous group interactions, although it is now manifested in the form of Internet tools such as e-mail, chat rooms, bulletin boards, and "list-servs". These technologies tend to serve distance education and virtual communities rather than virtual teams in organizations.

The 1980s saw the development of more sophisticated forms of computer-based technology that exploited each of the combinations of time and place. Ventana's Group Systems was designed to create an electronic meeting room to enhance support for face-to-face meetings. It provides features such as anonymous communications and support for various group process activities such as idea generation and voting. Later it was extended to support other types of meetings, especially those which are synchronous but separated. Another software package that has probably had the biggest impact, in terms of numbers of users, on team work and virtual teams is Lotus Notes. It provides sophisticated asynchronous meeting support through "databases" that can store multimedia communications.

The idea that teams can utilize computer technology to enhance their work and group processes is often termed "computer-supported cooperative work" (CSCW). The products that support these activities are typically termed "groupware." Groupware not only enables a full range of meeting types, but also supports the flow of documents across work tasks, and builds an organizational memory that can be used to support future tasks. With the increasing bandwidth of the Internet, the full complement of document-based, audio and video support will be readily available on every worker's desktop and in their mobile computers. This can only increase the number of virtual teams that will be operating in organizations all across the globe.

Virtual Organizations

The purpose of organizations is to enable groups of people to effectively and efficiently coordinate efforts and resources at their disposal in order to achieve stated organizational goals or objectives. Organizations rely on a structure to achieve their goals or objectives. The structure of an organization can be defined as the sum total of the different ways in which it divides its labor (people) and other resources (technology, capital equipment, databases etc.) into distinct tasks (processes) and then achieves coordination among them (Mintzberg, 1979). Traditionally, organizational managers have used a hierarchical structure with well-defined lines of command, control, and communication to coordinate the optimal assignment of people and other resources to processes. However, dynamic competitive forces in industry, including global competition, strategic alliances, re-engineering, total quality management, rightsizing and downsizing, all mandate a more dynamic assignment of available scarce resources to processes. The ability of IT to collapse distance and time provides a wider range of resources to draw from.

The problem can be formulated as: Demand for goods and services (information, travel, automobile) from an organization (Internet service provider, travel agency, car manufacturer) must be satisfied through the assignment and coordination of available resources (computer networks, databases, skilled personnel, IT, raw materials, capital equipment) (Mowshowitz, 1997). Assume for a moment that the Internet service provider is a multinational organization with headquarters in British Columbia but operations all over the world. Whereas a centralized command, control and communication structure may be suitable for the Internet service provider to assign and coordinate its resources to meet a service request in western Canada, a decentralized command, control and communication structure may be suitable to provide the same service in South Africa or Australia. The same could be said of the travel agency or the car manufacturing company. A virtual organization structure can provide an optimal dynamic allocation of resources to meet the demand requirements as long as there is a logical separation of customer demand, resources needed to satisfy that demand, and the decision makers who allocate the resources (Mowshowitz, 1997). A virtual organization structure will provide the Internet service provider with the agility and flexibility required to meet consumer demand anywhere anytime in the world. It can be said that in the virtual society, organizational structure follows demand and performance requirements.

Organizations competing in volatile technological and business environments must be agile, flexible, responsive and boundaryless (Eichinger and Ulrich, 1995), which is possible under a virtual organization model. In a virtual organization the assignment of resources, control and coordination are achieved through the use of telecommunications, e-mail, telework, groupware, teleconferencing, e-cash, the Internet, Intranets, Extranets, EDI systems and related technologies. The organizational theory literature labels agile, flexible, responsive or dynamic organizational forms as "fuzzy" models that are organic as opposed to crisp or mechanistic structures. Fuzzy structures are appropriate for organizations that need to cope with conditions of uncertainty (Buchanan and Boddy, 1992). The dynamic nature of the technological and business environment in a virtual society favors fuzzy organizational structures. The virtual organizational structures qualify as a fuzzy structure.

According to Mowshowitz, the optimal assignment of resources to processes required in virtual organizations influences managerial decision making, and management relations with its employees, external organizations, suppliers and the community. Flexible assignment of resources "favors temporary relationships based on explicit rather than implicit agreements" (Mowshowitz, 1997, p. 37). Propensity toward temporary relationships means that a virtual organization will be characterized by: shorter-term contracts with its employees, a greater use of teleworkers, outsourcing to external organizational activities that fall outside the organization's core competencies, and ability to switch from one supplier to another in order to obtain cost-effectiveness.

These characteristics would cause the local community in which the organization operates to have negative perceptions of the actions of the virtual organization management. However, such feelings and perceptions would abate as we achieve a critical mass of virtual organizations and move toward a virtual society.

Virtual Communities

Virtual communities have emerged from a surprising intersection of human needs and technology. When the ubiquity of the telecommunications network is combined with the information-structuring and storing capabilities of computers, a new communication medium becomes possible. Virtual community is a term commonly used to describe various forms of computer-mediated communication, particularly long-term, textually-mediated conversations among large groups. It is a group of people who may or may not meet one another face-to-face and who exchange words and ideas through the mediation of computer networks and bulletin boards. The range of activities is immense. People chat. They argue. They exchange property, ideas and gossip. They plan, make friends, even fall in love. They do everything people do when they get together face-to-face but, by using computers, they do it separated in space and time. Electronic interactions in which people don't know others make new kinds of communities possible.

This section discusses three arrangements and practices of virtual communities, namely: tele-democracy, virtual museum and tele-medicine. Tele-democracy deals with how voters can further their interests and participate in the politics and governance of their community. Virtual museums deal with the use of home-based PCs to link into vast collections of paintings, sculptures, drawings, prints, architecture, photography, film and video without regard to distance or time. Tele-medicine deals with the use of advances in medical and telecommunication technologies by the clinical community to provide health care information and services to people living in remote and under-served areas.

Tele-democracy

The rapid evolution of information and the new potentials for communication, particularly the unprecedented global telecommunications and information networks explosion, and the trend toward a global social society will have profound impacts on various phenomena such as work, social life, entertainment, education, and democracy (Becker, 1997).

Tele-democracy is a generic term that combines the understanding of the way citizens are empowered with the enabling technologies of computer networking and associated hardware, software, services and techniques (Keskinen, 1995). The major change that tele-democracy has brought to societies is to ensure that political decisions be made in accordance with the people's attitudes and desires. Tele-democracy has the potential of facilitating personal and community evolution by enabling them to build social value structures and to make their own future (Koumirov, 1994).

Tele-democracy has grown due to the demands of three constituencies: citizens (or voters), elected leaders and societal demands for voicing public opinion and communicating with potential leaders vying for political office. First, increased citizens' or voters' participation in the information revolution has caused substantial changes to their perception of the role of government. In modern societies, citizens want to shift from being "the governed" into "self-government." They want to be actively involved in the political work instead of being mere subordinates. They want to have more power, authority, and control over their own lives. Ordinary citizens can play a major role in helping to decide what kind of society they want to live in. They can take an active role in socio-political decision making in order to make their lives better and to manage their own affairs. They can participate in agenda setting, planning, and policy-making. They ask for the power to be handed back to them. Technology, now, can easily empower them. It promotes a new form of direct citizen participation and direct democracy—tele-democracy.

Citizens can use IT to share information about issues and priorities vital to their future, and to be informed about the critical trends and choices facing communities, nations, and the planetary society. IT can provide documentaries and investigative reports that will give them an in-depth understanding of the challenges they face. A vibrant civil and democratic society flourishes on a well-informed citizenry (Elgin, 1994). The increased number of informed citizens may increase the need to create a more conscious direct democracy.

Additionally, citizens also need to know what other citizens think and feel about different issues and priorities. When citizens understand what others think about key issues, then they can mobilize themselves into a collective interest group with singleness of purpose and action.

Elected leaders are the second constituent contributing to the demand for tele-democracy. Due to availability of electronic means of communication and social changes and demands, elected leaders need to realize critical political transformations that may redistribute their political power. They should know that the next generation of citizens are more informed, knowledgeable, and enthusiastic. They should understand that citizens can and should take an active role in socio-political decision making. Elected leaders need to use IT to communicate with citizens, colleagues, and government agencies. In so doing, they can variously persuade, negotiate, listen, and question to meet their stakeholders' desires.

Citizens' wishes can push elected leaders to adopt tele-democracy. Tele-democracy can also improve the relationship between citizens and policy-makers and decrease the gap between the governor and the governed. Citizens can interact electronically with their elected leaders and hold weekly or monthly electronic meetings. These meetings can establish some account-ability between the public and their elected leaders. Citizens can also give timely feedback to elected leaders by providing inputs to those who govern. Holding electronic town meetings may provide a forum for citizens to build a working consensus on major issues and priorities (Elgin, 1994). Here, elected leaders meet with groups of citizens to explain and/or defend their agendas and policies. These may assure that citizens feel engaged, involved, and invested in decision making and responsible for society and its future.

Societal demands for voicing public opinion and communicating with potential leaders vying for political office is the third factor contributing towards the demand for tele-democracy. Governments may need to increase their funding for telecommunication infrastructures to generate the level and quality of communication needed to support tele-democracy in its process of choosing a sustainable future. Faster, cheaper, more diverse, and more interactive communication have the potential to increase citizen participation and involvement in the democratic process in terms of voicing their opinions and electing the "right" leaders. Local information networks should be designed to promote civic participation by offering government information and communication at little or no cost. This may increase citizen interest in other community activities, thus tightening communal ties and increasing participation in community governance. However, this may necessitate changes in the role of government as we know it today.

Perhaps a more dramatic change for the future will be a shift in governmental processes. Traditionally, a representative government is used so that people are able to elect those they believe will perform governmental rules effectively and represent their interests. In this setting, elected represen-tatives are agents of those who elect them. In a virtual society, however, these agents may no longer be necessary because people could perform govern-mental functions virtually (i.e., virtual voting on issues, tele-democracy, Ross

Perot's suggestions for virtual town hall). While we foresee an increase in electronic meetings for global commerce, we expect an even greater impact will be made by simplified distribution in the government and political arenas.

Tele-democracy allows citizens who wish to make informed choices concerning candidates, government policy, or regulation to retrieve information from government databases (Koumirov, 1994). Citizens can be engaged in more thorough and substantive discussions rather than merely listening to a brief advertisement or sound bite. They can also vote electronically for candidates and issues.

However, there are some issues that need to be addressed: (1) *Access to computers*: A broad-based access to computers must be ensured. There is a large portion of the society that does not own computers or have access to external sources. It is imperative that everyone have access either from home or from a community location. (2) *Security and privacy:* Unsecured transmission is often a main deterrent for rapid growth of tele-democracy. Here, security includes authentication, integrity, accuracy, and confidentiality. We need to verify the identity of the participants while the information transmitted should not be modified. Citizens need also to ensure that the information is confidential and private and only the participants know the content. Individuals also need to have protected "anonymity." (3) *Mechanism for coordination*: The system should ensure that different viewpoints are presented with impartial refereeing of messages and automated negotiation.

Several projects have been initiated to examine tele-democracy in several countries. In November 1996, the Dutch province of North Brabant conducted an experiment to test the applicability of an Internet-based software for public debate. They invited 100 residents and organizations to discuss aspects of land use for the region under the banner. They debated the issue using an Internet-based application, which allowed moderated discussion, periodic polling of participants, and voting (Jankowski, Leeuwis, martin, Noordhof and van Rossum, 1997). Norway's Telenor Research and Development developed a communication system to support local politicians. The system allowed elected leaders to make calls, set up telephone conferences, use e-mail, and exchange documents between them and other government offices (Ytterstad, Akelsen, Svendsen and Watson, 1996).

The government of Costa Rica, with the help of an American university, is experimenting with voting systems using the Internet (*New York Times*, 1997). Their objective is to increase electoral participation and efficiency while reducing the cost of national elections. They plan to implement such voting systems by the year 2002. Other countries have also started to develop systems that will allow their citizens to vote directly on legislation at the national level—Denmark (Erne, et al., 1995; Schimdt, 1993); UK (Bartle, 1997). For more information on tele-democracy experiments in various countries visit http://www.auburn.edu/tann/tann2/report.html).

Virtual Museums

A virtual museum allows users to use their PCs to walk through and explore digital representations of various artifacts in virtual three-dimensional space on the Internet. The user can use a mouse or joystick to move around. The aim is to make the museum exhibits more accessible and visitor friendly. Visitors use the index home page to get an introduction to the collection highlights. Visitors who need more detailed information can dig deeper by choosing the specific detailed items they wish to explore. Virtual museums contain interactive databases which have many collections of different things on different subjects such as art, science, history, zoology, music, archeology, and biology. Virtual museums provide a new way for people to access vast collections of paintings, sculptures, drawings, prints, architecture, photography, film and video without regard to distance or time. The Virtual Library of Museums, http://www.icom.org/ulmp/, includes a list of links to various museum sites throughout the world. The site includes more than 400 museums in North America.

For example, if you visit the Metropolitan Museum of Art in New York (http://www.metmuseum.org) the index web page provides you with an overview of works currently on display in various galleries in New York. When you select a specific collection, you can also choose the floor you want to visit. A floor plan is then provided for you to select the images you want to see. The site also offers you an on-line gift and bookshop, various educational resources , a calendar of special exhibitions and other planned museum activities. For some of the collections, sound samples are available in RealAudio, WAV and AU formats. Other collections provide QuickTime clips of selected information.

The French Ministry of Culture has helped create a virtual museum that contains more than 130,000 paintings from the great art museums of France. The original project was started 25 years ago and was text based. In 1994 web pages were added to allow visitors to see the pictures and virtually navigate through the different collections. People are allowed to make digital or hard copies of the museum work to build their own private collections or use in the classroom, but are prohibited to make or distribute them for profit or commercial advantage. Visitors can view the museum collections in French or English at http://www.culture.gouv.fr/culture/exp/exp.htm.According to

Mannoni (1997), in real life, legal limitations or poor physical condition of the paintings and sculptures would have made it impossible to put all the paintings in the same place.

The Boston Computer Museum allows you to walk through the museum in real time (O'Rourke, 1996). The index home page requires you to fill in a quick survey that establishes you as a visitor. This allows you to communicate with other visitors in the museum through the "Who Is Out There" feature. You virtually talk with others and get a sense of almost being there.

You can virtually learn how a desktop computer is put together or design your own robot. The ability to dance on the keyboard, dive into a microprocessor or control a robot over the net is the next best thing to being there (O'Rourke, 1996).

However there are limitations. Current technology limitations do not yet provide an aesthetic experience. The pictures are not of the right scale and lack vitality. The information provided about the collections may not be detailed enough for serious scholarly work. Scholars needing more detail will have to wait— only the layman benefits from the current technology. This means lots of images need to be digitally scanned to meet scholars' needs. Intellectual property rights create further complications. The true value for the museum materials is yet to be established. There are also bandwidth problems.

Tele-Medicine

Tele-medicine is the use of telecommunication technologies by competent medical specialists to provide medical information and services to clinicians and patients living in remote and under-served areas. Early applications in tele-medicine began 35 years ago when it was mostly used for clinical applications, mostly tele-psychiatry consultations. Telephones and fax machines were the first to be used due to their relative cheapness and availability. Later applications used closed-circuit television systems. For example, a closed-circuit television system was implemented between Massachusetts General Hospital and a Veteran's Administration hospital 25 miles away, using a high resolution, black-and-white video technology supplemented with close-up lenses. This system was used for remote consultation and diagnosis in a variety of fields including dermatological, optical as well as psychiatric examinations. Now clinicians are incorporating more complex technologies such as remotely assisted surgery and patient monitoring.

In the USA, 25% of the health care providers use some form of tele-medicine technology. Given current developments in medical and information processing technology, hospitals and integrated health care organizations are realizing that tele-medicine will not only provide a more effective allocation of scarce medical resources, but also could become a valuable tool for increasing market share. There is also a realization that tele-medicine can help them tap into the potentially lucrative international health care market (Campbell, 1997).

Tele-medicine applications encompass:

1. the transfer of medical records, faxes, on-line text references and e-mail over the telephone,
2. transmission of X-rays and other images and the use of telemetry and still images,
3. interactive video and the use of satellites and microwave transmission of images, and
4. the use of a smart glove by a surgeon to carry out an operation at a distance (Ziegler, 1995).

In tele-medicine, clinicians engage in tele-diagnosis, tele-mentoring, tele-monitoring and/or tele-presence activities. Tele-diagnosis is the detection of disease by evaluating data transmitted electronically to a receiving station from instruments monitoring a distant patient. Tele-mentoring is the use of audio, video, and other information processing technologies by a medical expert to provide individual guidance or instruction to a clinician in a new medical procedure. Tele-monitoring is the use of audio, video, and other information processing technologies to monitor patient status at a distance. Tele-presence is the use of robotics and other devices to allow a medical expert (e.g., a surgeon) to perform a task at a remote site by manipulating instruments and receiving sensory information or feedback that creates a sense of being present at the remote site.

Overall, the integration of current technology into tele-medicine is still at the experimental stage. In 1996, the US Department of Health and Human Services (HHS) established an HHS tele-medicine initiative aimed at preparing the US healthcare system for the information age. HHS allocated $42 million to 19 tele-medicine projects affecting rural, inner-city, and suburban areas. In New Jersey, Blue Cross and Blue Shield and IBM are developing a communication system linking hospitals, physicians, suppliers and payers in order to facilitate the sharing of records, claims, lab requests, and administrative functions. The Kaiser Permanente Group in northern California has implemented a tele-medicine system whereby it no longer summons its radiologists to hospitals at night to read digital images, i.e., CT scans and MRI. Images are transmitted to the radiologists at home instead.

Despite the apparent benefits of tele-medicine, a number of problems constrain the overwhelming adoption of tele-medicine (Campbell, 1997). First, most information about the successes and failures of tele-medicine is anecdotal. Few empirical studies have documented the efficacy of tele-medicine in terms of systems being used, services available and their acceptability by patients, and overall clinical outcomes. For more information please visit http://www.telemed.org/. Second, no attempts have been made to match existing technology to medical needs. Most available technology is not user friendly and most providers with interactive television-based systems don't have e-mail capability— thus they can't send documents and text at the same time. Third, the set-up cost of equipment and telecommunication hardware and software is too high for the time being. Lower end systems cost between $100,000 and $500,000. High end systems cost anywhere from $3 million (Campbell, 1997). Maintenance and training costs are also high. Fourth, there are legal and social issues that need to be resolved. Those include providing services in an age where there are few legal precedents for remote liability and licensing across states and nations. There is a need for state and national governments to establish policies and laws that are compatible with tele-medicine. Data communication standards need to be established to allow various medical hardware devices and software applications to communicate with each other. States and national governments also need to establish payment and reimbursement procedures. Finally, transborder data flow regulations need to be established to allow the flow of patient information but to maintain privacy, security, and confidentiality.

DILEMMAS AND IMPLICATIONS OF THE VIRTUAL SOCIETY

Coincidental to the driving forces, the onset of the virtual society has far-reaching implications for governments, researchers, educators, businesses, individuals and society in general.

Global Policy and Economics

It is generally agreed that the technical backbone of the virtual society is Internet electronic commerce. The Internet upholds an open culture in which information is freely exchanged and no accounting for transactions is required. This environment has been in existence since the introduction of the Internet, but increased commercialization and globalization make this openness inefficient, and policies to balance openness and market efficiency are difficult to formulate (Press, 1994). In a survey of business executives conducted by the American Electronics Association (AEA), the majority of responses identified the need for government regulation as one of the two primary obstacles to the creation of a national information infrastructure for effectual information exchange (Widdifield and Grover, 1995).

Politics and Policy

Access rights, primarily censorship and intellectual property, are becoming increasingly important policy issues for global businesses. Security and privacy and the creation of methods for rendering monetary tender for transactions are also coming under scrutiny by countries, businesses and users of global services.

Although a number of countries have adopted national policies that support globalization, issues related to access rights, specifically censorship and intellectual property need to addressed on an international basis. For example, copyright laws in the United States are 20 years old and some say they are not appropriate for interpreting fair use issues that arise in an electronic world (Miller, 1996). Inappropriate or unfair use court rulings may hinder electronic commerce. Individual countries may resolve problems of access within their borders, but resolutions need to cross global boundaries. World governments need to enact international laws and policies that foster electronic distribution and dissemination of data yet protect the creators of the data. They also need to address the problem of transborder data flows.

Internet security and privacy remain elusive. The Internet was initially designed by researchers to share information electronically after a nuclear disaster, and security was not a design constraint. Expansion of the Internet revealed serious security flaws as evidenced by Internet-based intrusions such as the theft of passwords from service providers in 1993-94, "IP" spoofing attack on the San Diego Supercomputer Center in 1994, and theft of funds from Citibank in 1995 (Bhimani, 1996).

Bhimani (1996) states that an adequate security and privacy solution needs to uphold five fundamental requirements: (1) maintain confidentiality to the parties involved in the transaction, (2) authenticate the parties involved in the communication, (3) provide data integrity, (4) provide for future non-repudiation by parties involved in the transaction, and (5) include, if necessary, the selection of parts of a transaction which should be hidden from viewing by a party or parties. Confidentiality is typically provided through data encryption. Authentication, data integrity, and non-repudiation are enabled through digital signatures and public-key certificates. Although various governments and businesses have established their own data encryption standards and privacy laws, there is a need to address these issues at a global level. The International Telecommunication Union (ITU) should be given the responsibility of bringing together national governments and industry to adopt international protocols that support Internet security and privacy.

There is also a need for a global policy governing monetary exchange methods. The status of electronic payments is still ill defined and fraught with technological and institutional problems (Panurach, 1996). Insecurity, primarily anonymity, is the primary technical issue. Institutional constraints are (1) government regulations that could easily bring the downfall of electronic payments, (2) resistance from financial institutions which face a reduction in investment funds by adopting these new payment technologies, and (3) resistance from consumers who must accept the new methods.

Enlightened and Diversified Population

It is true that the world population is becoming more computer and information literate. However, people won't use a technology unless they are sure their transactions are secure and private. Issues related to employee monitoring, the right to obtain and correct information, and the right to authorize the use of one's information continue to occupy individuals, businesses and governments. Although universal laws that protect individual rights to privacy are not envisaged in the near future, this is an issue that the virtual society will have to grapple with.

Moreover, people tend to resist technologies that impact their behavior negatively. Virtuality means less physical interaction. Social and psychological ramifications of virtual societies are therefore eminent. Since we spend about one-third of our productive life at work, the consequences of workplace redesign related to virtual organizational structures should be examined. For example, a few years ago, it was a status symbol to carry a pager. A pager signified that one had critical knowledge or skills or was wired in to important people. Today, some workers view a pager as a leash so they can be led around by their bosses anytime and anyplace. Researchers need to examine the effects on people when an 8 a.m. to 5 p.m. workday is no longer the norm or when a telework contract can require someone to work awkward hours.

The role of human behavior as a driving force toward a virtual society cannot be overemphasized. Most people are social beings and derive satisfaction in their lives through interactions with other people. Researchers need to study the effects of these altered social designs, i.e., temporary work contracts, dehumanization, minimal face-to-face interactions, and information overload, as well as how people resist the forces that will propel us into a virtual society.

The process of education has changed very little since the advent of computer technologies underlying the virtual society (Alavi, Wheeler and

Valacich, 1995). New methods of education may change the way people learn but current research has not yet fully explored the effect of technology on the outcomes of education taking into consideration the models of learning and the methods of teaching (Leidner and Jarvenpaa, 1995). Future research should concentrate on issues of educational delivery by applying existing learning theory to understand the effect of technology on learning. There is also a need to evaluate whether education should be the sole responsibility of the individual or whether there is an effective mix of organizational and individual education.

Ideally, a virtual organization should be able to consummate temporal contracts with skilled workers who have proven track records anywhere in the world. Such contracts would be meritorious and should not consider country of national origin, race, religion or sex. Whereas this presents great opportunities for organizations and information technology literate workers, it also has implications for wealth distribution between the technological haves and have nots. It is up to national governments to establish policies that will protect wealth distribution within their national boarders and implement affirmative measures that provide equal opportunity for all their citizens.

Information Technology

While IT provides faster transmission of information, it affords the logical separation of work from work processes and the resources required to perform the work processes. This gives managers the flexibility to focus on effective accomplishment of the work requirements objectively. As noted previously, the flexible allocation of resources (e.g., labor, time, hardware, software) to work processes favors a virtual organizational structure. The virtual organizational structure, in turn, favors ephemeral labor contracts, telework, short-term supplier contracts, and outsourcing. Given the long-term nature of existing organizational arrangements, it is natural for there to be resentment from employees, suppliers, and the labor community. For example, one of the grievances in a recent labor strike between General Motors and the United Auto Workers labor union (June 1998) centered on the outsourcing issue. There is a dearth of research on the impact of such resentment on emergent virtual organizations.

Another challenge for the virtual organization is how to reduce switching and contract costs and how to handle temporal alliances and partnerships in order to protect company secrets such as special formulas or marketing strategies. These two problems are formidable since few or no studies exist for companies to learn from. However, as we move into the virtual society, virtual organizations will have to find solutions to such problems.

At the micro level, individuals should have the ability to become perpetual learners and apply knowledge to new situations. As technology changes, so will the need to master and use the new technology. The rate at which individuals and organizations are able to learn and apply new knowledge to new situations may become the only sustainable competitive advantage in the virtual society (Stata, 1989). Studies will be needed to evaluate the psychological and social impact of increased burdens on people to be knowledgeable about various technologies and to learn continuously.

SUMMARY AND CONCLUSION

This chapter provides important insights into the forces, dilemmas, and implications of the oncoming virtual society. We identified and discussed the main forces and exposed the issues and complexities involved. Additional research is needed to examine the relevance of such forces and issues in a virtual societal context. The framework provided in Figure 1 was aimed at organizing our knowledge from prior literature and identifying the boundaries of the "virtual society" phenomenon. The arrangements covered are seen as specific occurrences or manifestations of the virtual society. We hope that this chapter contributes to our understanding of the issues and complexities involved in our evolution to a virtual world and will stimulate research in field settings on the driving forces, issues, dilemmas and prospects facing the virtual society.

REFERENCES

Agres, C., Edberg, D. and Igbaria, M. (1998)."Transformation to Virtual Society: Forces and Issues," *The Information Society*, (14:2), 71-82.

Applegate, L. M., McFarlan, F. W., and McKenney, J.L.(1996). *Corporate Information Systems Management: Texts and Cases*, 5th Edition, Irwin, Chicago.

Alavi, M., Wheeler, B.C. and Valacich, J.S.(1995). "Using IT to Reengineer Business Education: An Exploratory Investigation of Collaborative Telelearning." *MIS Quarterly,* 19(3), 293-312.

Bartle, M.(1997). *Parliament Beware! The UK Is Coming On-Line,* URL http://www.auburn.edu/tann/tann2/bartle.html.

Becker, T.(1997). True Tele-democracy. [TAN+N and You] URL http://www.auburn.edu/tann/tann2/editor.html.

Bell, D.(1973). *The Coming of Post-Industrial Society: A Venture in Social Forecasting*, Basic Colophon, New York, NY.

Beniger, J.(1986). *The Control Revolution: Technological and Economic*

Origins of the Information Society, Harvard University Press, Cambridge, MA.

Bhimani, A. (1996)."Securing the Commercial Internet." *Communications of the ACM*, 39(6), 29,35.

Buchanan, D. and Boddy, D.(1992). *The Expertise of the Change Agent, Public Performance and Backstage Activity*. Prentice Hall, New York, NY.

Campbell, S.(1997). "Market memo: Will tele-medicine become as common as the stethoscope?." *Health Care Strategic Management,* 15(4), 1, 20.

Chon, K.(1996). "Internet inroads." *Communications of the ACM*, 39(6), 59-60.

Collins, R.(1979). *The Credential Society: An Historical Sociology of Education and Stratification.* Academic Press, New York, NY.

David, G. (1997).Technological Change, Globalization, and Productivity, Speech delivered to C-SPAN on December 26, 1997. George David is the CEO for United Technologies Corporation.

DeSanctis, G., and Gallupe, R. B.(1987). "A Foundation for the Study of Group Decision Support Systems." *Management Science*, 33(5), 589-609.

Drucker, P.(1969). *The Age of Discontinuity.* Harper and Row, New York, NY.

Eichinger, R. and Ulrich, D. (1995). "Are You Future Agile?." *Human Resource Planning,* 18(4), 30-41.

Elgin, D.(1994). *The Awakening Earth: Global Communications and The Social Brain* Morrow, New York. URL http://www.auburn.edu/tann/tann2/elgin.html.

Erne, R., Gross, A., Kaufmann, B. and Kleger, H. (Eds.)(1995). *Transnational Democracy,* Zurich: Realotopia. URL http://www.auburn.edu/tann/tann2/gross.html.

Fernandez, J.P.(1991). *Managing a Diverse Work Force.* Lexington Books, Lexington, MA.

Hiltz, S. R., and Turoff, M.(1978). *The Network Nation: Human Communication via Computer.* Addison-Wesley, Reading, MA.

InterNic News(1996). *Registration Services Performance Measures for June 1996.* URL http://rs.internic.net, July 28, 1996.

Jankowski, N., Leeuwis, C., Martin, P., Noordhof, M. and van Rossum, J.(1997). *Tele-democracy in the Province: An Experiment with Internet-based Software and Public Debate*, Paper prepared for Euricom Colloquium. URL http://www.socsci.kun.nl/maw/cw/publications/tdinprov.html, June 19-21.

Johansen, R.(1988). *Groupware: Computer Support for Business Teams.*

Free Press, New York.

Johnston, W.B. and Packer, A.H.(1987). *Workforce 2000: Work and Workers for the 21st Century*. Hudson Institute, Indianapolis, IN.

Keskinen, A.(1995). Introduction to Tele-democracy and Information Networks. In Auli Keskinen (Ed.), *Tele-democracy - on Societal Impacts of Information Networks*. Helsinki, Finland: Painatuskaskus. URL http://www.auburn.edu/tann/tann2/auli.html.

Koumirov, V.(1994). Tele-democracy. [Helsinki University of Technology]. URL http://www.tcm.hut.fi..

Leidner, D.E. and Jarvenpaa, S.L.(1995). "The Use of Information Technology to Enhance Management School Education: A Theoretical View." *MIS Quarterly*, 19(3), 265-291.

Mai-Dalton, R.R.(1992). "Managing Cultural Diversity on the Individual, Group, and Organizational Levels." In Chemers, M. and Ayman, R. (Eds.), *Leadership Theory and Research: Perspectives and Directions*, Academic Press, New York, NY.

Mandviwalla, M., and Olfman, L.(1994). "What Do Groups Need? A Proposed Set of Generic Groupware Requirements," *ACM Transactions on Computer-Human Interaction*, 1(3), 245-268.

Mannoni, B.(1997). "A Virtual Museum." *Communications of the ACM*, 40(9), 61-62

Martin, J.(1978). *The Wired Society*. Prentice-Hall, Englewood Cliffs, NJ.

Metcalfe, S. (1995)."The Economic Foundations of Technology Policy; Equilibrium and Evolutionary Perspectives". In Paul Stoneman (ed.), *Handbook of the Economics of Innovation and Technological Change*. Blackwell, Oxford, UK.

Mintzberg, H.(1979). *The Structuring of Organizations*. Prentice-Hall, Englewood Cliffs, NJ.

Mowery, D.(1995). "The Practice of Technology Policy." In Paul Stoneman (ed.), *Handbook of the Economics of Innovation and Technological Change*. Blackwell, Oxford, UK.

Mowshowitz, A.(1997). "Virtual Organization." *Communications of the ACM*, 40(9), 30-37.

NY Times (1997). "Costa Rica to Try On-line Elections." *New York Times*. URL http://www.nytimes.com/library/cyber/week/102797/costarica.html, October 22.

O Rourke, J.(1996). "Virtual Museum: Computers on Computer." *Rural Telecommunications,* 15(5), 10.

Panurach, P. (1996)."Money in Electronic Commerce: Digital Cash, Electronic Fund Transfer, and E-cash." *Communications of the ACM*, 39(6),

45-50.

Press, L.(1994). "Commercialization of the Internet." *Communications of the ACM*, 37(12), 17-21.

Pyle, R. (1996). "Commerce and the Internet." *Communications of the ACM*, 39(6), 23.

Schimdt, M.(1993). *Direct Democracy*. URL http://www.auburn.edu/tann/tann2/marcus.html.

Stata, R.(1989). "Organizational Learning- The Key to Management Innovation." *Sloan Management Review,* 30(3), 63-73.

Ullrich, R.T.(Ed.)(1997). "New National Survey Reports Sharp Rise in Telecommuting," in *AT&T News On-line*. URL http://www.att.com/press/0797/970702.bsa.html.

US Bureau of Census(1992). *Statistical Abstracts of the United States:* (112th Edition). Washington, D.C., 387-388.

Widdifield, R. and Grover, V.(1995). "Internet and the Implications of the Information Superhighway for Business." *Journal of Systems Management,* May/June, 16-21.

Wright, P.C.(1993). "Telecommuting and Employee Effectiveness: Career and Managerial Issues." *International Journal of Career Management*, Vol. 5, 4-9.

Ytterstad, P., Akselsen, S., Svendsen, G. and Watson, R.T.(1996). *Tele-democracy: Using Information Technology to Enhance Political Work.* URL http://www.misq.org/discovery/articles96/article1/, September.

ENDNOTES

1 Information technology comprises computer software and hardware of all types, workstations, computer networks, robotics, and smart chips.

2 In the USA, the information society emerged in the mid-1950s when more than 50% of the workforce was engaged in information and service-related activities. The information society is also known, among others, as the post-industrial society (Bell, 1973), knowledge economy (Drucker, 1969), wired society (Martin, 1978) or credential society (Collins, 1979).

Work
in the
Virtual World

Chapter 3

Am I Doing What's Expected? New Member Socialization in Virtual Groups

John E. Galvin
Indiana University - Indianapolis, USA

Manju K. Ahuja
Florida State University, USA

INTRODUCTION

The small miracle of telecommunications that Alexander Graham Bell brought to society in 1876 continues to transform our lives today. A technology that business was reluctant to embrace in the 1880s has now been embedded in the very fabric of organization life to such an extent that to exclude it is next to impossible. Today, communication technology allows people to work together even when they are physically far apart. In its most extreme use, businesses can operate without the employees ever meeting each other or their customers, thus creating a "virtual workplace" where time, space, and structure become tools for the individual rather than constraints of the organization.

A recent editorial page cartoon depicted a family of four relaxing at the beach while each of them was connected to another activity through telecommunications —faxing, checking e-mail, participating in an on-line conference and arranging travel schedules. Does this picture represent a positive or negative image of working in a virtual setting? Has the use of modern communication technology released us from the bounds of office walls and domineering organization hierarchies? Or, has it made us more dependent on our coworkers in order to perform our own work effectively, in addition to making us unable to have any time away from work? Has it made us more isolated or more connected? Positive advances are often accompanied by unexpected side effects that were not thoroughly considered or even anticipated by their proponents. For instance, individuals who work in a virtual workplace may have less visibility to their managers, co-workers, and peers. This might lead to feelings of greater isolation from the organization, lower levels of social interaction, a decreased sense of shared culture, and a greater dependence on technology rather than developing their own individual skills.

Consider the problems facing individuals working in a virtual workplace where there is a mix of new and experienced workers who are dependent on each other for the overall performance of the group. While some type of information that would be relevant to members of a co-located group is rendered irrelevant in a virtual setting, other types of information can be relevant to both co-located and virtual groups. For example, the local style and code of dress has little meaning to virtual group members since they are in different locations. However, these same individuals still need to understand and adhere to group deadlines, preferred task practices, and other group norms. In general, over time, experienced workers have developed an understanding of the needs, skills, practices, tools, processes, and informal structures that characterize the operational "equilibrium" of the team. When a new member is added, it disrupts the equilibrium of the group, until the new member is integrated into the team. The experienced members need to share their knowledge with the new member just as the newcomer has to learn what the expectations of the group are in order to perform effectively. Without access to co-located team members to help make sense of their work environment — including the task environment as well as the social environment — can technology adequately facilitate the socialization of newcomers into a virtual workplace? If so, what are the mechanisms that might make it easier for newcomers to become effective potential contributors? These are the questions we seek to address in this chapter.

THE VIRTUAL WORKPLACE AND SOCIALIZATION

A virtual group is a "group of people who collaborate closely even though they are separated by space, time, and organizational barriers"

(Lipnack & Stamps, 1997). Typically, these groups use information technology as the predominant communication means for achieving their common goal(s). Managers of virtual groups are able to configure team structures based on the best set of available skills regardless of the location of the individuals; likewise, virtual group members are able to handle their work activities without being physically present with the other members. Location has become irrelevant—or has it? One of the key challenges in the management of virtual groups is the adjustment and adaptation of group members to their new environment. Adjustment and adaptation are key because group activities, by definition, involve actions on the part of more than one person (Steiner, 1972). In a virtual environment, the exchange of facts, ideas and emotions is no longer tightly integrated with the social contact of others, but more likely conveyed through the sterile media of telecommunications.

Communication allows group members to work together. In its most basic form:

"Communication is the glue that holds the group structure together; it is the enzyme that allows the group process to function. Without communication, groups could not exist; without communication, people could not interact" (Applbaum, Bodaken, Sereno, & Anatol, 1974).

If communication is important to all groups, its importance is further magnified in virtual groups. In these settings, where those face-to-face interactions we have become so used to are limited, the communication technologies must become the primary context within which members convey information to one another (Poole & Hirokawa, 1996). This chapter explores the use of one such technology – e-mail – as the primary means for socializing new members into a virtual team.

Newcomer socialization in any group needs to occur within two broad contexts—task-oriented or technical (knowledge and skills required to perform effectively) and social (expectations and norms of the group members) (Comer, 1991; Morrison, 1995). Member schedules, task assignments, status reports, and technical "discussions" all represent task-oriented information that needs to be communicated explicitly and made available to all group members who need it. This can be accomplished relatively clearly through less rich (i.e. electronic) media because the task-oriented content is less ambiguous in nature (Daft & Lengel, 1984; Daft, Lengel, & Trevino, 1987). Most of us are used to reviewing this type of information—sales plans, product specifications, production schedules, service call reports, etc.—on the computers and typically have little trouble understanding the facts.

Social information, however, presents a different scenario. Since social information communicates expectations and attitudes in addition to tangible facts, it is more likely to be informal and tacit (and ambiguous) in nature (Morrison, 1993a). We rely on a wide variety of senses – sight, hearing, touch, taste, and smell—to interpret the social information. We walk into the office, see members of our group convened in the break room, smell the aroma of fresh coffee, and catch the sound of laughter. How should we respond? Join in, stand around to listen, make a beeline for our office or desk and begin work, ask the group what's going on? Most likely the action we take will depend on the previous experiences we've had in similar circumstances. If we're a long-standing member of the group, we know what to do because we've "been there, done that, and know what's expected". If we're a newcomer, we might not be so sure. Instead, we have to go by cues that are embedded in a specific setting. In this scenario we have the smell of coffee, the laughter of our team members, the break room setting, etc. So we can use all of our senses and decide how to respond. We might be wrong in our conclusion that the group is taking a coffee break when we decide to join, but it does seem logical. And, if we are wrong, we can always talk to someone later to understand what was going on so we don't make the same mistake again.

In a virtual setting, when electronic exchange (e-mail) is the medium of communication, the information is received only through the sense of sight (or hearing if the communication is read out loud). In such a limited forum, for information to be used in a way that effectively guides individual actions towards the common goal(s) of the group, it needs to be related to a context within the group so that a mutual interpretation and understanding can be achieved (Krauss & Fussell, 1991; Weick, 1995). This is a challenging task to accomplish. When we walk into our office no one else is there. Do we check with the others to see if it's coffee break time? Do we send an e-mail to everyone about the great weekend we just had? Or, do we just "get to work?" While co-located members can observe the behavior of others or seek information from their peers, virtual group members are limited to electronic exchange to gain their social knowledge—and it's difficult. If we have been with the group for a while, we also have the benefit of past experience to help guide us. Newcomers, however, are at a disadvantage because they have no common setting to observe and no common experience to draw upon. Here's another example to illustrate this point.

The expectation that IBM employees wear white shirts was never written anywhere, it was just expected. Employees learned about this expectation the day they walked into the office and saw that everyone had on a white shirt (*tacit communication*). They may or may not receive comments on their unique (non-white shirt) color coordination (*explicit communication*). Although this specific example no longer applies in today's environment, similar unwritten rules still exist and are a part of the identity of a group, which is related to its overall effectiveness. How long would we continue using our own dress code if there was no one else around to guide us? And how would we know if it really mattered? We might not learn about the problem until our first performance review, which is much too late. Since there is no one around to compare with, we don't even know enough to ask the right question. So, as virtual group structures become increasingly significant in organizations (Grenier & Metes, 1995), it is important to explore how *established* and *new* group members use electronic communication for socialization and task accomplishment.

SOCIALIZATION IN A VIRTUAL GROUP

One way to understand how electronic communication is used in virtual groups is to examine, in-depth, the experiences of an existing virtual group and then extrapolate their results to others. The "virtual group" chosen for this examination represented a collaborative effort between academia and industry. The consortium of universities and corporations involved individuals that did not share a single, physical space since its members were spread throughout the world and whose goal was to develop a general purpose artificial intelligence system. Since the common goal of the group was to design a system that could be used in a variety of settings, they were required to communicate and coordinate the task-related activities of its members.

We focused on the group's electronic exchange[1] since this provided a rich source of data on "who talks to whom" and "about what" in the virtual group and analyzed their e-mail messages from a three-month period. Particular insights that emerged from the study addressed the following questions: a) *How do newcomers use an electronic medium as a means of socialization into the group,* and b) *How do established members adapt the medium to help integrate the newcomers into the group?*

We looked at member status, information exchange (seeking versus providing), and information exchange content in this virtual group. Member status is simply whether the individual is a *new* member to the group or an *established* member of the group. Information exchange (seeking versus providing information) indicates whether the individual is using communication to *ask* for information or to *give* information that has been requested. Information exchange content reflects the type of information (procedures, norms, facts, issues, decisions, etc.) included in the individual's communication exchange. The information exchange content was categorized according to the organizational contexts of normative, regulative, or cognitive (Scott,

1995).

Normative context refers to activity focused on understanding what the group values and expects. This type of information concerns what it means to belong to the particular team and the expectations that go along with that sense of belonging. It is the means for finding out what behaviors are "normal" and those that are outside the range of "normal" for the team. *Regulative* context refers to activity focused on establishing or acting within specific organizational rules. Regulative information concerns the structure, procedures, or processes that currently exist or are being instituted within the group. This establishes a set of rules for the team and a framework for how activities are accomplished. Finally, *cognitive* context refers to activity focused on the construction of information meaning based on the social reality of the group and its members. It concerns the exchanges relating to resolution of group decisions, issues, and concerns. This is the most involved communication activity within a group because it involves the group's history in terms of its task-oriented and organizational issues and their resolution.

An examination of each of the above three factors—member status, information exchange, and information exchange content—and their relationship with one another will allow us to understand how virtual teams facilitate socialization of new members and help them learn about task accomplishment, rules, regulations, norms and expectations.

MEMBER STATUS, INFORMATION EXCHANGE, AND INFORMATION CONTENT IN VIRTUAL GROUPS

Member Status

When it comes to obtaining relevant information, should status of the person providing that information make any difference? Technically, a certain piece of information has the same value whether someone of lower status or higher status sends it. However, we all have experienced situations where one individual had more "influence" because of their position in the organization or group. In meetings, when the boss speaks, others are reluctant to disagree. When issues are discussed, senior members are listened to more than junior members. So, status does seem to matter. In fact, this observation has been born out by other studies. When examining the activities of health-care professionals, the content and network of communication among physicians, administrators, and nurses were significantly related to their occupational status (Saunders, Robey, & Vaverek, 1994). This was also confirmed in more general team populations where it was found that an individual's status within the group did in fact influence their interactions with other team members (Cohen & Zhou, 1991).

Newcomers to the group are faced with a need to adjust and adapt to a new and uncertain environment. In a situation where opportunities for face-to-face contact are scarce, one way to help reduce environmental uncertainty is to seek information from other members (Morrison, 1993b) concerning the norms, values, and expectations of the group (Comer, 1991; Mignerey, Rubin, & Gorden, 1995). Established members of the group then, who have the knowledge and experience necessary to perform the group's tasks, typically provide the information sought by newcomers (Morrison, 1993b). By acting as repositories of information required for the accomplishment of group goals, these established members act as keepers of organizational memory. Having been a part of the group for a period of time, they understand the rules, processes, and structures of the group (Tuckman, 1965). These established or "senior" members are able to provide task-oriented as well as social information to the newer members of the group. Thus, in general, newcomers are more likely to seek information and established members are more likely to provide information.

Our study reinforced the expectation that newcomers will engage in greater *information seeking* behavior than *information providing* behavior. In this specific group, they did so by almost a 2:1 margin. Out of the 86 newcomer e-mail messages, 55 of them were primarily involved with information seeking. Established members also met our expectation of engaging in greater *information providing* behavior than *information seeking* behavior and did so by more than a 2.5:1 margin. Out of their total of 587 e-mail messages, 424 focused on information providing.

While these observations may be intuitive to many, it points to a need for virtual group managers to provide explicit and accessible channels for newcomers to ask questions about situations of which they are uncertain. Formal mechanisms such as an on-line Frequently Asked Questions (FAQs) facility that addresses common newcomer issues and concerns can be extremely helpful.

The evidence shows that the role of the established team members in virtual groups is one of information provider. This indicates that the established members spent a significant amount of time responding to requests for information. While some information certainly represents unique situations, or simply those that are difficult to define, most of the routine information can be provided through somewhat formalized channels such as FAQs or bulletin boards. This will contribute to the efficiency of the group and allow senior members to focus on other group tasks and on socialization efforts that cannot be addressed through formal mechanisms. By providing more formal and structured mechanisms for newcomer socialization, the group's productivity can be improved by saving valuable time for these exchanges. Newcomers have an available resource to independently look for information that is common to the group, department, division, company, etc., without involving others.

Information Exchange Content – "What Is Being Said and Who Says It?"

At this point we can examine the content of the information exchanges as a way to better understand how normative, regulative, and cognitive information is exchanged in this virtual group.

First, let's look at normative information exchanges. As we have already established, senior members, who are already familiar with the group norms and expectations, should be the ones providing this information and its interpretations to newcomers. Newcomers can be expected to seek this information from the senior members.

Figure 1 shows how information seeking messages are distributed based on member status. Two interesting observations can be made concerning the use of information seeking behavior. One, a very small proportion of

Figure 1: Information Seeking Behavior by Member Status

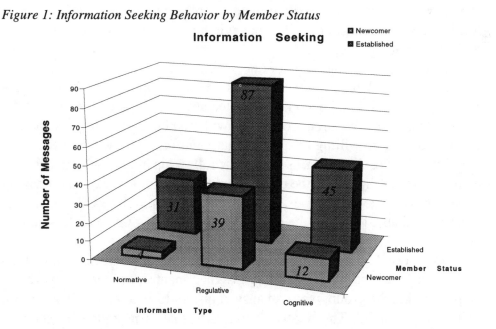

information seeking exchanges was related to normative inquiries (only 35 messages out of 218). And second, established members sought normative information significantly more than did newcomers (31 times out of 35). Both of these observations are contrary to our expectations. How can this be explained and what are the implications of this behavior?

The first observation, that few normative information exchanges occurred, might reasonably be explained as follows: *Normative* information seeking is more difficult to explore through public e-mail because it focuses on transferring tacit understanding between group members. Having to use a written communication form (e-mail), over a broadcasted medium (distribution list), and being identified to all in the list (e-mail address) may present an uncomfortable situation for many. Instead, the individual might use a more private medium (e.g., telephone) for these types of inquiries or use private e-mail with a peer. Normative information is also more ambiguous in nature and could require multiple exchange to reach a full understanding. Newcomers, who are trying to become a part of the team, will tend to avoid questions that might reflect poorly on them. They are usually more concerned about making a good impression and as such are unwilling to take risks by asking questions that may be perceived as unintelligent or unwise. As a new member, would you want to broadcast a message to the group asking, "What color shirt should I wear to work?" or "What time does the team take a coffee break?" where everyone could read and remember who asked? Probably not! You would more likely wait until you could get this information from a more private source – a friend, written material, observing others, etc. It's also likely that you would continue this behavior until you were comfortable with the others in the group.

This, then, may help explain our second observation—that established members engaged in normative information seeking more than the newcomers. Once an individual becomes accepted as an established member of the virtual group, they are not as concerned with making a good impression and are therefore more willing to seek normative information when needed.

Overall, the e-mail data, as well as the follow-up interviews, suggest that no matter who is involved, the use of a public, electronic medium for asking about norms, behaviors, values, and expectations is minimal. Other channels must be available for use if the group members are to gain an understanding of these important group characteristics.

One way to facilitate socialization regarding normative information then is to pair up each newcomer with an assigned mentor, or at least an official contact within the group, who can answer questions in a more private forum than group e-mail. The relative anonymity that is provided by such an arrangement should be beneficial also. Being able to seek information in a more private interaction minimizes the personal risk to newcomers' sense of dignity. Further, it should encourage newcomers to ask questions they may feel uncomfortable asking in a public forum, thus expediting the socialization process.

Again, this may be viewed as an intuitive result, but it is one that is often not acknowledged in virtual groups. Rather than take a reactive approach to socialization, it might be helpful to proactively pair newcomers with an experienced team member, even if they are not in the same location. By providing a direct link to another team member, the newcomers will have someone with whom they can build a relationship and from whom they can get advice and help while they are learning the information related to task accomplishment as well as cultural norms. Mentoring has long been used as a way to help individuals during their careers (Kram, 1983, 1985) and it's reasonable to extend this approach to helping newcomers in virtual teams.

So if virtual group members do not use e-mail for normative exchanges, do they use it for the regulative and cognitive information exchange? Let's first look at our group's use of the electronic media for regulative information. Since this is the type of data that helps all group members understand the structure, procedures, and processes that currently exist or are being instituted within the group, it's reasonable to expect all members – newcomers and established—to engage in regulative information exchange. However, there should be differences in their roles in this exchange. Established members, who already understand the rules of the group, may help transfer this knowledge to newcomers in the group. This type of information is especially important for new team members since the rules and regulations are strong guides for task accomplishment. As such, newcomers in virtual teams would be expected to seek a high amount of regulative information exchanges.

The data from this group supports our expectation in this regard. Regulative information exchanges represented the predominant type of communication among the group members. As the information seeking chart shows, this type of exchange represents the highest number of messages for newcomers and established members alike (39 out of 55 and 87 out of 163). Figure 2 shows how information providing messages are distributed based on member status.

Figure 2 shows that regulative exchanges represent the highest number of messages for newcomers and established members alike (14 out of 31 and 171 out of 424). This certainly supports the notion that individuals will use electronic media for less ambiguous types of information and will do so regardless of their status within the group. Information regarding regulations,

Figure 2: Information Providing Behavior by Member Status

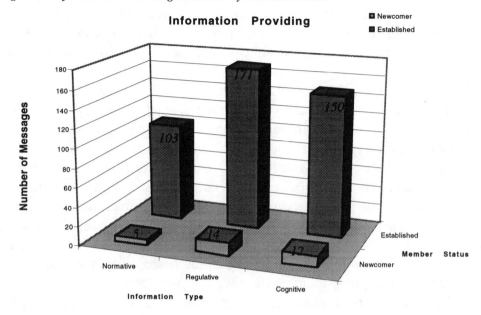

processes, specifications, structure, etc. tends to be factual in nature and can be easily written down, communicated, and interpreted by others. Newcomers are typically expected to ask about this type of information, and therefore, they are not reluctant to openly engage in exchanges regarding regulative information. Our expectations that established members are more likely to provide regulative information than seek it (171 versus 87 messages) were also met. The converse was true for newcomers–they sought more information than provided to the group (14 versus 39).

Cognitive exchanges relate to issues concerning discussion and resolution of task ambiguity. Because current information is interwoven and linked with past activities, interpretations made without this knowledge can be misleading (Langley, Mintzberg, Pitcher, Posada, & Saint-Macary, 1995). Newcomers were expected to participate in this type of exchange to a lesser extent than established members who possess the historical knowledge associated with the group. As expected, established team members participated in cognitive exchanges significantly more than newcomers. They were four times more likely to seek information (45 versus 12) and twelve times more likely to provide information (150 versus 12). This certainly suggests that newcomers do not involve themselves in this type of discussion.

CONCLUSIONS

This in-depth examination of a virtual group supported the notion that the process of socialization consists of newcomers seeking information and established members providing it to them, thus enabling a virtual group to transfer knowledge and information in an efficient manner.

Differences were found in communication patterns for established members versus newcomers in the group. Along with a preference for a particular type of exchange behavior, differences were found in the *content* of information exchanges depending on whether *information seeking* or *information providing* was being used. Newcomers were willing to use electronic communications for regulative information inquiries but not for normative information seeking. Established members showed high levels of regulative and cognitive exchanges but not as much for normative exchanges. If these results are typical of how most virtual teams behave, then the differences help provide a direction for future research – Are there different communication technologies that would improve the exchange of normative information? Was the quality of information exchanged adequate for both types of users, established and newcomer? While it's not possible to investigate these questions based on this study, there are some implications that can be inferred.

By taking advantage of the natural difference in information seeking and information providing behavior due to the team members' status, groups can provide an environment that supports the needs of their members and makes it easier to accomplish their work. The ability of group members to access information, and each other, provides the means for resolving uncertainty and ambiguity in the work environment (Russ-Eft, 1996). Without communication, coordinated group activity would be difficult to accomplish since each individual would be acting independently, unconcerned with the effect of their actions on others. Within the group, communication with other members is usually intended to guide actions that lead towards goal accomplishment. Some examples of this are: receiving the work product of another individual to review, interacting with others to resolve a technical project issue, or informing a team member that their behavior is outside the team norms.

Managers should realize that newcomers to a group might feel uncomfortable using electronic communication for exploring normative types of socialization information. Our study suggests that newcomers did not use electronic communication to acquire this type of information. This implies that alternative means should be considered to meet the socialization needs of the newcomer. Since much of the normative information traditionally flows from those who have "been there" to those who are new, one way to promote learning of this information might be to partner newcomers directly with an established member. This might provide a communication linkage that would be more comfortable for the newcomer and may ease their socialization process into the group. Another approach might be to create an on-line *water fountain* or *break room* where members could visit with each other during break times. Much like chat rooms on the Internet, this could provide a means for newcomers and established members to socially visit with each other.

The large amount of information exchange activity in this group suggests the importance of having a person focused on managing the flow of information through the group. For example, if newcomers don't know who the appropriate person is for obtaining a particular type of information, they may be able to contact a coordinator for help. A list of experts acting as resources in their respective fields may be very beneficial to newcomers. Thus, an internal coordinator and external liaison role may help improve the effectiveness of socialization process in virtual groups.

Many additional issues remain unaddressed with respect to newcomer socialization in virtual groups. First, is it a good use of time and effort on the part of established members to engage in newcomer socialization? Or, would it be better to leave the newcomers to their own devices for a short period of time during which the task-related expectations from them are minimal. During this "socialization period", the new members can simply "lurk" and observe the group interactions through electronic media. In all of these, there is no single right answer. When established members take time away from their activities to help a newcomer, their individual productivity might suffer in the short run. However, in the long run, they build an interpersonal relationship with the newcomer, which may lead to future collaborations. Further, this process certainly has benefits for the group as a whole –the newcomers gain a sense of belonging, and in time, become contributing members of the group. On the other hand, there may be other ways to approach socialization. For example, newcomers can be a great source of socialization support for each other. Given the time and resources to interact with each other they may become more comfortable asking each other rather than each of them individually going to senior members for answers. What works best will probably be a combination of senior member involvement and newcomer-specific support mechanisms.

Virtual groups tend to exhibit high member turnover. Can effective socialization reduce this turnover? It may very well be that individuals are more likely to leave or abandon the virtual team if they don't have a sense of belonging to the group. Group cohesion has been recognized as a contributor to group effectiveness (Vinokur-Kaplan, 1995) and to members remaining committed to the group (Seashore, 1954). Improving socialization may strengthen the individual's feeling of belonging and thus their willingness to stay with the group.

Finally, is socialization related to improved "organizational memory" and performance in virtual groups? We certainly think so! Socialized members are more likely to stay with the team, which means that they can become potential contributors to the group. Higher turnover will distract the virtual group away from its task-related activities and towards those related to recruiting and training. This is bound to diminish performance. Keeping new members is much like keeping customers in a retail store for a longer time – it's cheaper and more cost effective than getting new customers. Socialization helps strengthen the bond between the individual and the group.

At this point, virtual group research has just begun to scratch the surface. Much work needs to be done before researchers and managers learn to effectively manage the socialization process in virtual groups. Though there are many questions and hurdles, one fact remains: Virtual teams will continue to increase in prevalence throughout the organizational world. By investigating how to support these teams in all aspects with communication technology, we can help improve their performance and effectiveness.

REFERENCES

Applbaum, R. L., Bodaken, E. M., Sereno, K. K., & Anatol, K. W. E.(1974). *The Process of Group Communication,* Science Research Associates, Inc., Chicago, IL, .311

Cohen, B. P. & Zhou, X.(1991) "Status Processes in Enduring Work Groups," *American Sociological Review* (56:April), 179-188.

Comer, D. R.(1991). "Organizational Newcomers' Acquisition of Information from Peers," *Management Communication Quarterly*, 5(1), 64-89.

Daft, R. L. & Lengel, R. H. (1984). "Information Richness: A New Approach to Managerial Behavior and Organization Design,". in *Research in Organizational Behavior,* L. L. Cummings & B. Staw (Eds.), Vol. 6, JAI Press, Inc. Greenwich, CT, 191-233.

Daft, R. L., Lengel, R. H., & Trevino, L. K.(1987). "Message Equivocality, Media Selection, and Manager Performance: Implications for Information Systems," *MIS Quarterly*, 11(3), 355-366.

Grenier, R. & Metes, G.(1995). *Going Virtual: Moving Your Organization into the 21st Century,* Prentice Hall, Inc., Upper Saddle River, NJ, 320

Kram, K. E.(1983). "Phases of Mentor Relationships," *Academy of Management Journal*, 26, 608-625.

Kram, K. E.(1985). *Mentoring at Work: Developmental Relationships in Organization Life,* Scott, Foresman, Glenview, IL.

Krauss, R. M. & Fussell, S. R. (1991). "Mutual Knowledge and Communicative Effectiveness," in *Intellectual Teamwork: Social and Technological Foundations of Cooperative Work,* J. Galegher & R. E. Kraut & C. Egido (Eds.), Lawrence Erlbaum Associates. Hillsdale, NJ, 111-145.

Langley, A., Mintzberg, H., Pitcher, P., Posada, E., & Saint-Macary, J. (1995). "Opening up Decision Making: The view from the black stool," *Organization Science,* 6(3), 260-279.

Lipnack, J. & Stamps, J. (1997). *Virtual Teams: Reaching Across Space, Time and Organization with Technology,* John Wiley & Sons, Inc., 262.

Mignerey, J. T., Rubin, R. B., & Gorden, W. I.(1995). "Organizational Entry: An Investigation of Newcomer Communication Behavior and Uncertainty," *Communication Research,* 22(1), 54-85.

Morrison, E. W.(1993a). "Newcomer Information Seeking: Exploring Types, Modes, Sources, and Outcomes," *Academy of Management Journal,* 36(3), 557-589.

Morrison, E. W.(1993b). "Longitudinal Study of the effects of information seeking on newcomer socialization," *Journal of Applied Psychology,* 78(2), 173-183.

Morrison, E. W.(1995). "Information Usefulness and Acquisition During Organizational Encounter," *Management Communication Quarterly,* 9(2), 131-155.

Poole, M. S. & Hirokawa, R. Y. (1996). "Introduction: Communication and Group Decision Making," in *Communication and Group Decision Making,* Second ed., R. Y. Hirokawa & M. S. Poole (Eds.), Sage Publications, Inc. Thousand Oak, CA, 3-17.

Russ-Eft, D.(1996). "Hurrah for Teams or Teams-Schmeams: So, What is the Impact of Teams?," *Human Resource Development Quarterly,* 7(4), 305-312.

Saunders, C. S., Robey, D., & Vaverek, K. A. (1994). "The Persistence of Status Differentials in Computer Conferencing," *Human Communication Research,* 20(4), 443-472.

Scott, W. R. (1995). *Institutions and Organizations,* SAGE Publications, Inc., Thousand Oaks, CA, 178.

Seashore, S. E.(1954). *Group Cohesiveness in the Industrial Work Group,* University of Michigan, Ann Arbor, 107.

Steiner, I. D.(1972). *Group Process and Productivity,* Academic Press, New York, NY, 204.

Tuckman, B. W.(1965). "Developmental Sequence in Small Groups," *Psychological Bulletin*, 63(6), 384-399.

Vinokur-Kaplan, D.(1995). "Treatment Teams That Work (and Those That Don't): An Application of Hackman's Group Effectiveness Model to Interdisciplinary Teams in Psychiatric Hospitals," *Journal of Applied Behavioral Science*, 31(3), 303-327.

Weick, K. E.(1995). *Sensemaking in Organizations,* SAGE Publications, Inc., Thousand Oaks, CA, 231.

ENDNOTES

1   Electronic exchange, here, refers to e-mail exchange.

Chapter 4

How Are You Going to Keep Them in the Classroom After They've Seen MTV? Online Education in a Virtual World

Fred Niederman
Saint Louis University, USA

Bruce Rollier
University of Baltimore, USA

INTRODUCTION

Education is a vital activity in our society.   It involves many things, including (1) the transfer of knowledge from experienced to less experienced individuals; (2) the creation and storage of information for a wide range of individuals known and unknown to the creator of knowledge; (3) social engineering to create skills for people to play productive roles in the future; (4) opportunities to change one's major life activities and financial prospects; and (5) the prospect of the fun of discovery (and/or the sweat of drilled memorization).

An educated citizenry has always been essential for any society, but for much of history the necessary knowledge was largely acquired through experience and self study. The "book learning" provided by prestigious universities was primarily designed for the elites (and almost exclusively for males). Abraham Lincoln, a highly educated man and one of the greatest of U. S. presidents, was largely self-taught; he had less than a year of formal schooling (Donald, 1995).   A century ago, in even the most advanced industrial countries, most jobs required long hours, vigorous physical labor, and minimal formal education. In industrialized countries, the routine jobs in both agriculture and manufacturing have been mechanized, and workers in those occupations comprise a very small segment of the total work force. Service jobs predominate, some of which are routine and require little schooling, but the fastest growing and most lucrative categories are the so-called "knowledge workers".

Today, largely from the impact of technology, the nature of work is much different.   In the latest employment projections of the Bureau of Labor Statistics, the five fastest growing U.S. occupations between 1998 and 2008 are predicted to be computer engineers, computer support specialists, systems analysts, database administrators, and desktop publishing specialists. All of these, and most of the next fastest growing occupations, usually require at least a bachelor's degree for an entry level position, and increasingly a master's degree is preferred by employers.

Organizational success in the 21st Century will surely require an emphasis on lifelong learning.   Throughout the world there is an increasing mismatch between the level of education being attained by the majority of the population and the needs of employers. Most of the available jobs, especially the jobs that provide a living wage and prospects for advancement, require knowledge and skills that the majority of people have not attained. The degree of skill needed for low-level jobs is increasing, and high-skill employees require continuous retraining (Chute, Thompson, and Hancock, 1999). For all job openings projected to 2008, more than 30% will require some type of post-secondary training (Bureau of Labor Statistics, 2000).

This is a severe problem in the United States as well as most other industrialized countries.   The lack of education is even more critical for the developing countries of the world, that desperately need educated managers and workers to lead the countries out of poverty. In any country, rich or poor, education is increasingly a continuous process.   The pool of necessary knowledge is constantly growing, skills quickly become obsolete as technologies change and, in general, educational institutions have not adapted to this more complex environment. Increasingly, potential students may live in every part of the world, may be fluent in multiple languages, and may work at jobs that require them to travel frequently or to change their residence location frequently. They may wish to take classes at the workplace, as they travel, or at home.

Is it possible for technologies, particularly the Web and other distance-learning tools, to help alleviate this crisis? Can technology make education more attainable for those on the lower economic levels? If so, this might raise the standard of living for everyone, not just the poor, because their increased income would enable them to consume more goods and services and share more of the tax load. Can technology make education more available to those who cannot conveniently take classes at a fixed time and place? Can it meet the needs of busy professionals for frequent upgrading of their skills? Is teaching online and at a distance as effective as classroom teaching? Can all students learn through this medium, and if not what type of student can most benefit? Will it meet the needs of the MTV generation, who have become accustomed to acquiring most of their knowledge from a television set? What are the most promising technologies that will improve the effectiveness of distance learning? We will explore these topics in this chapter, commencing with some thoughts about the impact of technology in the learning process.

THE PROMISE OF APPLYING TECHNOLOGY TO EDUCATION

The number of universities catering to a single gender of students has shrunk markedly in recent decades to the point where choices for such a program are now rather limited. Will technology do the same thing to traditional programs? Most of the new buildings, at least for business schools, boast the most advanced possible educational technologies, often in every classroom. Students at some time in the future may not be able to find schools that present materials exclusively with chalk and blackboards. Some schools have begun requiring that all students have personal computers. This provides at least three benefits: First, students can organize and maintain a permanent record of their work, notes, musings, and acquired materials that can provide them their own personal 'knowledge-base'. Second, students have an opportunity to learn and use technologies that are likely to be useful in their careers. Third, a common technology platform allows students to more freely interchange information with peers and instructors.

Why would we imagine that technologies could be applied to enhance educational opportunities? Technologies represent opportunities to address the limits of other teaching approaches. Traditional classroom teaching has inherent limits in the numbers of students who can be simultaneously served and for potential students who cannot conveniently attend at a fixed time and place. Moreover, presentations are not inventoried—they are presented once and disappear. Pre-computing technologies, such as television and radio broadcasting, address these issues by their availabilities to large numbers of people and to being stored for rebroadcast (witness the success of *Sesame Street*). However, these early versions provided almost no interactivity. Students could not communicate with instructors to ask questions or to make comments. They could not communicate with other students nor engage in group activities or experiential exercises.

Modern telecommunications, computers, and innovative software can greatly enhance the educational capabilities of the broadcasting technologies. Separately, each technology has great limitations, but in combination and with creative design they can provide a rich learning experience and can make education available to a much wider population. Courses on the Web can be offered asynchronously, enabling people in remote areas or with busy schedules to take them from any location and at convenient times. Professionals can upgrade their skills or learn new ones without committing to a formal program in fixed classrooms. However, it has not yet been demonstrated, for the currently available technologies, that they can be effectively used under all conditions for all students. Much of the rest of this chapter will be devoted to examining the conditions and students for whom application of new technology to education will be most helpful. In a larger sense, though, the most basic impact will be to give learners more options and increase the range of alternatives available to them. Through discerning use of these technologies, the overall set of educational opportunities available to learners, educators, and parents should only improve.

POTENTIALS AND PREDICTIONS FOR ONLINE EDUCATION

It seems likely that, over time, face-to-face presence will become much less important for education, as it has in many other areas. Twenty years ago it was virtually impossible to hold an effective meeting unless the participants were in the same physical location. With today's sophisticated videoconferencing technology, the participants might be at widely separated locations, executive time and travel expense is saved, and meetings can be scheduled more spontaneously. Ten years ago, an office was in a specific physical location, but today's executives, sales representatives and maintenance engineers have "virtual offices" that enable them to spend much more time with customers while still keeping in touch with administrators. In education, the advantages of face-to-face contact are primarily due to the intimacy of a classroom environment. An experienced instructor can see the nodding heads when students suddenly grasp a difficult concept and the dazed looks when they do not. The instructor can see the fidgeting and the quick glances at watches when it is time for a break and can more spontaneously and effectively illustrate a concept on the board or conduct an impromptu exercise. Students and instructors can more quickly become comfortable with each other and soon know each other by sight and by voice.

This degree of awareness and intimacy is not yet possible with current online learning technologies. In teaching courses on the World Wide Web, the instructor and the students are neither visible nor audible to each other, and the students cannot see or hear each other. Asynchrony is often seen as an advantage for this medium because the students and instructor can perform their tasks at different times, but interaction is very severely limited. Some interaction can be provided with chat rooms, but these are often more chaotic than they are instructive. Almost all communication is through the keyboard, and students (or instructors) who lack good touch typing skills may be at a disadvantage.

The video broadcast technologies can more closely simulate a face-to-face environment. Students can see the instructor; instructors can communicate by voice rather than through a keyboard; and students can hear each other. The asynchrony capability is lost, however. Often the audio is of poor quality, and in some implementations the communications are one-way only, requiring the instructor to open a switch for a particular remote classroom to speak, which cuts off the instructor audio. Students cannot spontaneously speak out and be heard by the instructor or the other sites. There is no way for the instructor to determine that the students are paying attention to the lecture unless they are called on by name and their microphones activated. On the other hand, if the system is designed with two-way voice capability, the result may be chaotic because everyone may try to speak at once. In most such systems, the instructor controls what the student can see on the video screen, and this is usually limited to one image at a time. They can see the instructor, or they can see what the instructor is demonstrating, but not both at the same time. Typically the audio is two-way, with land-based transmission, but with one-way video transmitted by satellite.

It would be extremely expensive to have satellite uplink facilities at several sites, which would be necessary for video transmission of the student images, but the uplink from the instructor studio can be broadcast to all sites within the satellite's range. In such implementations the instructor cannot see the students and can get to know them only through their voices. Another disadvantage is that there is an 8-second delay in the video transmission so that the audio is not synchronized with the image seen on the screen, which can be confusing and disorienting for the viewers. The number of receiving sites is limited because the downlink equipment is also expensive, and a large number of sites would be very difficult for an instructor to control. Therefore these technologies are not flexible enough for students to take courses from their homes; it is necessary for them to travel to the nearest receiving site.

The technologies are improving rapidly, however, and costs are decreasing. Moore's Law, which has been valid for 40 years, predicts that the power of computer chips will double every 18 months (Zelnick, 1999). Bandwidths are increasing, also very rapidly, bringing transmission costs down. Fiber optics and other digital media allow for graphics, sound, and text to be transmitted together rather than through separate cables. The result will be to merge the best capabilities of both the Internet technologies and the video broadcast technologies. Within a few years we should see courses that will be accessed through the Web that will have multiple images on the screen so that the instructor will be able to see the students in real time and interact with them in real time.

WHAT FORMS OF DISTANCE LEARNING ARE THERE?

The first education involving students who were geographically separated from the instructor was correspondence courses, conducted through the mail. One example of this was the International Correspondence Schools (ICS), which provided home study courses. Non-technical correspondence courses have been available for self-paced learning since early in the last century (Schreiber and Berge, 1998). Courses delivered for credit via radio were conducted by universities as long ago as 1925. When television became widely available, instructional television was offered by such universities as Iowa State and Stanford, and by the Public Broadcasting Service (PBS). In the 1980s, the term "distance education" began to be applied to the transmission of courses by satellite. "Satellite communications, originally launched in the mid-1960s, matured and became readily available in the 1980s to those organizations that could afford them. Corporations, including Xerox, Hewlett-Packard, and the National Technological University, used commercial and proprietary satellite networks to successfully broadcast seminars and training courses globally" (Schreiber and Berge, 1998, pp. 6-7).

With the rapid spread of the Internet in the 1990s, many instructors started using the World Wide Web in their courses: for attachment of course materials such as readings and assignments, for Web board discussions of cases or assignments with the instructor or with each other, and for chat rooms to hold interactive discussions. It was soon discovered that the Web provided a sufficiently robust environment so that, at least for some courses, part of the class could be conducted on the Web, with students communicating through e-mail or Web boards. Before long, many universities and university consortia, such as Western Governors University (Johnstone and Tilson, 1997), were offering entire programs on the Web. Several universities (e.g., NYU, Duke) have spun off private corporations to offer such courses commercially. Courses and other educational services are increasingly being offered across national borders, offering the possibility, for example, of studying French in Chicago or Buenos Aires from an instructor based in Paris (Downes, 2000).

Delivering courses via the Web offers some advantages, particularly for students who are working at times when preferred courses are offered, are required to travel frequently, or are living in locations without easy access to their preferred educational programs. The courses are generally designed to be asynchronous so are ideal for students who desire "different time, different place" instruction. However, at the present time there are some major disadvantages: The level of interaction is typically very low, especially between students. It can be very difficult to evaluate a student's performance or even to ensure that the person performing the assignments is the same one who enrolled in the class. Development of innovative materials and assignments and the need for high volumes of communication with students can make the workload for a conscientious instructor much higher than for a classroom course. The older broadcast technologies, with special studios from which video images can be broadcast and students can participate in real time, are still very important also. We believe, as noted above, that the two technologies will merge. As transmission costs come down rapidly, special studios will no longer be required and both video and sound can be transmitted to the desktop via the Internet. The new environment, which will provide both synchronous and asynchronous capabilities, will greatly improve the interaction possible in Web-conducted courses, while retaining the ability to communicate at different times.

HOW WELL DO STUDENTS LEARN WITH THESE TECHNOLOGIES?

Information technology can affect a learning program in at least two ways. It can deliver some routine activities more efficiently and it can facilitate engaging, participatory activities for students.

Routine activities include presentation of well-known structured information. This is generally done through reading and lecture. Reading materials can easily be delivered online. Where materials are already in electronic format, they can be stored on a Web-server for student retrieval through Web browsers (or analogous methods for proprietary networks) or sent by e-mail or attachment to e-mail to one or more students. Students can read such materials on-screen or may, with relative ease, print these materials for reading at the time and location of their choice. Many Web pages and much Web-based information suffer from the trend to short single-page bursts (e.g. they may break up ideas into small chunks without necessarily showing the appropriate level of complexity or interconnection with related ideas). In a dedicated learner program this problem can be easily overcome by presenting the whole work and letting the student choose how best to approach the reading of it. While this raises issues and opportunities for textbook writers, publishers, and distributors, from the perspective of the learner this should not be problematic.

Lecture material presents some other issues and opportunities. Some teachers have the gift of developing wonderfully stimulating presentations that they may deliver nearly verbatim time and again. Fairly straightforward media technologies such as audio and videotaping can record those presentations, freeing faculty for other tasks. Rarely are such videotapes considered more than a poor substitute for an actual course. Such tapes tend to be slow in pace and unable to generate interest or enthusiasm among students. Radio and television shows such as PBS geography programs provide wonderful learning opportunities. However, it is rare that these tackle subjects with sufficient method and detail to be considered the equivalent to a course. The value of the "course" is that it aims to cover all significant aspects of a topic area in an organized manner so that the learner is left with a coherent organizing framework that includes both facts and the relationships among them.

While there are some issues with reading and lecture, it is not hard to imagine online courses providing reasonable substitutions for or delivery of these traditional routine activities. How does online education fare in terms of addressing nonroutine education?

One of many examples of the use of the Internet for nonroutine education is the Jason project (Soloway et al., 2000). Founded by Robert Ballard, who discovered the wreckage of the Titanic, Jason allows children to conduct scientific "expeditions" in the classroom. "Using live-feeds, video cameras, and telecommunications technologies, students can see and talk with deep-sea divers, archaeologists, and others. There are currently 750,000 children, up from 300,000 two years ago, utilizing Jason" (p. 22). (See this project for yourself at www.thejasonproject.org). The authors have seen no evidence that projects such as this one will not continue to flourish, grow in number, and gradually be assimilated into more extensive overall educational programs.

However, engaging as it is, this program is not a traditional educational experience that will necessarily result in overall understanding of basic geography. For the more adventurous, it is not programs like the Jason Project that need to change, but our understanding of the goals of education. A provocative paper on distance learning suggests that we can, indeed must, reengineer the learning process. Mundviwalla and Hovav (1996) propose applying the approach of business process reengineering to the design of learning programs. Additionally, they identify three key processes: questioning, discussion, and document processing, though arguably there are more. Experimenting, experiencing, abstracting, as well as receiving and interpreting feedback come to mind. But the idea of considering learning as a 'business' process is a fascinating one. What are the elemental steps? Do they occur in a particular order? Are there fewer than millions of permutations, variations, and contingencies?

In addition to routine and more customized educational approaches, we must also consider a number of additional concerns with online education from the learner's perspective. These include: (1) Is it possible for technology to make education "too easy"? (2) How will learners deal with "information overload" and verifying the quality of information? (3) Will learners be able to transfer knowledge from one domain to another? and (4) Is online education effective for all types of learners?

Is it possible for education to be too easy? Online education may allow for the creation of what appears to be an equivalent educational result (e.g. a term paper) with significantly less effort. To the extent that this consists of less busy work (e.g., manually searching for articles in stacks, driving to distant libraries to find an article, or hand copying quotations or citations) this would be a valuable efficiency gain. But if it means being able to cut and paste ideas and text without necessarily understanding the contents and implications of each, the task may have become "too easy".

Is there inherent value in putting forth effort? We have observed that on occasions when a goal takes extraordinary effort, the achievement of that goal seems more fulfilling than when it was easy. Doesn't this create an incentive to make goal achievement more difficult rather than less? On the other hand, if achieving the goal becomes easier, should the saved time be used for achievement of additional goals? We must be careful that technologies do not allow the creation of results that resemble learning to become so easy that the "learning muscles" are not developed sufficiently for the learner to take on substantial challenges.

Australian researchers S. Nielsen, L.A. von Hellens, A. Greenhill, and R. Pringle (1998) have observed three main motivators for students entering the information systems profession. These are: escapism and leisure, secure employment and status, and flexible work arrangements. Apparently some students feel they can continue to enjoy computers as they have as consumers without recognizing the implied changes in responsibility when shifting to a provider. Playing computer games and surfing the Web, while both fun and educational in their own ways, are actually quite limited in the lessons offered. Students, for example, often don't realize that underneath the Web pages of a commercial site like Schwab or Amazon are extraordinarily complex database management systems and elaborate data processing mechanisms. They often don't realize that software that allows for the quick placement of icons, menus, and pop-up windows on a screen really provides the "easy" part of helpful user-oriented computer interfaces. Demonstrating this to students and showing how they can move beyond these limits is, of course, the "fun" part of teaching systems analysis and design.

One of the challenges for using the Internet as a free-form educational device (learning through net surfing) is the amount and variety of information that can be presented. The sheer volume of information already posted to the Web is staggering and frequently leads to information overload. It can be discouraging when search engine requests generate tens of thousands of possibilities, and one may be tempted to give up the search rather than attempting to refine it. Of course one criterion for screening Internet information is the quality with which the material was presented. In using literature from libraries there is the presumption that some authority has screened at least the most egregious materials from publication. This is probably a great weakness as well as a great strength. There is the risk of excluding the genuinely correct as well as the risk of including the egregiously false.

What is the impact of technology on the transfer of knowledge from one domain to another? It is a common complaint that what students learn in writing classes is often not applied on marketing or human resource management term papers. Clearly, in the computer-based information environment, data from one file can be cut and pasted into another file easily enough. In systems development we call this developing a library of reusable objects. The tricky parts are (1) the object had better be perfect or its flaws will simply be spread around; (2) the writer needs to know which items from the other file are relevant; (3) the writer needs to know how to find these items in a manner that is less costly (perhaps in time rather than dollars) than simply starting in again; and (4) the writer needs to be able to tailor the integration of the object into the new context, if needed. It is generally true that it is easier to edit than to create. Perhaps information technology can shift the burden of creating reports from generation of new material to editing of pieces. But at what point will the repackaging of existing ideas become exhausted and require the generation of new ones? Would a fully online educational program compared to traditional modes have any impact on the tendencies of learners to be able to generate novel approaches as well as to recombine bits and pieces from cyberspace?

One final issue regarding full online learning pertains to the range of students for whom it will work. In surveying human resource managers regarding the training methods they use for teaching skills on new software, one frequently mentioned critical success factor for all education on an individual or asynchronous basis was the motivation and persistence of the learner. Where the learner is not self-motivated, the value presented by tutorials, correspondence courses, and online learning appears to be quite dependent on existing learning skills. Consider the possibility that this is a robust finding supported by future more extensive research. If it becomes too expensive to pay for both a traditional and an electronically mediated, information technology-enabled educational system, can we afford to have one that works well only for a subset of learners?

COSTS OF ONLINE LEARNING PROGRAMS

Just because a phenomenon can be achieved doesn't guarantee that it will be achieved. Providing rich levels of information and human interaction is an expensive proposition (Young, 2000c). Some university administrators appear to be emphasizing online learning programs because of their belief that the offerings will be less expensive. We believe that a high quality online learning experience may cost even more than face-to-face classroom courses. This position is reinforced by a seminar convened to investigate this issue by the University of Illinois. Their study concluded, "Because high quality online teaching is time and labor intensive, it is not likely to be the income source envisioned by some administrators. Teaching the same number of students online at the same level of quality as in the classroom requires more time and money" (University of Illinois, 1999, p 2).

What are the costs of providing a high quality program? Again, if we consider the two parts as assembling world-class information and providing interaction, there are three types of costs. The first involves quality text, graphics, sound, and visual materials. How much does it cost Disney to produce a 2-hour animation? Why would it cost any less to produce Disney-quality multimedia for education? The second involves staffing. Clearly the productivity and quality of existing faculty is mixed. The third type of cost is technical infrastructure. In addition to providing the mechanisms for creating content (e.g., sound studios) there are also servers, data storage, security and backup, and mechanisms for updating myriad Web sites.

Students have accumulated the effects of many years of exposure to broadcast media. This exposure affects the way the learner sees the world. For example, the professional quality of information delivery through these media changes the expectations and evaluation regarding educational materials. All but the most charismatic lecturers will appear wooden and one-dimensional in contrast to the fast tempo and exciting presentations that can be manufactured with thoughtful expenditure of large budgets on materials designed for reuse across many settings and learners. The line between education and entertainment, though not erased, becomes fuzzier. Education without an entertainment component becomes excruciating. However, the entertainment component is not free. It costs some overhead as a percentage of the total message. It also involves significant additional costs of producing educational materials for all but the especially gifted educators whose internal stimulation burns through even their most off-the-cuff remarks.

The limits, as in the world of business data processing, will not be hardware and software packages, but rather content. By the time Microsoft (or equivalent) spends large amounts on a Tom Cruise-level production regarding ways to integrate spreadsheet techniques into the decision-making environment, there is an upgraded spreadsheet with another score of new features and significant interface changes. The half-life of knowledge at any significant level of detail will strongly affect the payoff timeframe for high quality educational materials.

The need to present material in a highly entertaining, as well as factually correct manner, will very much affect the role of the faculty member and the skills needed to teach. In order to take full advantage of online education, a different set of skills will be required of faculty. Assuming that some percentage of time will still be devoted to traditional activities such as lecture and Socratic examination of student observation and inference, the range of skills will require broadening. These skills will have to include facility with the technology itself, ability to scan for new technology opportunities, ability to prepare material down numerous branching alternatives, ability to integrate material and react to ad hoc additions by students, and, not least, to manage the classroom in a less hierarchical environment.

For institutions that wish to provide superior online learning and are willing to devote sufficient resources to ensure high quality, it can be done.

One effective approach is to have some online components but also to require students to spend some time in face-to-face contact. An example of how this might work is the Global Executive MBA (GEMBA) program at Duke University. This is an exemplary program filled with world-class instruction, intensive face-to-face interactions, worldwide student internships or continuing management activity, and apparently excellent results. It is not, however, inexpensive, and tuitions are quite high. Distance learning might also be used to provide lower quality education at lower cost. This might be significantly helpful where students are located in low-density areas that make it impossible to attend urban classrooms or where states providing education face ever-increasing costs and increasing levels of demand from potential students. Then again, lower costs are concrete and levels of quality are difficult to measure. Another potential advantage is in alleviation of crowded conditions on some campuses; Carnevale (2000a) reports that to cope with increasing enrollments at the already-crowded California State campuses the schools are being urged to add distance education programs.

THE FUTURE OF THE VIRTUAL UNIVERSITY

At the time of this writing in May, 2000, there are already entirely virtual universities operating without buildings or walls and with classes conducted entirely in cyberspace. Dunn (2000) reports that there are 11 distance-education mega-universities in various parts of the world; the largest is in China, the China Central Radio and Television University, with more than 3 million students. Will traditional universities disappear? Probably not, although it will not be surprising if traditional universities increasingly contain higher numbers of electronically adapted classrooms and use increasing amounts of technology-supported materials. In this section, we explore some of the possible scenarios for the future development of online learning capabilities.

The University of Maryland University College (UMUC) was founded more than 50 years ago to serve adult, part-time students throughout the world. It was originally established after World War II to provide classes for military personnel stationed in various areas of the world. It operates classroom sites in Maryland and at over 100 overseas locations. UMUC has long pioneered in development of classes conducted at a distance, including correspondence courses, interactive classes broadcast by satellite, and courses on the Web. As of Spring, 2000, they have more than 20 complete degree programs offered online, and their Web site claims that "UMUC students around the world can complete their degree without having to set foot in a classroom." (University College, 2000). In an article in the *Baltimore Sun*

(Hill, 2000), the President of UMUC, Gerald Heeger, is quoted as saying that "I think there will only be four or five universities in the world that will become world-class virtual universities. Our goal is to make sure UMUC is one of them." (p. 6A). In the same article, Gary Smith, director of Pennsylvania State University's World Campus, agrees: "Ultimately, only a few institutions will have a significant impact using the Web to serve students beyond their own campuses. That's because only a few institutions are prepared to do all the things you need to do to support students beyond their campuses."

Will such predictions come true? Certainly there are doubters. Carol Twigg of Rensselaer Polytechnic Institute says: "When you think of all the colleges and universities there are in the world today — about 3,600 in the United States alone — the notion that there will be only three or four survivors is ludicrous. That's like saying everybody will go to Yale or Harvard. There's tremendous diversity in the market. What the Internet and technology allow is an explosion of universities." (Hill, 2000, p. 6A). Our crystal ball is a bit out of focus, but we suspect that there is some truth in both of these extreme positions. We would agree with Twigg that there are likely to be many more than a few universities with large and thriving Web programs. However, there is also merit in the argument that the majority of these will be focused on niche markets. The all-encompassing, global, truly comprehensive virtual universities are likely to be quite large and rich enough to devote major resources to marketing, course development, faculty training, and student support.

Market share is much more important on the Web than in traditional businesses. Since location is no longer a factor, proximity to customers is not an advantage, particularly in a service business such as education that does not require warehouses. Successful e-commerce ventures seem to result in oligopolies: e.g., Amazon and Barnes & Noble, E-bay and Amazon. A large firm has a major marketing advantage because it can spend more on advertising than its competitors but at a lower percentage of revenue. The largest virtual universities of the future will offer programs in almost every discipline, at every level, and will compete for students at every level, in every locality, perhaps even in every language. We suspect they will be more like today's Ohio State or Penn State than like Harvard or Yale, and not all of them will be headquartered in the United States. Just as many global corporations have, these schools will gradually lose their identification with a particular country.

The elite schools, as well as most others, will adopt a niche strategy (as most universities have always done). They will compete in those markets for which they perceive a competitive advantage, or markets thought to be underserved. Some of the characteristics of virtual universities of the future may include the following:

- They will utilize a combination of technologies, both asynchronous and synchronous.
- Wireless will also be a major communications technology, offering the opportunity not only to do assignments at home, but also to do them at the beach, or sitting on a park bench. Initially, the mouse and the keyboard will predominate as input devices, but the use of voice for both input and output will increase rapidly. Students will have access to interactive video which will allow them to see and hear the instructor and each other.
- Much greater interaction will be possible than with today's technologies. When Internet2 arrives, digital video will be available, bringing such possibilities as large-scale indexed video archives of television broadcasts and digital-videoconferencing (Olsen, 2000).
- Such technologies as virtual reality and realistic simulations will be available (Ives and Jarvenpaa, 1996).
- Markets will be much more competitive, so the perception of quality from prospective students and from prospective employers of those students is vital. In the long run, such perceptions must be based on real quality and on continuous improvement. Researchers in a study sponsored by the National Education Association have compiled a list of 24 benchmarks that may be used in distance education programs to ensure high quality (Carnevale, 2000b).
- More emphasis on the reuse of content, rather than using the content once for a particular lecture and then discarding it.
- It will be no surprise to see coalitions of universities across continents offering integrated programs, and not just on international or global themes. Just as many global corporations have, some of these schools will gradually lose their identification with a particular country. Not all of them will be headquartered in the United States.
- Students will demand the ability to transfer credits easily from one institution to another. This will force the institutions to move toward increased standardization of programs and of individual courses.

As Tsichritzis (1999) points out, professors can deliver lectures to more than one university at the same time with little additional overhead. Universities can also "import content from specialists or distinguished scientists without having to pay them a salary, or give them a permanent position." (p. 95). Universities will become increasingly like brokers, providing facilities for buyers and sellers of educational services to meet virtually.

Mergers, joint ventures, and strategic alliances will be increasingly common (Makri, 1999). Already, a growing number of states are centralizing services for distance education, claiming that such collaborations save money and provide more choices for students (Young, 2000b). Collaborations between universities in different countries can provide obvious benefits to both. Such alliances will lead to an emphasis on standardization of course definitions, syllabi, and perhaps even grading policies and examinations. Some 28 "virtual universities" recently signed an agreement pledging to encourage student transfers and other types of collaboration, with the goal of eventually making it possible for students to transfer credits easily between the institutions (Young, 2000a).

CONCLUSIONS

As information technologies continue to provide changes to the wide range of environments, methods, and strategies for education, the landscape begins to look more like a patchwork than a coherent whole. At some point the accumulation of change will lead to the realization that the domain has transitioned into a genuinely new one. In that new learning-teaching environment, several extremely basic notions will be called into question and will require new thinking. The learning community will need to conceptualize at least three things: What is learning? What differentiates more valuable from less valuable learning? How do we know (and certify) that learning has taken place? In the age of spell checkers, how important is accurate spelling? In the age of calculators is there any reason to calculate square roots by hand? In the age of online atlases, is there any need to know what continent Cameroon is located on? If we move significantly to the behavioral, skill-oriented side — learning is the ability to do increasingly complex things, in less time, with more accuracy — do we need to measure or certify that? Do we have to account for ability to problem solve or the performance of problem solving (with motivation a key differentiator of those who excel at the former and fall down on the latter)?

With society moving into a knowledge age, whether we like it or not, the question of what knowledge should be proprietary and what should be public may become increasingly salient. This question will confront organizations that need to distribute knowledge to build a pool of people competent to enter their domain for task performance while retaining other knowledge to distinguish their ability to provide goods and services from those of other organizations. Individuals will need to grapple with retaining their own insights, inferences, and procedures in contrast to providing those to organizations, colleagues, and competitors at the risk of diminishing their advantage or employability.

In all, if the rate of change of computer processors continues to follow Moore's Law and network value continues to follow Metcalfe's Law, we have seen only the tip of the iceberg of technological capabilities. We will see the continual accumulation of pedagogical methods and materials and we will eventually be living in a decisively new educational paradigm about which we can speculate, but by which we will probably be quite surprised.

REFERENCES

Bureau of Labor Statistics: http://www.bls.gov/news.release/ecopro.t06.htm. (2000)

Carnevale, D. "Crowded Cal. State U Campuses Are Asked to Add Distance-Education Programs", *Chronicle of Higher Education* (XLVI:30), March 31, 2000a, p. A48.

Carnevale, D. "A Study Produces a List of 24 Benchmarks for Quality Distance Education", Chronicle of Higher Education (XLVI:30), April 7, 2000b, p. A45.

Chute, A. G., Thompson, M. M., and Hancock, B. W. *The McGraw-Hill Handbook of Distance Learning.* McGraw-Hill, New York, 1999.

Donald, D. H. *Lincoln.* Simon & Schuster, New York, 1995.

Downes, S. "The Internet and Transnational Education", *Chronicle of Higher Education Online*, May 3, 2000.

Dunn, S. L. "The Virtualizing of Education", *The Futurist*, (34:2), Spring 2000, pp. 34-38.

Hill, M. "State's University College Plans Future as 'Virtual U'", *Baltimore Sun*, May 1, 2000, pp. 1A and 6A.

Ives, B., and Jarvenpaa, S. "Will the Internet Revolutionize Business Education and Research?", *Sloan Management Review*, (37:3), Spring 1996, pp. 33-47.

Johnstone, S. M., and Tilson, S. "Implications of a Virtual University for Community Colleges", in *Building a Working Policy for Distance Education*, C. L. Dillon and R. Cintron (eds.), Jossey-Bass Publishers, San Francisco, 1997.

Makri, M. "Exploring the Dynamics of Learning Alliances", *The Academy of Management Executive*, (13:3), 1999, pp. 113-114.

Mandviwalla, M. and Hovav, A. \'93Redesigning the Questioning, Discussion and Document Processes,\'94 Proceedings of the Special Interest Group on Computer Personnel Research, M. Igbaria (Ed.), Denver, Colorado, 1996, pp. 326-337.

Nielsen, S.H., von Hellens, L.A., Greenhill, A., and Pringle, R. "Conceptualizing the Influence of Culture and Gender Factors on Students' Perceptions of IT Studies and Careers." In *Proceedings of SIGCPR*, R. Aggarwal (Ed.), Boston, MA, 1998, pp. 86-95.

Olsen, F. "Internet2 Effort Aims to Build Digital-Video Network for Higher Education*", Chronicle of Higher Education*, (XLVI:33), April 21, 2000, p. A49.

Schreiber, D. A., and Berge, Z. L. *Distance Training: How Innovative Organizations are Using Technology to Maximize Learning and Meet Business Objectives*. Jossey-Bass Publishers, San Francisco, 1998.

Soloway, E., Norris, C., Blumenfeld, P., Fishman, B., Krajcik, J., and Marx, R. "K-12 and the Internet", *Communications of the ACM*, (43:1), January 2000, pp. 19-23.

Tsichritzis, D. "Reengineering the University", *Communications of the ACM*, (42:6), June 1999, pp. 93-100.

University of Illinois, "Teaching at an Internet Distance: the Pedagogy of Online Teaching and Learning" *The Report Of a 1998-1999 Faculty Seminar*, December 7, 1999.

University College (2000). URL: virtuniv.html" www.umuc.edu/gen/virtuniv.html.

Young, J.R. "Virtual Universities Pledge to Ease Transfer and Encourage Other Kinds of Collaboration", *Chronicle of Higher Education*, (XLVI:35), May 5, 2000a, p. A49.

Young, J. R. "Citing Benefits, 2 More States Plan Virtual Universities", *Chronicle of Higher Education Online*, May 3, 2000b.

Young, J.R. "Faculty Report at U. of Illinois Casts Skeptical Eye on Distance Education," *Chronicle of Higher Education*, January 14, 2000c.

Zelnick, N. "Optimizing Networks", *Internet World*, December 1, 1999.

Chapter 5

Meeting Current Challenges for Virtually Collocated Teams: Participation, Culture, and Integration

Gloria Mark
University of California - Irvine, USA

INTRODUCTION[1]

The term 'virtual team' is becoming increasingly more visible in the news media, due to recent trends of corporate mergers, global markets, and interdisciplinary teamwork. A number of different technologies are currently being tried out in the workplace to support both real-time and asynchronous communication and interaction. These technologies include more well-known support such as e-mail and audio-conferencing, as well as newer technologies such as desktop conferencing, media spaces, and chat.

The goal of this chapter is to describe certain challenges for teams who engage in virtually collocated work. Numerous challenges face these teams who are expected to perform as physically collocated teams: to provide deliverables, meet project schedules, and to generate feasible and even innovative problem solutions. And yet all this must be done at a distance. Team members stem from different departments, organizations, countries, and sometimes even competitor companies. Sometimes teams meet face-to-face on a regular basis, sometimes rarely, often not at all. How can team members be expected to be motivated to attend meetings, to develop trust, or even to adopt the technology when social pressures from a distance are weak?

Even management and technical support for these teams at the local level may also be weak; managers may consider such teams to be a part-time activity, and local sites may lack gurus, champions, or even compatible hardware.

In this chapter, I distinguish the topic of virtually collocated teams from a general discussion of the problems involved in distributed work. The key word of my argument is *teams,* and I will focus on how the development and sustainability of social processes in the group are affected by the use of technology. The challenges that these teams face are directly tied to the limitations that the technology imposes on the communication of relevant social information, believed to be essential to the effectiveness of teams.

It is widely believed that a well-functioning team needs to forge common goals, working procedures, and rules of interaction. Researchers are accumulating evidence that suggests that the ability of a distributed team to function depends on such factors, and not only on the capability of the technology to enable communication and data-exchange. In the next sections, I describe the role of interaction in developing perceptions of membership of a social/working group and explain challenges that arise when teams do not have the opportunity to meet face-to-face often during their formation process. I illustrate these challenges with examples found in virtual meeting interaction. I then discuss future directions for technology development and social research to support virtually collocated work.

DEVELOPING AS A "WELL-FORMED" VIRTUAL TEAM

My hypothesis in this chapter is that limitations due to technology and distance make it difficult for geographically distributed teams to develop certain social processes in order to function as a "well-formed" team. However, a "well-formed" team, especially one that is geographically distributed, is hard to define. Originally Lewin (1948) proposed that a group becomes a social system when members' goals and their means to attain these goals become interdependent. Rabbie and Horwitz (1988) elaborate on this idea by adding that not only is the perceived interdependence of individual members essential to forming a group, but they must also experience a common fate. However an alternative view by Tajfel and Turner (1986) explains that members can still perceive themselves as a group even though their goals may not be interdependent. Rather, the process of emphasizing and defining social category differences defines a group for individuals.

Interaction among group members facilitates perceptions of interdependence or distinct social categorizations for the group. Most investigations of group formation have been performed with groups who are physically collocated, i.e., whose primary contact is face-to-face. Interaction enables individuals to slowly merge their attitudes and develop a new set of "group" attitudes, identifications, and behaviors, which becomes a collective structure (e.g., Weick, 1969). Interaction is especially critical in the initial stages of group formation. Through interaction, group members can evaluate each others' discrepant and conforming behaviors, and seek commonalities (Moreland and Levine, 1989).

With teams that are virtually collocated, it is not clear how interaction should be assessed. Communication in groups changes with the use of computer-media along a number of dimensions, e.g., the overall amount increases (Hiltz et al., 1986), back-channel responses decrease (O'Conaill, Whittacker and Wilbur, 1993), and meetings last longer (Gallupe and McKeen, 1990). Such changes certainly must affect the basic nature and style of interaction in a group, but how they do is still largely unknown.

That interaction plays a role in shaping a group's culture, norms, cooperative attitude, and identity is hardly disputable. But now we enter an era where individuals are meeting from a distance, and their interaction is both enabled and constrained by technological means. I attempt to define challenges for teams whose primary means of communication and operation is through technology. My claim is that basic group attributes are affected as a result of this communication, and I focus specifically on participation, culture, and integration into other work.

DRAWING FROM THE EXPERIENCE OF DISTRIBUTED TEAMS

The challenges that I describe in this chapter are well illustrated in a case study of virtually collocated team interaction, done at The Boeing Company (Mark, Grudin and Poltrock.,1999). In 1996, two years before the study began, mergers with two other large corporations nearly doubled the number of employees in the organization and expanded their geographic distribution to the entire country. This redistribution led to the development of geographically distributed teams. Along with this case, I will also include examples of virtually collocated team interaction from other studies which examined synchronous communication among distributed actors.

In the case that I describe, four geographically medium-sized distributed teams (8-15 members), which had existed for six months or longer in the company, were observed and studied during their weekly meetings for a three-month period. The teams used desktop conferencing technology combined with audio-conferencing to support their meetings. Most team members participated in the meeting from their desktop, and in two of the groups, some participants gathered in a conference room, where a large electronic whiteboard was networked to the computers of remote team members.

The four teams included: a scientific problem solving team, a voluntary team that solved real technical problems for the company; a Technical Working group, whose goal was devising standards for the company Web; a Distributed Staff, whose manager was located in another city and whose team goal was information exchange and planning; and a Best Practice team with the goal of designing vehicles better, faster, and cheaper. As we will see, the experiences of these teams are not unique to their domain of work, but are rather illustrative of basic interaction problems that many distributed teams face in different work settings.

THE CHALLENGES INHERENT
IN VIRTUALLY COLLOCATED WORK

To list all challenges that face distributed teams in this chapter is not possible. Instead I have selected key examples of team behaviors that are profoundly affected by computer-mediated interaction. My argument is that not only does technology use produce immediate behavioral effects in the group, but more importantly, these observable effects will have long-term consequences on the team development and effectiveness, and therefore must be considered seriously. The challenges for teams that I focus on are: 1) achieving a high standard of participation, which affects impressions, interaction patterns, and trust; 2) developing an appropriate group culture for high motivation and cooperation, and 3) integrating the remote team suitably into one's current working sphere. These challenges are not independent, but intricately related. For example, limited participation and discussion shapes the way that culture will be developed.

The challenges exist at different levels of granularity. This is to be expected, as teamwork is composed of a combination of individual and group effort, amidst a background of organizational constraints. I consider the participation challenge to exist primarily at the individual level. Social cues transmitted or restricted by the media and clarity of the channel affect individual perceptions. On the other hand, developing a suitable culture to promote engagement and motivation in the group is a challenge at the team level. On yet a broader level, integrating work from an interorganizational team into one's local working sphere is a challenge that may only be met through organizational change.

The Challenge of Participation

Virtually collocated groups communicating in real time via audio and video conferencing face a definite challenge in encouraging members to participate in the group meetings. The awkwardness of participation not only impedes the current discussion but also results in long-term cumulative effects for the group. I will first review several interaction phenomena observed with audio and video communication.

Transmission delays in videoconferencing can have a negative impact on group interaction, resulting in collisions, unnecessary rephrasings, and misapplied feedback (Ruhleder and Jordan, 1999). Even though video cues are available, these problems can still occur. Ruhleder and Jordan stress that when different actors hear different conversational segments due to delays, the actors' different expectations and interpretations inhibit the construction of a shared meaning.

Interaction can also suffer during audio-conferencing meetings from not knowing who is present, and by awkward turn-taking (Ackerman, Hindus, Mainwaring and Starr,1997). These types of interaction difficulties also occurred with the Boeing teams, who additionally had problems in identifying remote speakers. In the large distributed organization, actors often did not know which organizations the speakers in their teams belonged to.

An example of awkwardness in turn-taking and the problem of not knowing identities or who is present is shown here, from distributed teams in the case study. These kinds of exchanges are heard often during the team meetings:

Remote: I'd like to make a suggestion.
Leader: Is this Anita?
Remote: Yes.

M: Everyone clear so far? [one "yeah" is heard].

Dan: I have a quick question. Paul, are you still here?
Al: Who is this speaking?

Carol: I'm Carol, I work at——; my area is data exchange.
[long pause]
Carol: Is everyone still there?
[a few say yes]
Carol: Because I didn't hear the background noises and didn't know if everyone is still there.

In face-to-face conversation, communication mechanisms exist which manage conversational flow, through a rich and varied set of behavioral cues. These include intonation, gesture, gaze, and back-channel responses, which serve to turn conversation into a smooth dance among partners, without bumping into each other, so to speak.

It is questionable whether video images provide a real advantage for coordinating interaction. Video has been found to be advantageous for communicating nonverbal expression and reasons for pauses yet has been found disadvantageous for turn-taking and floor control (Isaacs and Tang, 1993). Sellen (1995) concluded that there are no observable effects on turn-taking and synchronization when adding video to audio.

In the short term, these effects of the technology impact the group by limiting the richness of discussion. In distributed video presentations, audience members are less likely to ask follow-up questions or clarifications, compared to face-to-face interactions (Isaacs et al., 1995). In the case study, it was discovered from observations, and confirmed from interviews, that team members at remote sites find it hard to interject. Nonverbal cues serve for them as signals that a conversation turn has ended; without such cues, remote members prefer to err in favor of not speaking, and thus not interrupting.

Few researchers have considered the long-term impacts for a group in experiencing communication delays, awkwardness in turn-taking, and not knowing who is present, who the speakers are, the meaning of pauses, and whether others are listening. In the long term, they create expectations for a certain type of interaction which can easily become a pattern for the group. It is not even clear whether distributed groups can develop norms to regulate conversation flow and establish positive interaction patterns. In one longitudinal study, group members did develop norms to regulate their conversational exchange (Ackerman et al., 1997), but other studies did not find this to be the case, even among people who were experts in using the technology (e.g., Ruhleder and Jordan, 1999). One difference is that in the Ackerman et al. study, cooperation was continuous, among a well-defined set of team members. In the case study, communication in the media space was discontinuous, with larger numbers of people. This in fact may be more representative of the type of virtual meeting interaction that can be expected in large organizations.

Another type of consequence as a result of the awkwardness of participation is that it inhibits spontaneous behaviors. Granted, in many face-to-face formal meetings, especially those run by strict meeting protocols or facilitation, spontaneity is also not encouraged. But in the case study, during most parts of the meetings, free discussion was encouraged, for example, in posing questions to a presenter, in offering relevant information to the group, or in problem-solving discussions. And yet spontaneity was often not observed among the members, and its absence was described in interviews.

Many of the team members in the study expressed in interviews that it was difficult to interpret others' on-line conversations. They remarked that facial expression helps to establish a context for them, to understand in which light they should frame a comment. Understanding the context in turn helps them to formulate a response. As the users described:

I get extra feedback of the body language of a person. Having met that person, I have that in the back of my mind [during a desktop conferencing session]. Without it, something is missing.

Reflective looks means they are thinking. Silence on the line doesn't. People may say things sarcastically, but the expression on-line is confused. Many signals that you have in face-to-face are lost.

The "sterile" type of interaction pattern that forms in the group subsequently affects the potential for further group development. It creates expectations of the kinds of interaction possible in the group, for example that after a ten-minute monologue, no one in the group may be listening. Even worse, the limitations on the interaction and richness of discussion can lead to the formation of stereotypes of other group members, as opposed to a more multifaceted view of them. The danger of stereotypes was recognized by a team member who describes that face-to-face interaction helps him form a better model of the other:

It has value. When a person speaks, I attach a face and personality to him. When I hear a voice, I'm dying to associate the face with a voice. The only way to get good interaction is to represent the person. You have to interact with this person. Your stereotype of the person doesn't work on the program, the person works on the program.

Additionally, "impolite" behaviors such as nonresponse, silence on the line, and interruptions are often attributed to the individual, and the role of the technology in contributing to this is downplayed. This phenomenon is known as the fundamental attribution error, the tendency for people to attribute the cause of behavior to an actor, rather than to situational factors (Ross, 1977). This misattribution further impedes the development of the group as it can convey rudeness or lack of involvement, as shown in this example:

Leader: Susan, anything else?
[long pause]
Leader: Susan left us awhile back.
Susan: No, I haven't. [Susan then explains that she put two URL's in the chat window. The leader replies that he did not have the desktop conferencing shared application running.]

The team leader did not see what Susan was doing, i.e. that she was actively participating in the meeting by putting URL's into the chat window. He had instead assumed that she had left the meeting.

Another long-term consequence of the interaction difficulties is on the formation of trust in the group. Trust involves forming an expectation of reciprocation. Trust is explained by Gambetta (in Hinde and Groebel (1991) as:

…a particular level of the subjective probability with which an agent assesses that another agent or group of agents will perform a particular action, both before he can monitor such action (or independently of his capacity ever to monitor it) and in a context in which it affects his own action (p. 5).

Being able to assess or predict the actions of others involves learning about their behavior, preferably in as many varied situations as possible in order for the predictions to be robust. The lack of nonverbal behavior in computer-mediated communication, combined with inhibited participation, hinders people in developing robust predictions of others' behaviors. It is easy to understand how trust can be broken down in an audio-mediated conversation. If a delay occurs in the transmission, and the speaker does not hear a response, she may form an assumption about the others' reaction to her remark. If the speaker misspeaks, the facial expression is not visible in order for the speaker to repair the mistake.

Many of the team members expressed their intuitions about this relationship between their computer-mediated communication and building of trust:

You build relationships in face-to-face meeting. I notice that in the council time, the work in the group, and the social time, this all builds relationships. When you build trust with, e.g. top directors, then they are more likely to deal directly with you. It's easier to get through to them, and making contact with them is easier.

Trust is not a [desktop conferencing] issue. You build trust by working with the individual.

[Desktop conferencing] is possible only after trust is established. Problems are amplified by not meeting face-to-face. The real content of communication is not on the screen. If someone says something and then pauses, you can imagine anything.

Everyone has a public and hidden agenda. You can't get hidden agendas from [desktop conferencing]. Here [face-to-face meeting] I can see everyone, look at the body language.

Until roles and activities are well-shared, people will be suspicious. As experience with team members grows, the predictability grows. For example, are people disclosing agendas that are not apparent?

On the other hand, a few members do not expect that the distributed team should develop a high level of trust. One member differentiates between a high level of trust which is necessary for his physically collocated team, because he depends on them, and the virtually collocated team, which is "several organizational boundaries away". Another describes:

The level of trust that we have is appropriate for the group. It is not a close-knit team, as, e.g., a basketball team. Therefore, it is not so necessary.

Several members described that trust for them meant authenticating the knowledge of the others on the team, i.e., that they had competence in the context of their field. Keeping in mind that many of the members had not met each other and come from different organizations within the company, it is hard for them to judge the level of expertise and competence of others. And restricted verbal conversation is not sufficient for learning about the knowledge of other team members.

The Challenge of Developing a Team Culture

We think of culture with respect to a country or organization, but groups can have their own cultures. Although different definitions of culture have been offered for groups and organizations, I follow Schein's (1990) definition of the shared assumptions and beliefs that are held by members of a group that is a learned product of group experience. Now when discussing distributed groups, we are faced with the problem of establishing what a definable group with a history means. There may be a roster with a list of members, but who actually attends scheduled meetings may be variable and even unknowable, especially when presence is not announced. Schein discusses the importance of having sufficient common experiences to have developed a shared view. This creates a challenge for the distributed group whose members themselves may not be able to define who is a member of their social unit. This is especially the case if attendance at meetings is not regular and if the group does not have a long history of meeting face-to-face.

On the other hand, assumptions of mission and operation can be formed implicitly, and certain patterns of behavior can set in quickly. It can be misleading to presuppose that teams, because they are geographically distributed and victim to some of the interaction difficulties described earlier, lack a culture. There is a danger of fooling ourselves if we believe the solution to effective teaming is simply that of presenting a set of recommendations that the group can follow. By following these recommendations, the group can use the technology more efficiently and conduct better meetings. Wrong. We first have to discover whether a set of assumptions exists for the members, in order to change them. And change, once culture is set in place, does not come easily.

Culture in a group is affected by a number of factors: the group's history, its experience, its structure, the larger organization, the composition of its members, and the environment. However, additionally in a virtually collocated group, the nature and usage of the technology also plays a major role in shaping the group's culture. Deep-seated assumptions in a group can be manifest through its handling of artifacts, its products or creations, or overt behavior of the group members, as Schein describes. In a virtually collocated group, when, due to the technology use, patterns set in of interruptions, or of lack of engagement in the meeting, although these are not favorable cultural manifestations, they are observable traits by which the group operates. And they often reflect deeper assumptions by which the group functions. To illustrate this, I present the case of the Best Practice team. The members, who had been meeting for about nine months, developed the behavior of multitasking during the weekly desktop conferencing meetings. Multitasking refers to performing activities external to the meeting (e.g., reading email) during the desktop conferencing session. During the meeting, a spreadsheet scrolled down on the shared desktop conferencing display showing action items. The team member responsible for the action item would report on its status: done, or due date extended. The meeting had very little interaction among the members, influenced by the action item reporting practice. The members soon began to do multitasking, until their action item was reached or until they were called upon to comment about the action item. This seemed like a reasonable activity until every so often conversations such as the following surfaced, which was not atypical for the team:

Mark: Dan, that's your action item.

Dan: Sorry, I didn't catch that.

Mark: Jack, what's your comment? [long pause] Jack, are you there?

Jack: I had my mute button on.

Mark: Next is the rotocraft area, but he is not here.

Rob: We need communication. 80 hours is not the problem. I waste 80 hours talking on the telephone. It requires a tremendous amount of extra effort to clearly communicate. When someone says we're having a telecon, then we need to be on the telecon.... People need to be on the telecon. We need a schedule.

Joe: We all sit here and what are we doing? Is everyone trying to be on these telecons?......We have to decide on issues that we feel are important. Things can be done but we need to talk to each other and use these telecons.

Mark: Thank you, Joe. [Mark moved on to the next action item]

The multitasking resulted in a lack of engagement in the discussion and thus low commitment to the meeting. As in this example, the members sometimes did express frustration, yet the group leader did not try to counteract the problem. One possible interpretation of the group's practice is that they lacked a culture. I argue that the practice of multitasking during the meeting and the corresponding lack of engagement *was* the group culture. Contrary to the broader organizational culture, which promoted participatory decision-making and where group meetings were expected to have high engagement and contributions of the members, the assumption of this group was that only minimal involvement was necessary during a virtual meeting.

Although multitasking occurred to some extent in other groups that were investigated, in no other group did the lack of engagement approach the level found in this group. This suggests that lack of engagement is not a behavior that is found in all virtual meetings. Multitasking has also been found in a video broadcast setting (Isaacs et al., 1995). However, unlike a team meeting, audiences during a broadcast would not necessarily be expected to be highly interactive with the speaker.

In fact, the members gained benefits by multitasking. Since their main task was reporting on the status of an action item, they needed only to be peripherally (or not at all) aware of others' reports in the meeting and could conduct other work in their offices in parallel. In some occasions, they even met with others in their offices during the virtual meeting. Yet overall, this group, who was expected to design a virtual collocation program within their division, did suffer by the lack of involvement. The meetings took more time because people had to refresh members about previous discussions. Information was unnecessarily repeated. Sometimes hostility was expressed by different members, concerning lack of engagement and miscommunication. Since the action items were interrelated, directed toward achieving a common goal, learning about others' contributions could often have helped members with their own action items. Frequently the team leader asked people if they knew certain information; it was unclear whether the silence on the line was due to not knowing the answer or simply due to lack of involvement; for example:

> Leader: Has everyone the information? [long pause] I assume silence means yes.

The team displayed very different types of overt behaviors when they met face-to-face, in contrast to their virtual meetings. The different overt behaviors reflect different expectations that the members had for their face-to-face and for their virtual meetings. For example, in one face-to-face meeting, where members flew in from all over the U.S., the group used a facilitator. The purpose of the meeting was different than the typical virtual meetings of reviewing items; its goal was to prepare a charter. In contrast to the virtual meetings, the discussion was quite free, with many interjections that the facilitator had to cut off. There were jokes, clarifications, debate, nonverbal gesturing and facial expressions in response to comments—in short, a high degree of interaction and engagement by the members.

One way that the technology may have influenced the interaction style is through the provision of a shared reference in the desktop conferencing; i.e., all members had the same view of the information. In the face-to-face meetings, members often referred back to points discussed earlier. Here we can see an influence of the technology: the shared application defines the focus, or view, for the group. In a face-to-face group, people are focused not only on the information, but on each other. (Also, the members in the virtual meeting may not have paid attention to earlier items ,which could also explain why they did not refer back to points.)

It might be argued that the multitasking, and corresponding lack of engagement made the most sense for the group members, given the action item reporting format of the meeting. However, other models of interaction were possible in the group, and my claim is that the group would have benefited more had the members paid more attention at meetings. The interaction style that the group adopted was shaped by a complex interaction: The technology and the meeting format *interacted* with other factors, such as the history of the group, and composition of the members.

If we examine the group's history, we find that after the company merger, the team was formed officially by a vice president and assigned the goal of designing vehicles better, faster, and cheaper. The team was intentionally composed of representatives from all geographical areas of this company division, one person per site, spread across the entire United States. It is important to consider that the members stem from the different heritage companies and also different organizations within each of the former companies. The different members thus come from organizations that had different company cultures (e.g., participatory and tree-structured decision-making models) and different language codes (e.g., different acronyms). Since the group began, they had met about four times face-to-face. Given the members' differences, it is perhaps not surprising that this type of behavioral pattern set in. One team member even expressed that the meeting, and the technology use was not being used to its full potential. A final product so far had not been created by the group.

Thus, developing a shared set of assumptions to promote positive group behaviors is a challenge for a distributed team. Culture forms from a number of influences, and it is important to consider that the technology and how it is used, comprise a key factor in shaping a distributed group's culture.

The Challenge of Integrating Remote Work

The third challenge of virtually collocated teams is to discover ways that they can integrate the work of their virtually collocated team into their local working spheres. Work is continuous and complex. People move fluidly from one task to the next. The problem with virtually collocated teams is that the end of meetings often signal "out of sight, out of mind." Remote people and tasks are thus not part of the continuity of one's working spheres. Rather, as the team meetings in Boeing were, they fulfilled specific functions at specific points in time. In the words of the manager of the Staff, "it compromises the ability to get involved in things at the right time."

What does integration mean? It refers to more continual communication than just weekly or bimonthly formal meetings, with occasional telephone or email exchanges in-between. It refers to learning more about the other members on the team: their organizational homes, their expertise, their backgrounds, which currently is not the case in the teams studied. It refers to the exchange of results with selected team members to get feedback when the results are ready, instead of waiting for the formal meeting time. It refers to building a shared repository of common team materials, e.g. a shared workspace, accessible to all from remote locations. Again, currently none of the teams have such a shared space for team materials. Web sites exist, but it is not easy for team members to upload information. Integration refers to engaging in informal as well as formal communication, which can even lead to building relationships outside of the formal meeting structure. In all the interviews conducted, only one member from the Scientific Team reported contact with another remote team member outside of the formal meeting time, based on finding common interests. The Technical Working group used chat during the meetings, where informal communication took place. A member reported that it helped the team bond. It may in fact have served more a purpose of "breaking the ice" during the meeting than of bonding.

The lack of integration of the remote team work into the members' local working spheres became manifest in different ways in the organization. First, one consequence for the lack of integration is found with adoption of the technology. Remote team members in the case study had problems in adopting the desktop conferencing technology. These problems included downloading the software, securing the appropriate computers to run the software, and learning how to use the technology. One reason cited was that the team was viewed as a part-time activity and therefore assigned less importance than other tasks with people with whom one is collocated. This was also true of the members' local site managers. They viewed the team as part-time and were reluctant to fund appropriate equipment needed for the software.

Second, another consequence we might expect of the lack of integration is that members may not give high priority to the assigned tasks for the virtually collocated group. We see evidence of this from the large numbers of action items in the Best Practice team that were delayed.

MEETING THE CHALLENGES HEAD-ON

We are moving into an era where distributed teams are not expected to have single encounters, but rather long-term relationships. In this chapter I have focused on challenges that distributed teams will face over a long time. Contrary to this idea, much research on the effects of computer-mediated communication in groups has focused on identifying the immediate communication difficulties that people experience. It is my hope that the challenges that I have outlined in this chapter can spark more thinking about longitudinal research on the effects of technology and distance on team building. Dissecting the process of team development identifies a number of social processes in the group, such as the development of participation patterns, culture, norms, refinement of roles and procedures, cohesion, identity, motivation to perform, trust, and leadership.

In considering team participation, not only does interaction via computer-mediated communication present immediate interaction difficulties, but it also has consequences on the long-term development of group processes. Not knowing who is present, not knowing identities or organizations, misattributions of behavior, inhibited participation from remote members, and the lack of nonverbal behavior to help interpret on-line speech all affect the group development. I have argued that they contribute to expectations and patterns of certain participation behaviors, as well as impeding the building of trust.

Virtually collocated teams can have their own unique cultures, shaped by the use of the technology. The assumptions shared by the group members may be different for a group, depending on whether they meet from a distance, or face-to-face. In the case of the Best Practice team, the lack of engagement of the members was much higher than in the other teams observed. It seems reasonable to argue that the structured meeting format, use of desktop conferencing, and interorganizational homes all contributed to the members' multitasking behaviors. Although it brought the members benefits, the price in the long-term was a set pattern where low commitment and lack of engagement in the meeting was accepted. Certainly multitasking brings advantages: It enables people to attend and monitor more meetings while working in parallel. Yet practitioners need to reflect on whether multitasking should be promoted rather for peripheral meeting participation than for people who are core group members.

As with the groups described here, many virtual meetings are highly structured. But this meeting style produces a paradox. Virtually collocated team members are expected to produce high quality deliverables on schedule.

Yet group members limit their main involvement to the formal meetings. Many teams would in fact benefit from more continuous communication and involvement with each other and with the task. Rather than more formal involvement, teams need more regular informal communication. The value that this can provide to teams is in helping them get to know one another, a first step toward building trust.

The integration challenge applies at two levels. First, it addresses how people can seamlessly integrate their remote team activities into their current activities. Secondly, more broadly, it is a challenge to make remote sites more of a presence in an organization. Ultimately, the goal would work toward creating one company culture.

Because of their origins in distributed companies or parts of the organization, team members in virtually collocated teams are diverse, which makes the integration challenge even more difficult. Organizational rewards are given at the individual level: Members of cross-unit teams do not get salary reviews; members of local teams get salary reviews. Further, team members give distributed groups less priority than groups at their local sites. These views are held not only by team members, but also by managers, many of whom may be reluctant to provide funding for the equipment necessary to run the appropriate meeting technology.

THE NEXT STEP: FUTURE DIRECTIONS AND TECHNOLOGIES FOR VIRTUALLY COLLOCATED WORK

Since this study was conducted, I have discovered many other researchers and industry practitioners who share the same central hypothesis that I describe here. The combination of distance and use of low-bandwidth technologies imposes a considerable burden on teams who are commissioned to work together with little or no face-to-face interaction. I have discussed this topic with others at workshops, conferences, in industrial settings, and over email (with people I have never met face-to-face). I am continually surprised at the consensus that I am finding.

Research needs to address two aspects of virtually collocated work: developing new technologies that can convey the essential type of social information to aid a team in its formation and maintenance, and understanding the competencies that are needed by distributed teams to engage in their work.

New technologies can certainly help to meet the challenges of developing a positive team culture and integration of remote and local work. Poltrock and Engelbeck (1997) articulate the requirement of supporting opportunistic interactions through a combination of e-mail, telephone, and awareness mechanisms. Synchronous and asynchronous awareness mechanisms can help inform team members of each others' current and past activities, can spark discussions, and provide them with a context for their own. Chat can have great value in supporting informal communication in distributed teams. Shared repositories of information for the group would be beneficial, such as a shared workspace, where all can enter and download material. In this way, members need not wait for the scheduled meeting to view the results. They can have the results at hand when they are ready and could even discuss them prior to the meeting. In fact, meetings consisting of action item reports may not even be necessary, if the action item status could be made available to all in a shared workspace. In this case, the meeting time could be used for other purposes, such as creating a final product, as one member proposed. Another fruitful area of technology research is to discover ways to capture and convey nondisruptive signals online, showing people's remote behaviors to others during a meeting.

Research is called for to understand new roles necessary in distributed teams: e.g., appropriate forms of leadership and facilitation. Although it is costly to create new roles, on the other hand, if communication and technology use become more efficient, then it becomes an overall gain. The problems of not knowing who is present speaking, difficulty in turn-taking, and interpreting silence on the line can be alleviated through appropriate forms of facilitation, as we discovered (Mark et al., 1999). It is worth considering a role of technology meeting "producer" for the team, who can ensure that members receive appropriate visual and audio information about others during a meeting.

The schedule of face-to-face meeting in distributed teams also needs to be understood. Studies of group development suggest that the early phases of group formation are the critical time for interaction: At this time, information exchange, the accommodation of the group to the individual (and vice versa), and settling of roles takes place. However, in some cases it is impractical for geographically distributed teams to meet face-to-face. Research is needed to better define face-to-face schedules, such as when "booster shots" may be needed. The meeting itself may be restructured so that certain tasks can be better accomplished face-to-face, while other tasks, e.g., those which have less dependencies among the members, can sufficiently be accomplished from a distance.

As we enter the age of virtual teamwork, we need to revise our notions of what teamwork actually means. People have acquired competence in working together face-to-face, and this competence has many components. It includes establishing relationships with one another, remaining aware of the overall work activities and progress, engaging in smooth interaction in group discussions, and producing high quality group products. All of these are examples of competencies that are strained when team members are geographically distributed. Members of such groups need to develop new ways (i.e., competencies) to work and develop together as a team. They also need to become technically competent—not just in understanding how to operate the technology, but in knowing how to use it to interact effectively and how it can benefit the development of the team. New competencies are needed in all areas of virtually collocated work: new team roles, new forms of meeting facilitation, new leadership styles, an awareness of remote team members, new interpersonal skills, new social conventions, and skill in integrating remote work with other working spheres.

But even as we find ways to meet current challenges of participation, developing cohesive cultures, and smoothly integrating remote and local working spheres, new challenges will continually arise. The development of new technologies may solve some immediate problems for teams, but as we know from experience, they may result in higher order effects. For example, a technology that conveys activity information about remote team members may increase the overall amount of coordination needed by the team. New technologies may create a "virtual" team leader or facilitator, which may in turn create new challenges for team members in adapting to this new form of leadership. We are only at the beginning of a new era of virtually collocated work and can expect far more interesting technology developments and unforeseen social challenges. Technology is shrinking the world, but the understanding of how teams can adapt to the new technologies and new form of virtually collocated team structure is not yet keeping pace.

REFERENCES

Ackerman, M. S., Hindus, D., Mainwaring, S. D., and Starr, B. (1997).Hanging on the 'wire: A field study of an audio-only media space, *ACM Trans. on Computer-Human Interaction,* 4(1), 39-66.

Gallupe, R. B. and McKeen, J. D. (1990). Enhancing computer-mediated communication: An experimental investigation into the use of a group decision support system for face-to-face versus remote meetings. *Information and Management,* 18, 1-13.

Hiltz, S. R., Johnson, Kl, and Turoff, M.(1986).. Experiments in group decision-making: Communication process and outcome in face-to-face versus computerized conferences. *Human Communcation Research,* 13(2),

225-252.

Hinde, R. A. and Groebel, J. (1991). *Cooperation and Prosocial Behavior.* Cambridge: Cambridge University Press.

Isaacs, E.A., Morris, T., Rodriguez, T.K. and Tang, J.C.(1995). A comparison of face-to-face and distributed presentations, *Proceedings CHI'95,* Denver, ACM Press, 354-361.

Isaacs, E. A. and Tang, J. C. (1994). What video can and can't do for collaboration: a case study. *Multimedia Systems,* ACM Press: Anaheim, CA, 2, 63-73.

Lewin, K.(1948). *Resolving social conflicts: selected papers on group dynamics.* New York: Harper.

Mark, G., Grudin, J. and Poltrock, S. (1999). Meeting at the desktop: An empirical study of virtually collocated teams. In S. Bødker, M. Kyng, and K. Schmidt (eds). *Proceedings of the 6th European Conference on Computer-Supported Cooperative Work,* Copenhagen, 159-178.

Moreland, R.L. and J.M. Levine.(1989). Newcomers and Oldtimers in Small Groups. In *Psychology of Group Influence,* P. Paulus (eds.), Lawrence Erlbaum, Hillsdale, NJ, 143-186.

O'Conaill, B., Whittaker, S., and Wilbur, S. (1993). Conversations over video conferences: an evaluation of the spoken aspects of video-mediated communication. *Human-Computer Interaction,* 8, 389-428.

Poltrock, S. E. and Engelbeck, G. (1997). Requirements for a virtual collocation environment. *Proceedings of ACM Group '97,* Phoenix, AZ, New York: ACM Press.

Rabbie, J. M. and Horwitz, M. (1988).Categories versus groups as explanatory concepts in intergroup relations. *European Journal of Social Psychology,* 18, 117-23.

Ross, L. (1997).The intuitive psychologist and his shortcomings: Distortions in the attribution process. In L. Berkowietz (ed.) *Advances in experimental social psychology,* Vol. 10, New York: Academic Press, 173-219.

Ruhleder, K. and Jordan, B.(1999). Meaning-making across remote sites: How delays in transmission affect interaction. In S. Bødker, M. Kyng, and K. Schmidt (eds). *Proceedings of the 6th European Conference on Computer-Supported Cooperative Work,* Copenhagen, 411-429.

Schein, E. H.(1990). *Organizational Culture and Leadership,* San Francisco: Jossey-Bass.

Sellen, A. J.(1995). Remote conversations: The effects of mediating talk with technology. *Human-Computer Interaction,* (10), 401-444.

Tajfel, J. and Turner, J. C. (1986). The social identity theory of intergroup behavior. In S. Worchel and W. Austin (eds.), *Psychology of intergroup relations,* Chicago: Nelson-Hall, 7-24.

Weick, K. E. (1969). *The Social Psychology of Organizing*, Reading, MA: Addison-Wesley.

ENDNOTE

1 This chapter is based on "Some challenges facing virtually collocated teams", in Proceedings of the IFIP WG 8.2 International Conference: The Social and Organizational Perspective on Research and Practice in Information Technology.

Chapter 6

Succeeding in the Virtual World: How Relationships Add Value on the Web

Diana Burley Gant
Indiana University, USA

As organizations race to stake their claim on the information superhighway, many are finding that the World Wide Web is not only a place for selling products and providing information, but it is also an effective tool for managing their relationships with other organizations. Without downplaying the importance of electronic commerce, a cursory surf of the Web reveals that the majority of Web links, which move Web site visitors from one organization space to another, are not mechanisms of active coordination. Instead, organizations strategically create many of these links to reinforce and/or promote a relationship with another organization. The links reflect a strategic choice on the part of the organization (Jackson, 1997).

Across a variety of industries, organizations are using the Web to reinforce strategic alliances, to promote joint ventures, to endorse partnerships, and to manage their public image. For example, the Geico Insurance Company uses its Web site to promote its business partnerships by including links to the Web sites of its partner organizations. And the American Red Cross provides links on its Web site to highlight joint disaster response efforts with other nonprofit agencies. By including these links on their Web sites, Geico and the American Red Cross are able not only to provide access to additional products and services but also to reinforce their relationships. They are not alone. By late 1995, approximately twenty percent of all organizational Web sites contained some type of link to another organization (Bray, 1996), and this number has increased more than twofold since then.

Clearly, organizations are using the Web to manage their relationships, but the question is why. What value does Geico gain by including a link to the American Dental Hygienists Association on its Web site? Why would the American Red Cross include a link on its Web site to CNN? Perhaps Geico wants its customers to learn about good dental hygiene. A noble thought, but is Geico in the business of dental hygiene? Certainly organizations are motivated by more than just the technical ability to create these links, but what is driving their behavior?

In this chapter, we explore why organizations create Web links to other organizations by looking at the set of relationships among a group of disaster response organizations. We discuss how these organizations add value to their Web sites by using use Web links to reinforce their interorganizational relationships – solidifying exchange relationships and promoting normative ones. Our observations deal primarily with the set of organizations responding to the 1996 flooding in western Pennsylvania. For these organizations, we compare the relationships displayed on the Web to those reported between the organizations during the actual disaster response. This comparison allows us to draw conclusions about why the organizations created Web links and how they use these links to manage their interorganizational relationships and add value to their Web sites.

MANAGING DISASTER RESPONSE

Hurricanes, floods, oil spills, and other natural and technological disasters occur all too often in our society. When they do, a host of organizations appear on the scene almost instantaneously, ready to help the victims. For some organizations, like the Federal Emergency Management Agency (FEMA) or the American Red Cross, disaster response is their mission. These agencies are responsible for overall success and for coordinating the other organizations participating in the response.

However, organizations from several other industries also respond. Mass care and religious organizations like the Salvation Army come to provide victim support. Military and civil defense units keep order and are often called upon to provide protection for victims, their abandoned belongings, and assistance workers. Hospitals send out teams of emergency health care workers. Schools and hotels temporarily house both victims and emergency workers. Private businesses provide supplies and monetary donations. And media organizations keep the public informed through broadcasts of the disaster response effort.

Given the varied roles organizations play in disaster response, it should not be surprising to learn that the size of a typical disaster response ranges anywhere from several dozen to several hundred organizations. These organizations face time pressure, limited resources, multiple levels of authority from local, state and national agencies, uncertain and volatile conditions, different priorities, and public scrutiny. Given this level of environmental complexity, organizations must work together and coordinate their activities. To a large extent, their success depends on the formation of strategic partnerships to stabilize the exchange of such resources as personnel or information. Additionally, faced with the strong norms and rules of appropriate behavior during a disaster response, organizations find that they must also form partnerships in response to environmental pressures.

Stabilizing Resource Exchange

During a disaster response, needs are complex and resources are scarce. The American Red Cross never has enough people to clear roadways, enough space to provide shelter, or enough food to serve hungry victims. Nevertheless, the tasks must be accomplished. This situation also holds true for the host of other organizations participating in the disaster response. Working alone, the response organizations do not have sufficient resources to meet the needs of victims. Therefore, organizations form relationships to aid in resource exchange (Pfeffer and Salancik 1978).

The complexity of the response environment requires that they manage several different relationships simultaneously. In addition, faced with intense time pressures, organizations have little time to manage their existing relationships and even less time to create new ones. Therefore, in order to be effective, organizations must form relationships during non-disaster periods and rely on the efficiency of their relationship management strategies to maintain these relationships.

Organizations use a variety of strategies to maintain their relationships. For example, high-ranking bank officials are often asked to serve on the boards of nonprofit organizations to both provide financial guidance and to increase access to necessary funds. These directorate interlocks often work to stabilize resource exchange (e.g., Boyd 1990). Other agencies form joint ventures (e.g., Alter and Hage, 1993) to share in both the costs and the rewards of the tasks. This is a particularly popular strategy among human service and mass care agencies. And still others form strategic alliances (e.g. Barley, Freeman and Hybels, 1992) that allow companies to benefit from each other without explicitly linking their ultimate success or failure.

Satisfying Normative Expectations

Organizations that respond to disasters are, perhaps more than any other group of organizations, held up to intense public scrutiny. With every hurricane or chemical spill, the directors of FEMA, the American Red Cross, and state emergency management agencies are in front of cameras updating the public on the status of the response. They describe the event, the work effort and the partnerships.

These appearances have little to do with resource acquisition. Rather, their actions are to a large extent guided by societal pressure (e.g., DiMaggio 1988, Meyer and Rowan 1977). Organizations behave in accordance with environmental norms in order to be perceived as legitimate. Employees wear the proper clothes, they set up operations in the correct location, and they partner with the right agencies. Because they adhere to the norms of appropriate behavior in disaster response situations, the public sees these organizations as legitimate (DiMaggio 1988, DiMaggio and Powell, 1983).

In a disaster response, organizations follow both formal (i.e., mandates) and informal (i.e., norms) rules of interaction. The government mandates not only which organizations should interact, but also which organizations are responsible for providing certain resources. The American Red Cross is responsible for coordinating mass care efforts, and FEMA is responsible for coordinating assistance from private industry. These rules of interaction stabilize the environment by creating routines and procedures that reduce information-gathering costs (Zucker, 1987).

Adherence to informal norms also plays an important role in shaping public perception. Although there is no official document that dictates that grassroot community groups work with media organizations to provide meals for victims, that is, in fact, often what happens. These partnerships arise in response to environmental pressures that the media do more than simply report the news, but also take part in the response effort (Gant, 1998).

When an organization's operating environment changes frequently and their legitimacy (or reputation) is an important factor in their success, relationships formed in response to both resource exchange and normative pressures provide a powerful source of stability. Again, given that disaster response organizations operate in complex environments where tasks are often beyond their scope, they must maintain a host of interorganizational relationships. Efficiently managing these relationships is key to their success.

Enter the World Wide Web. The ease with which organizations can maintain relationships on the Web makes it ideal for helping to manage relationships among the disaster response organizations. Links on an organization's Web site are cheap to maintain and easy to manipulate. Once the American Red Cross creates a link to the Salvation Army, the link is there until they decide to remove or alter it. The Web is far reaching. At no additional cost, the American Red Cross can use links to provide information on response partners to visitors from around the globe. Using Web links, organizations like the American Red Cross can efficiently reinforce existing relationships and promote new ones. Organizations use links to gain value from their Web sites by increasing control over exchange relationships, promoting strategic partnerships, and highlighting normative relationships. To further illustrate the value of Web links, we report the activities of the set of organizations that responded to the 1996 floods in western Pennsylvania.

1996 WESTERN PENNSYLVANIA FLOODS

On Friday, January 19, 1996, severe flooding began in western Pennsylvania. Heavy snowfall followed by abnormally high temperatures caused the rapid thaw of more than 30 inches of snow around the region. This quick thaw, coupled with several inches of new rainfall, overwhelmed creeks, streams, and rivers with the equivalent of one month's worth of rainfall in one day. The flood of 1996 was the seventeenth largest flood in the region's history and the largest flood to occur in two decades.

Damage was widespread and severe. A total of 18 citizens died. More than 200,000 citizens were evacuated, 11,000 homes were destroyed or received major damage, and another 40,000 homes received minor damage. Approximately 2,000 businesses were destroyed or damaged. In addition, the flooding caused severe damage to state infrastructure. More than 200 bridges, 2,000 water systems, 1,400 roads, and 78 parks were damaged. Within days, the area was declared eligible for federal disaster aid. The largest city in western Pennsylvania, Pittsburgh, sustained major damage to infrastructure and parks. The most noticeable damage was in downtown Pittsburgh at Point State Park (the point at which the Ohio River is formed from the Allegheny and Monongahela rivers)—where the park and fountain were completely immersed in water. Additionally, ice jams clogged the Allegheny River and increased the level of damage by displacing and redirecting runoff water.

A disaster of this magnitude necessitated that over 100 organizations participate in the response and work together to meet the needs of victims. Government and mass care agencies worked with local hospitals, schools, businesses and media organizations to provide relief. They exchanged information and shared personnel. The national military worked with local police departments to clear roads and secure property. Private organizations provided supplies which nonprofit agencies then delivered to victims. And churches and volunteer organizations formed partnerships to feed and care for victims.   In general, the relationships between organizations during the response reflected resource exchanges of personnel, information, physical supplies and money, and relationships mandated by law in the *Federal Response Plan[1]* .

Web Links and Their Significance

"I have many off-line relationships which are reinforced by on-line links...They're a natural extension..." (Deputy Director of the Office of Emergency Information and Media Affairs, FEMA, 5/20/97).

What motivates organizations to establish relationships on the Web? Organizations use the Web to solidify resource exchange relationships, to satisfy normative expectations, and to promote business partners.

As the interview excerpt presented above suggests, FEMA exploits the power of the Web by strategically creating links that reinforce their relationships. FEMA is not alone. In fact, 63 percent of webmasters surveyed for this study state that their organization uses the Web to reinforce existing exchange relationships and 42 percent of the webmasters indicate that they include links to satisfy Web site visitor expectations.

These response organizations use their Web links to reinforce partnerships and information exchange relationships. FEMA uses Web links to reinforce the exchange of information between itself and agencies like the National Humane Society and the National Weather Service. According to FEMA personnel, these links solidify critical relationships. Other organizations use Web links to reinforce exchange relationships as well. For example, several local nonprofit agencies included links to area banks from which they get a substantial amount of funding and area businesses with which they have volunteer programs in place. These links, whether reinforcing personnel exchanges, information exchanges, or monetary exchanges, all add value to the organization's Web site by reducing the information-gathering costs of Web site visitors and by adding more control over the flow of Web site visitors.

Response organizations also create Web links to help shape public perception. For example, Mellon Bank includes Web site links to community partners and to sponsored community events like the Mellon Jazz Festival. These links provide information on special events. Equally as important, the links reinforce Mellon's relationships with community organizations. Similarly, Pittsburgh National Bank includes links to its community partners. These links also demonstrate an organization's adherence to environmental norms. The public believes that local financial institutions should work with community organizations. These links satisfy these normative expectations by showing that they do have these relationships. They add value to the organization by promoting trust and goodwill.

Still other response organizations use Web links to promote businesses on whose success they have a stake. This was often the case for local governments. Local governments use Web links to promote businesses in their metropolitan areas. The City of Pittsburgh, for example, uses links on its Web site not to reinforce relationships with local merchants, but rather to promote them and encourage their patronage. The same holds true for the State of Pennsylvania. Similarly, television media provided Web links to their radio counterparts (and the reverse) in order to highlight these strategic alliances and promote their partner organizations.

According to the webmasters of the local and state governments, they view one of their primary roles on the Web as that of a regional promoter. They add value by providing information about local organizations to the general public. Further, they act as an information resource for the region by providing access to national organizations through their Web sites. For example, the Sewickley, PA webmaster encourages regional organizations to link to their Web site to provide Web site visitors with access to various federal government sites, rather than "cluttering up" their own Web site with dozens of links.

Clearly, the response organizations are using Web links to reinforce existing relationships and, in turn, add value to their Web sites. They are using Web links not simply to provide information, but to promote joint ventures, highlight strategic alliances, and manage their public image.

CONCLUSION

This chapter examined how organizations gain value from their Web sites by using Web links as a relationship management tool. What do the results of this study suggest for the changing nature of work in the virtual world? In order to be successful in the new virtual world, organizations must not only define their Web strategies, but also consider how their Web site will add value to their business. Organizations in this study were able to use their Web links to reinforce their existing relationships by increasing their ability to control Web site traffic, to legitimate their existence, and to promote their strategic partners.

Among the most exciting features of the World Wide Web is the ease with which users can move through the Web simply by clicking on a button. It is fun to travel around the virtual world, clicking buttons and going to new places and spaces. And although some might argue that this pattern of links is somewhat haphazard, a closer look at the structure of the Web suggests the opposite to be true. The Web is developing in systematic fashion because organizations are strategically creating these links to manage their relationships.

As organizations hone their Web strategies, they are likely to continue using these interorganizational links to help manage their relationships and add value to their organizations. This chapter investigates some of the specific factors that might motivate organizations to create these links and takes us another step closer toward understanding the emerging culture of the World Wide Web.

REFERENCES

Alter, C. and Hage J. (1993). *Organizations Working Together,* Sage Publications, Newbury Park, CA.

Barley, S. R., Freeman J., and Hybels R. C.(1992). "Strategic Alliances in Commercial Biotechnology," in *Networks and Organizations: Structure, Form, and Action.* N. Nohria and R. Eccles (eds.), Harvard Business School Press, Boston, MA, 311-347.

Boyd, B.(1990). "Corporate linkages and organizational environment: A test of the resource dependence model," *Strategic Management Journal* (11), 419-430.

Bray, T. (1988). "Measuring the Web," *The World Wide Web Journal,* 1(3).

DiMaggio, P. J.(1988). *Nonprofit Enterprise in the Arts: Studies in Mission and Constraint.*

DiMaggio, P. J., and Powell W. W.(1983). "The Iron Cage Revisited: Institutional Isomorphism and Collective Rationality in Organizational Fields," *American Sociological Review*, 48, 147-160.

Gant, D. B. (1998). "The Web of Affiliation: Theoretical Motives for the Strategic Establishment of Inter-organizational Relationships on the World Wide Web," Unpublished Doctoral Dissertation, Carnegie Mellon University.

Jackson, M.(1997). "Assessing the Structure of Communication on the World Wide Web," *Journal of Computer-Mediated Communication*, 3(1).

Meyer, J W. and Rowan B. (1977). "Institutionalized Organizations: Formal Structure as Myth and Ceremony." *American Journal of Sociology*, 83(2), 340-363.

Pfeffer, J. and Salancik G. (1978). *The External Control of Organizations: A Resource Dependence Perspective,* Harper and Row, New York, NY.

Zucker, L. G.(1987). "Institutional Theories of Organization," *Annual Review of Sociology*, 13), 443-464.

ACKNOWLEDGMENTS:

The author would like to thank the Natural Hazards Center for funding a portion of the study discussed in this chapter. In addition, Jon P. Gant and Kathleen Carley provided many helpful comments.

ENDNOTE

1   The Federal Response Plan, enacted in January 1992, is an official U.S. government document which outlines the procedure for responding to national disasters.

Play
in the
Virtual World

Chapter VII

Online Poker and the Individuals Who Play It

Ramesh Venkataraman
Indiana University, USA

INTRODUCTION

The emergence of the Internet has started to transform society along various dimensions. While news regarding the way the Internet is affecting business captures headlines on a daily basis, its impact on various aspects of day-to-day life also cannot be ignored. In particular, the Internet has had a clear impact on the way people spend their leisure time. For example, people (users) spend substantial amounts of time online trying to find the cheapest airline tickets to our favorite destinations, booking hotels and rental cars, etc. Users are also spending greater amounts of time shopping for everything from clothing to groceries to cars online.

Increasingly, one of the key activities that users are engaging in during their leisure time is the exploration of or participation in one or more of the many forms of online entertainment options available. Examples of these online activities include reading books and magazines, listening to music, listening to radio and TV broadcasts, engaging in chat room conversations etc. The list of online entertainment options available is truly mind boggling. Add to this the fact that a number of these activities require a relatively low amount of monetary investment by the user (usually none) and you have very potent mechanism that is shaping the future of society.

One of the most popular categories of online entertainment options available to users is games. Every major portal has a games section where players can engage in games ranging from resurrected versions of popular computer-based games such as Hangman, Tetris, Solitaire, etc., to TV-style games such as Jeopardy and Wheel of Fortune. These sites also feature intellectually challenging games such as chess and crossword puzzles. However, it can be argued (based on sheer number and variety) that the largest category within online games is casino-style games. Part of this popularity might be attributed somewhat to the growth of gambling and casinos in the US (Davis, 1992). According to the final report of the National Gambling Impact Study Commission (1999), casinos operate in 28 states. These include casinos in Nevada, Atlantic City, and approximately 100 riverboat casinos and 260 Indian casinos. The growth in the number of on-line casinos also might be a reason for the popularity of casino-style games on the web (Barry, 1998). For example, a search on Yahoo resulted in 295 on-line casinos being listed (www.yahoo.com/games).

Typical of the casino-style games supported on web sites are different versions of slot machines, roulette, blackjack, craps etc. All these games have the following common features: a) they are pure games of chance, and b) they pit the individual player against the house (which in this case is the computer). Thus, the actions of other individuals are irrelevant to the outcome of the game. Most of these sites also support Video Poker, which also pits a player against a machine. However, very few of these sites support "true" poker games, i.e., games that pit a group of players against each other. The lack of "live" poker games on web sites is not really surprising considering that of all the games played in a casino, poker is arguably the one game where being able to see an opponent's mannerisms is critical to the way the game is played. Also, a poker game (unlike the other games listed) cannot be played without a minimum number of opponents being available. In this sense it is similar to a chat room in that its viability depends on the existence of a strong base of customers.

Is it possible to support poker games that require participation from multiple players across the Internet? What kind of infrastructure will be needed to support such a game? Is such a game sustainable over the long run? How will individual players perceive online games compared to live poker games in terms of other players' skill level, commitment to the game etc.? In order to answer these questions, we studied two of the most popular forms of the game currently supported on the Internet: Internet Relay Chat (IRC)-based poker and e-mail-based poker.

In this chapter, we trace the evolution of the two types of online poker games, characterize the players who play them and examine the reasons for the success of both these online games. The data and observations presented in the chapter are based on: a) personal observations, b) comments from players in response to open-ended questions posed online, and c) a survey that examined the attitudes of players towards online poker. By examining factors such as the characteristics of the medium, the background of the players, and the players' attitudes towards the game we hope to be able to draw some conclusions regarding how a game that inherently requires face-to-face contact is able to thrive in an online mode.

The rest of the chapter is structured as follows. We begin by presenting a brief description of the medium (IRC) that is used to support the IRC-based poker game. This section is followed by a basic description of how the IRC-based game is played. We then share some observations about the evolution of the software used to support the game as well as how players were able to adapt to the characteristics of the existing medium to make the online game closer to a real-life game. The subsequent section describes an alternative version of online poker (e-mail-based), which is followed by a section that presents a summary of results from an exploratory survey that examined players' attitudes towards both types of online games. We conclude by describing the real-life get-togethers that have emerged as an important aspect of the online community as well as the emergence of online alternatives to IRC-based poker.

IRC

Internet Relay Chat (IRC) is the precursor to modern day chat rooms. Whereas current day chat rooms are hosted at a particular server, e.g., Yahoo! or AOL, an IRC network consists of a number of general IRC servers connected together to form a network. The primary purpose of these servers is to exchange messages (sent by users) in a synchronous manner. Each network of IRC servers provides users with the ability to log on to any of the individual servers and instantly communicate with other users logged on at any of the other servers on the same network. Each network supports a number of channels (created by users). Users can register with and send messages to more than one channel at the same time.

IRC users exchange two types of messages: public and private. A public message is a message that is sent to a particular channel and hence is visible to every other user who is logged onto the particular channel. A private message on the other hand is sent to an individual(s) who is currently logged onto an IRC network. In the early 1990s, there were only two major IRC networks in place, EFnet and Undernet. As the number of users (and correspondingly the traffic) on these networks grew, the need for newer IRC networks became apparent. Currently, there are five major networks (and an even larger number of smaller ones) for users to choose from. The major IRC networks currently in place are, EFnet (the original IRC net, often having more than 50,000 people at once), Undernet, IRCnet, DALnet, and NewNet (http://www.mirc.co.uk/).

Each IRC user has to specify a nickname in order to be able to log onto an IRC network. This nickname must be unique within the network that they are logging onto. Users use an IRC client to log onto the network. The client software is either completely text-based, e.g., on Unix machines, or has a Windows-based interface, e.g., mIRCII, a shareware program for IRC connections (http://www.mirc.co.uk/). All a user needs to be able to connect to an IRC server is an IRC client, a TCP/IP connection and the name of an IRC server that serves the network they wish to connect to.

IRC POKER

An online poker community, consisting mainly of computing professionals, was started in the early 1990s. The game was (and is) supported using the Internet Relay Chat (IRC) protocol. It has been increasing in popularity (and subscribers) ever since its inception. There is no real money exchanged in any of the games and the operators of the game run it as a not-for-profit organization.

The IRC poker game is played on an isolated (i.e., it does not communicate with other servers on the network) server (irc.poker.net) that is on the Undernet IRC network. On this server, there are a number of channels, each dedicated to a different type of poker game. The number of poker channels on this server is controlled by the operators of the network, i.e., users cannot create new poker channels on the fly. However, they can create chat channels as desired. Each poker channel is served by a "bot" (short for robot). This "bot" essentially plays the role of a dealer and a floorperson. Thus, the "bot" deals the cards, asks for bets from the users, handles bets, raises, etc. It also takes care of (virtual) money management issues. Users signify their intentions by sending (private) commands to the "bot". The first version of the "bot" was created as freeware by Todd Mummert at Carnegie Mellon University who continues to maintain them (http://www.cs.cmu.edu/People/mummert/public/ircbot.html).

Figure 1 shows a list of channels available on the IRC poker network. It shows a user being connected to the IRC poker network using a specialized-client called GPkr (available for free download at http://webusers.anet-stl.com/~gregr/) and a nickname of "cardshark" (each nickname has an associated password that is used to authenticate it). A user connecting to the network for the first time gets a starting bankroll of $1,000. Every time a user goes bankrupt he/she gets another $1,000 (the number of bankrupts is kept track of by the bot). Each channel listing contains a brief description of the game as well as the minimum amount that a user needs to possess in order to be able to join a game. Users can only accumulate money by winning at poker games. Thus, the games that have higher starting limits usually have "better" players playing them. Games on IRC can be classified into two categories: regular games and tournament games. Each player has separate bankrolls for each of these games. Among the regular games, the two types of games that are dealt are Texas Hold'em and Omaha Hi-Lo[1]. Players' bankrolls for each of the regular games are also separate, thus allowing them to assess their ability and level of play in each type of game.

Figure 2 shows a sample screen from a Texas Hold'em game. The screen shot was taken at the end of a showdown. Users interact with the game through the various buttons shown in the left-hand panel. There are buttons for game related activities such as call, raise, fold, etc. The grid in the middle displays the current status of players in the game. Information such as who is next to act, how much money each player has contributed to the pot thus far, as well as the total money in the pot is displayed in this part of the screen. The area at the top center of the screen displays information regarding common cards (the board) as well as a player's private cards. The shaded text box in the

Figure 1 List of Poker Channels available

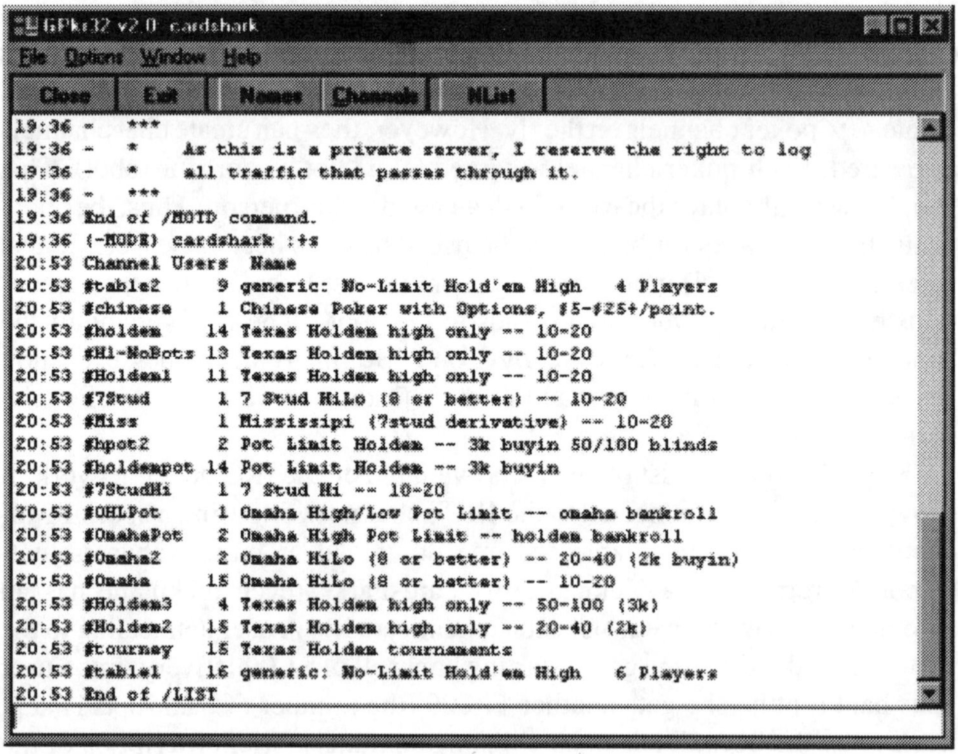

Figure 2: Client Interface to the IRC Poker Game

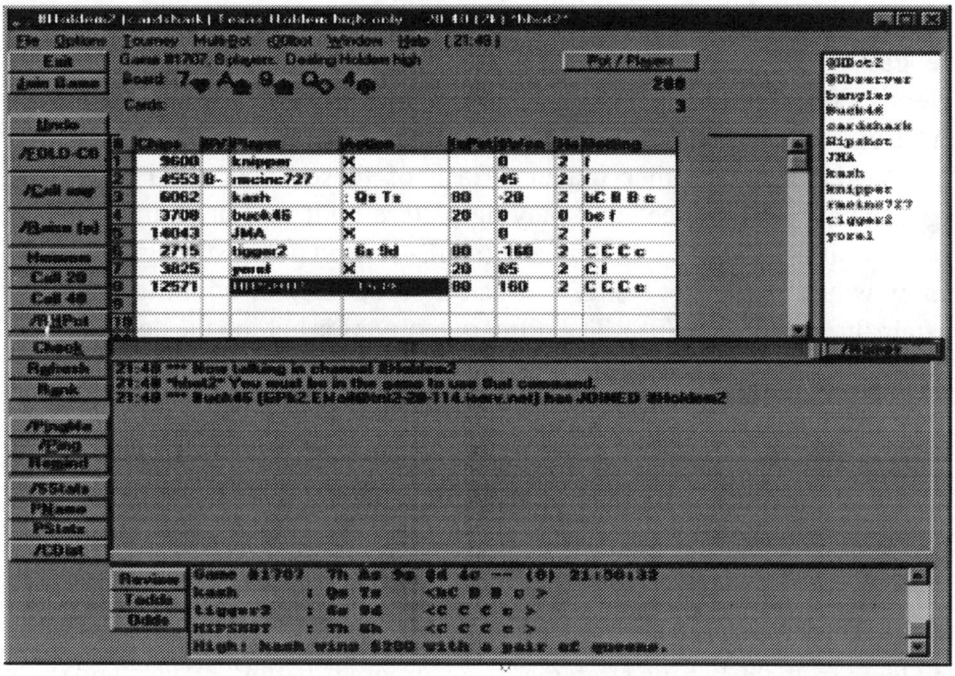

middle of the screen is used to type messages meant for the whole channel. Any text typed there appears in the box below and is visible to everyone who is part of the channel. Finally, the lowermost box on the screen displays information related to showdowns.

EVOLUTION OF IRC POKER

In this section, we present some insights into the evolution of a) the software used to support the IRC poker, b) online cues, and c) the "language" among the players in the online community.

Evolution of the "Bots"

The initial "bot" was capable of dealing only Texas Hold'em games. There were two channels supporting different stakes (10-20 and 20-40). As the popularity of the IRC poker game increased, more channels such as a 50-100 game channel and another 10-20 channel were added. After a few more months due to demand for the Omaha game a new "bot" was created that was capable of dealing that game. The final major addition to the software was the creation of a "bot" capable of dealing tournaments. Each major addition was a clear indication of the growing popularity of the game.

An interesting phenomenon occurred within a year of the introduction of the game. The online game became a simulation testbed for computer scientists with interests in poker. Thus, several player "bots" were unleashed on the various channels. As far as the dealer "bots" were concerned these other "bots" were simply other players. Each of these "bots" had their own algorithms, "intelligence" and playing pattern built in. For example, some "bots" would play almost every hand (an ill-advised poker strategy) whereas others would only play hands that had a probability of winning beyond a certain threshold, e.g., 70%. The primary motivation behind the development of these "bots" was to see if the simulated statistics found in many well-respected poker books (Skalnsky and Malmuth, 1999) actually hold up in the face of real play. The online game presented the perfect platform because the "bot" would be able to play upwards of 100 hands an hour and thus in a short period of time reach the high number of hands usually used in the simulations. Other aspects of the "bots" that were manipulated include the betting strategy and player profile (conservative vs. aggressive) (Lahey, 1998). Some of the player "bots" also had a learning component to them, i.e., they would observe and learn from the betting strategies used by some "better" players and try to adjust their own game based on the data collected. While the early "bots" were easily beaten by most players, the more intelligent "bots" actually ended up frustrating human opponents and beating the average or below average player.

Evolution of "Commands"

The initial set of IRC players were all members who worked in high-tech jobs or were members of the academic community (students, faculty members, etc.). The group's composition was primarily driven by the fact that during the period from 1992-1996 easy online access was available only to the people who belonged to this category. While the channels themselves were available 24 hours a day, several usage patterns could be observed. There were two peak times during working hours, the three hours surrounding the eastern time zone's lunch hour and the three hours surrounding the pacific time zone's lunch hour. This pattern suggests that people primarily played IRC poker during breaks in their work schedule, e.g., lunch time, down time on projects, etc. However, the large customer base ensured that games were sustained and available throughout the day (thanks in part to the somewhat more flexible schedules of the academic players). The games would usually wind down around dinner time in the east (which also coincided with the time some West Coast users would begin their commute home) and then pick up again at a vigorous pace around 9:30 p.m. or so East Coast time. The peak in terms of the number of users would be usually be reached (and sustained) between 10:30 p.m. and 1:00 a.m. eastern time

Initially, the "bots" had a very limited vocabulary, enough to support a basic version of the game. Thus, there were commands that allowed players to bet, fold, raise, etc. However, over time the set of available commands evolved to meet user needs. Tracing the evolution of the commands supported by the "bots" tells us an interesting story about the characteristics of IRC players and how they were able to play IRC poker while at work. As noted above, most early IRC players were in the high-tech arena, primarily software developers and engineers. These people had access to larger monitors (at that time a 17-inch monitor was a luxury) and were thus able to have IRC poker running on one of their windows while engaging in their primary work activity, e.g., debugging, on other windows on the screen. The evolution of many features in the software can be traced to this mode of activity. For example, the early version of the dealer program would only allow users to bet when their turn came around. However, this meant that players had to constantly monitor the game. To avoid having to follow the game closely, the beep feature (causing the user's machine to beep when it is their turn to play) was introduced. However, this still required players to act only when it was their turn, thus requiring them to closely monitor every hand (not to mention the fact that frequent beeps tended to attract the attention of co-workers). To accommodate this problem, the ability to place advance bets was introduced. This allowed players to indicate in advance their intended behavior, e.g., they were able to indicate their intention to fold in advance. Since typical poker players fold more often than engage in betting during a game, this turned out to be a very useful (and frequently used) feature. Another problem with the original version of the game was that frequently people would take a variable amount of time to act when it was their turn. This could happen either because the player left the game without logging out or due to network delays. Thus, a command to "kick" people out of an ensuing game was added to the list of commands understood by the dealer bot. For the most part (surprisingly) this command was not misused. However, online poker players were as impatient as their real-life counterparts when it came to waiting for people to make a decision regarding their intended action (the threshold was usually around 30 seconds). Thus, sometimes players with low tolerance for time delays would kick people out of the game prematurely. This would lead to considerable conflict and heated exchange of words (players seemed to really value their virtual money; see next section). Hence, the "kick" command was modified such that any kick action required two players' vote before it went into effect.

Finally, as noted before, there were times of the day when all the channels on the IRC server had games running at their maximum capacity. It was thus understandable that players who were already seated at a table placed a premium on their seats. However, this meant that players could not take short breaks, e.g., restroom breaks, to attend to urgent work-related matters, etc. Taking a break was an invitation to be kicked from the game, since the dealer "bot" would not be able to skip over the person on break, causing the game to halt temporarily, which would eventually cause other players to kick the person out. This, of course, meant that the "kicked" player could not get back in. To accommodate the need for people to take short breaks, a vacation command was introduced. This feature allowed users to indicate to the dealer "bot" that they were intending to take a short break ("go on vacation"). The dealer "bot" would simply skip over the players who were on vacation thus allowing the games to progress normally. Users on vacation were automatically "kicked" out after 0.5 hours. This allowed the users next on the wait list (maintained by the "bot") to get into the game.

Development of Online Cues

Poker is a game in which success in a game depends on one's ability to read "tells", i.e., mannerisms, from other players. In particular, when playing at a poker table, players' strategy is partially based on these "tells". Players use them to make guesses as to what kind of cards the player might have as well as whether a player is bluffing or not. At a real poker table, these tells range from easily observable ones such as sweating or trembling of the hands to subtle tells such as shifting of the eyes, biting one's lip, etc. It is clearly impossible to find replacements of this range of cues in an online medium. However, online players were able to develop their own set of cues based on a couple of key factors: *time to take action* and *observed pattern of individuals' behavior over time*. Players with substantial experience playing online believe that they can judge the actions of other online players simply by observing how much time elapses between when it is a player's turn to act and the time "bot" takes to implement their desired action. Players make judgement based on an understanding of the advance betting feature that is built into the dealer "bots". For example, when a player places an advance bet, e.g., for a raise or call, the player is in effect implying that no matter what happens before his or her turn he/she is willing to bet a certain amount of money. This clearly indicates a certain amount of "strength" in the player's hand. This knowledge, in turn, can be used by other players in the game to determine the relative strength of their current hand. However, depending solely on this cue is sometimes difficult (and error prone) since many players routinely place advance bets for "the fun of it". Experienced players are able to separate these players from the serious players based either on *prior observation* or *the basic statistics about a player* (for example, by looking at the number of times the frivolous players have gone bankrupt). They can thus combine this knowledge with any observable cues from the advance betting patterns and adjust their style of play accordingly.

Another common aspect of real-life play is that nonprofessional players tend to exhibit "tells" such as trembling hands or sweating when they hold a particularly good hand. Interestingly, a similar phenomenon seems to manifest itself in the on-line game as well. Players who routinely place advance bets on run of the mill hands will suddenly start betting very carefully and take their time to act when it is their turn during those rounds when their hand is really strong. Good online players are able to pick up on these clues and adjust their play accordingly. We believe that the development of these alternative cues is an important contributor to the continued success of the game.

Socializing Online

One of the aspects of a real-life poker game that makes long hours at the table enjoyable is the socializing that takes place at the tables. While it is customary not to talk when a particular round of betting is in progress, discussion of the hand that just finished is very common. These discussions revolve around issues such as did the winning player play the hand correctly, i.e., were they able to extract the maximum amount of money they could have from the other players, should the losing player(s) have stayed in the hand for as long as they did, etc. Other aspects of "table talk" at a live table include, discussion of non-poker related items (e.g., weather, sports, etc.).

"Table talk" in the online version of the game is accomplished through the use of textual messages. The range of topics discussed in the online version of the game is very similar to what is discussed in a live poker game. However, players tend to use a variety of acronyms for communication purposes. Some of these acronyms are used to indicate the emotional tone of a player. For example, lol is often used to indicate that an incident or joke was particularly funny. A few examples of such acronyms and their explanations are listed in Table 1. Many of these acronyms are common to chat rooms in general while some are specific to poker.

The IRC Poker Player

As indicated earlier, the typical IRC poker player was and is still relatively technologically savvy (despite the increased accessibility of the Internet to non-technical people) and is very likely to be in a profession where

Table 1 Acronyms Frequently Used During "Table Talk"

nh	nice hand
ty	thank you
g1	good one
rotfl	rolling on the floor laughing
str8	straight
bbl	be back later
brb	be right back
wb	welcome back
lol	laughs out loud
r00l	roolers, i.e., star players
s00ted	suited, when more than one card is of the same suit
argggh!	scream of frustration
doh	a stupid mistake
ttfn	ta ta for now

they have easy access to technology. Having access to the Internet at work still remains a key to a user's participation in the game. Users are known and addressed by their nicknames and for the most part conversations do not take an inflammatory or vulgar tone. Any time conversations begin to go down either of these paths, other players intervene and diffuse the situation relatively early. Whether this phenomenon is motivated by a general need for decorum or a desire to keep the game moving is an empirical question.

A large number of players spend upwards of 15 hours a week playing poker on IRC. At the outset, this may seem like a substantial amount of time. However, when one takes into account the fact that most poker players (in a live poker game) spend upwards of five hours at a stretch during a "session", this number does not seem excessive. The most often cited reason for why people spend time on IRC is a desire to improve their poker playing skills (based on an informal open-ended question asked online). The second most cited reason (again based on an open-ended question asked online) for playing IRC poker is entertainment. People use dead time either at work or home to simply log on, play a few hands, socialize a little, etc. An interesting consequence of the social nature of IRC poker is that after playing for a little while (among the regular players) one can almost predict who would be on at a particular time of the day/night. Players would often log on to simply say "Hi!" to their regular playing partners even if they did not have the time to play on that particular day. In this sense, over time, the IRC poker game becomes a forum for socializing and is very similar to some live poker games. For example, in casinos, low-limit games, i.e., games where the stakes are low, tend to be a gathering place for regulars to while away their time playing poker and catching up on other aspects of their life. Since by its very nature the amount of money exchanged is pretty low, the low-limit games in a casino have a much higher social interaction component to them when compared to the high-limit games. The same is true for the IRC game also. People playing the higher-limit games (50-100 and 20-40) tend to be more serious about the game itself and log on primarily for practice whereas the low-limit 10-20 game has a lot more table talk and a definite social flavor to it.

Perhaps one of the most interesting aspects of the online game is the fact that despite the lack of any real money being exchanged, players tend to be very protective and proud of their bankrolls. Recall that everyone starts with $1,000 and that the only way to increase one's bankroll is by winning at the various poker games. The very fact that there currently are several players who have amassed anywhere from a quarter of a million to a million dollars or more through years of IRC play clearly suggests that these players value their IRC bankroll and status. One might even speculate that for these players their bankroll is an indicator of their real-life poker-playing abilities.

The next section describes another popular forum for playing poker online and is followed by a discussion of online poker players' perceptions regarding both forms of the game.

AN ALTERNATIVE FORM OF ONLINE POKER (WRGPT)

The World Rec.Gambling[2] Poker Tournament (WRGPT) is a no-limit Texas Hold'em tournament in which all game activity takes place via electronic mail. The tournament is currently in its 9th edition. All one needs to play this game is a valid e-mail account. The game usually lasts around 9 months before a champion emerges. The rules of the tournament are very similar to the annual World Series of Poker tournament[3] played at Binion's Horseshoe Casino in Las Vegas. The intent of the electronic game is to provide players with the feel for playing a high-stakes tournament without spending any real money.

A special program acts as dealer and manages all aspects of the game. A rich set of commands allows users to indicate their actions in advance as well as take "vacations" from the game. This version of online poker does not require users to spend excessive amounts of time playing the actual game since a single hand may sometimes take many days to complete (depending on response times from users). Still this version of the game also continues to remain extremely popular. The current tournament has over 975 subscribers from many countries. As with the IRC poker game, this game is also absolutely free.

PERCEPTIONS OF ONLINE POKER PLAYERS

How does the online game compare to a live poker game? In this section, we present the results of a preliminary survey of IRC and WRGPT players. Our intention in reporting these results is not to draw conclusions from the data (since the sample size is relatively small). However, the data does provide us with some information as to how people perceive the two online poker games.

Table 2 summarizes the results from some of the key questions in the survey. As noted previously, the IRC version of the game seems to provide a forum for players to improve their skills (Question 3). The relative speed at which hands are dealt and completed per hour (> 100 online compared to < 20 in real life) means that players are able to gain a substantial amount of experience in a relatively short time for a great price (zero dollars). The second key observation is that the richness (or lack thereof) of the medium itself does not seem to be perceived as a problem in the context of "table talk" (Question 4). Players seem to perceive that the textual table talk is an adequate replacement for verbal talk in a live game. In fact, anecdotal evidence suggests that there is a substantially higher amount of table talk in an online game than there is in a live game. One reason for this could be the fact that the online medium allows players to engage in "table talk" without being a disturbance to others at the table.

Slow response times and lack of facial cues seem to be the aspects of the medium that clearly contribute towards players' perceiving the WRGPT game to be very different from a live tournament (Question 5 and Question 2, respectively). Both of these are understandable, with the latter being potentially a serious problem since "tells" are important in a high-stakes tournament. As noted in the section on online cues, players do develop heuristics when engaging in IRC poker that tend to act as surrogates for "tells" in a live game. However, it is interesting to note that despite the lack of cues, WRGPT players actually seemed to believe that they are able to judge their opponents' skill very well (Question 7). While this result may seem some-what surprising to a non-poker player, it is in fact easily explained by the fact players are playing in a tournament. As the WRGPT game progresses and showdowns occur they are posted on a common Web site. By tracing the

Table 2 Means for Selected Questions
        (Scale: 1 - Completely Agree .. 7 - Completely Disagree)

		IRC (n = 16)	WRGPT (n=15)
1	The electronic game is very similar to a real-life game.	4.0	5.0
2	Lack of facial cues makes IRC poker a different game.	3.9	2.7
3	Playing IRC poker has improved my poker skills.	2.4	3.7
4	Lack of table talk makes it a different game than a live poker game.	5.4	3.3
5	Difference in response time makes the game different when compared to a live poker game.	3.6	1.9
6	I play a lot more loosely when playing IRC poker.	3.4	4.7
7	I can evaluate opponents' skill level in online poker as well as I can in a live poker game.	4.5	2.3

actions of players involved in various showdowns as well as observing their reactions to "moves" (e.g., the betting of a substantial amount of money) made by others, good players can evaluate an individual's tournament playing tendencies and ability.

The answer to the question about how loosely players play (Question 6) also suggests that there are a reasonable number of players who play both games seriously. In summary, the results suggest that despite the obvious limitations of the medium players do not have very negative perceptions about the "realness" of either of the virtual poker games.

FROM VIRTUAL TO FACE-TO-FACE

An interesting aspect of this online poker community is that it is no longer a truly virtual community. After a couple of years of playing together on IRC, several members of the community thought that it would be a nice idea to meet once a year in Las Vegas to play poker face-to-face against each other (in a tournament). The get-together was christened BARGE (Big August Rec.Gambling Excursion). What started seven years ago as a small gathering (60 people) has now begun to attract upwards of 350 people to the annual meeting. It is billed as "our annual venture out of cyberspace into the Real World (shudder) in which we get together to meet our most favorite/notorious

Usenet personalities face-to-face, participate in several BARGE-private events" (http://www.conjelco.com/barge/). While the first couple of years players met only once a year in Las Vegas, as the online community grew players found the need to meet face-to-face more often. Thus, several other (regional) meetings were begun. These include: ATLARGE (ATLantic City Annual Rec.Gambling Excursion), FARGO (Foxwoods Annual Rec.Gambling Outing), MARGE (Mississippi Annual Rec.Gambling Excursion), and ES-CARGOT (Experimental Southern California Annual Rec.Gambling Outing and Tournament). The centerpiece of each of the above listed events is a poker tournament (open only to attendees of the event). However, several other social events, such as dinners and symposia (on poker, of course) are also organized. Several custom memorabilia such as T-shirts, individual poker chips, etc. are also distributed at each of these events. However, in keeping with the "free" nature of the online community, each of the events itself is not-for-profit. The organizers contribute their efforts on a volunteer basis with the sole objective being to provide a forum for the online poker players to meet each other face-to-face. The fact that these events are constantly growing in size is a clear indicator of the positive atmosphere created in the online game. When you add in the fact that most of the players attending these events do so at their own cost and many of them schedule their vacations during these events, it becomes very clear that the camaraderie developed during the online interaction is very positive. On the other hand, the growing demand for several "live" meetings a year suggests that the online community needs these real meetings to thrive and grow.

Finally, for proof regarding the perceived quality of the players engaged in the online poker game, one only has to look at the fact that each year one member from the online poker community is sent to participate in the World Series of Poker (WSOP) event in Las Vegas. An event nicknamed TARGET (The Annual Rec.Gambling Entry Tournament) is used to generate funds and elect a "representative" to participate in the World Series of Poker event. While there is no data as to whether someone from the online group has gone very far in the WSOP, it is clear that the players at least believe that they are capable of competing in this world-class event. The results from our survey suggest that they attribute at least some of their skill development to the free online tournaments available to them on IRC and/or WRGPT.

WHAT'S NEXT FOR ONLINE POKER?

The success of the online poker community described above would suggest that commercial options for playing online poker should have emerged by now. In fact, the games section of Yahoo! does have a poker game that looks very similar to the environment described in this chapter. The poker game at Yahoo! brings people from across the globe to the table through its games server. Figure 3 presents a screen shot of the poker game at Yahoo!. The games at Yahoo! are also free and currently only regular Texas Hold'em games are supported (since that is the most popular poker game played in a casino). Clearly, Yahoo!'s interface is a lot more appealing than the interface shown in Figure 2. However, the games at Yahoo! move at a much slower pace than they do on the IRC server. This could partially be a function of the population that plays the games at Yahoo!. For example, since these players may not be as technologically savvy as the typical IRC player, they are likely to: a) have slower connections to the Internet, and b) not be as comfortable using computers. However, the biggest reason for the slow pace is the lack of advanced betting options. Thus, despite the nicer display, the Yahoo! game is technologically at the level that IRC poker was in 1995. Several other commercial games (similar to Yahoo!'s game) also exist. However, none of

Figure 3: Poker Room from Yahoo !

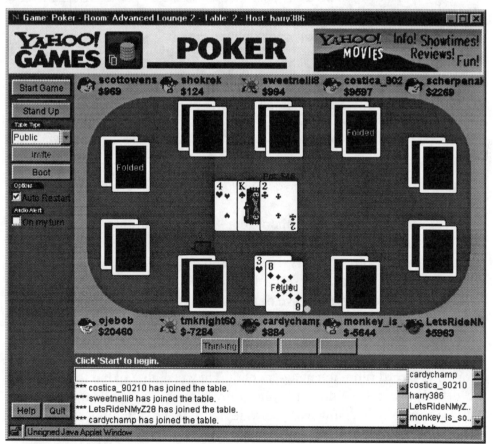

Figure 4: Poker Room Depiction from www.planetpoker.com

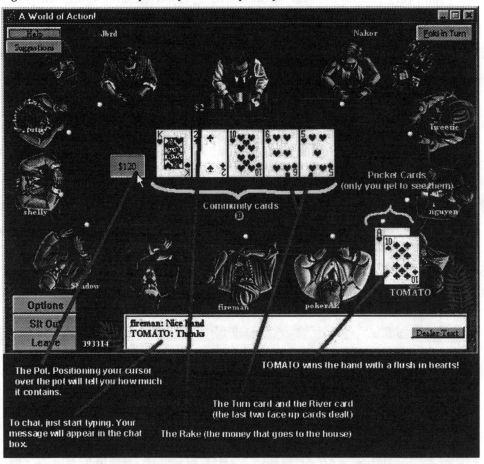

them (at this point) seem to have the strong customer base and support that IRC poker has.

While the poker game at Yahoo! simply provides an entertainment forum for players, there are at least a dozen online casinos that are offering play for real money against live players (Figure 4 shows an example screenshot from www.planetpoker.com). These casinos are betting (no pun intended) on online poker becoming the wave of the future. Given the relative success of the online poker community described above, one would expect that "virtual" casinos where people can play for real money would be very popular. Poker at a virtual casino has several advantages. For example, players do not have to drive to a card room to engage in play. They can also spend long hours at the virtual poker table while sitting in an environment (couch, bed, etc.) where they are comfortable. However, there are a number of stumbling blocks to the rise of such virtual casinos. First, there is the issue of whether playing in such casinos is legal (Robbins, 1996; Rose, 1998; Salbu, 1998; Starkman, 1998). Most of these casinos are hosted from offshore locations, e.g., the Caribbean Islands, and are thus legal establishments. However, many states in the US are beginning to impose restrictions on whether their citizens can participate in such casinos (Curry, 1998). Even if all the legal issues were resolved it is still not clear that poker players (especially technologically savvy ones) would flock to these casinos (Zinchiak, 2000). Interviews conducted with many of the current IRC poker players suggest that issues that they are most concerned about include: a) lack of knowledge of the opponents, b) lack of knowledge about the integrity of the software, c) inability to determine when two or more people at the table are colluding and thus cheating, and d) lack of trust in offshore establishments' financial dealings.

CONCLUSIONS

In this chapter, we described the characteristics of an online poker community and identified several factors that have led to the success and growth of the community. The key factors identified include: a) the availability of advanced software that has adapted to changing needs of the users, and b) the availability of an environment (through features of the software) that is conducive to the generation of online cues as replacement for cues available in a live poker game as well as the facilitation of social interaction among the players. A survey of online players indicates that most players found the online game to be a cheap and effective way of improving their playing skills. Players also seemed to take the online game very seriously and tended to view their bankrolls as an indicator of their poker-playing ability. The creation of real-life meetings where players from the virtual world were able to associate faces with nicknames was also identified as an important contributor to the success of the community.

What does the future hold for online gaming? Online games are likely to play a significant role as a mechanism for attracting customers to Web sites providing various types of content. According to Dale Crowley, CEO of NuvoStudios (http://www.nuvostudios.com), a content development company specializing in the creation of innovative web-based games and interactive entertainment products, many websites are offering several incentives such as prizes, points etc. for users to play games at their websites. These incentives provide a tangible reason for people to provide data about themselves in order to play the games. The data provided by these users can be captured in a database which can then be used for data mining and marketing purposes. The creation of games that capture user information and provide prizes, however, adds a level of difficulty because of the significant database interaction component. Most online games are created using Java 1.1 (due to its wide support on browsers). However, as support for Java 2 increases, game developers will move towards this platform to take advantage of its enhanced 2-D and 3-D graphics capabilities.

The majority of games available online currently are single player versions. However, the future of online games clearly seems to be multi-player online games (like IRC poker). For example, in addition to providing a single player version of their popular Who Wants To Be a Millionaire? game, abc.com also provides a multi-player version that provides users with the ability (via Enhanced TV) to play along with the show being aired at that time. Users can login to www.abc.com and compete with other online users in answering questions that are posed to contestants on the popular TV show. According to Dale Crowley, current technological challenges such as the inherent latency and lack of bandwidth in the current version of the public internet as well as the complexity of writing software that can handle large volumes of users and surges in use (at peak times) are holding back the emergence of multi-player versions of online games. However, he believes that these technological challenges will be solved in the very near future leading to a substantial increase in the number of multi-player online games.

Will the new gaming communities that emerge from the predicted increase in the number of virtual play worlds evolve in a manner similar to what was described in this chapter? Only time will tell. What is certain is that no matter the form they take, virtual worlds where users can "play" are here to stay.

REFERENCES

Barry, G. (1998). "Seven Billion Dollar Gambling Market Predicted," *Interactive Gaming News*, www.igaming.com.

Curry, T. (1998)."States Strive to Regulate Betting", www.msnbc.com/news/103424.asp.

Davis, B. (1992). *Gambling in America: A Growth Industry. An Impact Book*, Franklin Watts, New York.

Jones, L. (1994). *Winning Low-limit Hold'em*, ConJelCo.

Lahey, A.(1998). "Raising the Ante on Digital Smarts," *Canadian Business*, Aug., 71-73.

Larkey, P.(1997). Kadane, J.B., Austin, R. and Zamir, S. "Skill in Games," Management Science, 43(1),596-609.

National Gambling Impact Study Commission (1999). *Final Report.* http://www.ngisc.gov/reports/finrpt.html.

Robbins, N.(1996). "Baby Needs a New Pair of CyberShoes: The Legality of Casino Gambling on the Internet," *B.U. Journal of Science & Technology Law*, 2(7).

Rose, N.I. (1998). "Internet Gambling and Police Power," *Gaming Law Review*, 2(2).

Salbu, S.R.(1998). "Who Should Govern The Internet? Monitoring and Supporting a New Frontier," *Harvard Journal of Law & Technology*, 11(429).

Skalnsky, D. and Malmuth, M.(1999). *Hold'em Poker for Advanced Players*, Two Plus Two Publishing LLC, 3rd Edition.

Starkman, D.(1998). "U.S. Indicts 14 over Gambling on the Internet," *Wall Street Journal*, March 5.

Zinciak, M. (2000). "Exploring the Direction and Future of Interactive Gaming," *Interactive Gaming News*, www.igaming.com.

ENDNOTES

1 Readers unfamiliar with these games can read the rules at http://www.conjelco.com/faq/poker.html.

2 Rec.Gambling is a Usenet newsgroup

3 The premier poker tournament in the world

Chapter 8

Online Recreation and Play in Organizational Life: The Internet as Virtual Contested Terrain

Jo Ann Oravec
University of Wisconsin-Whitewater, USA

There are in fact very few activities which cannot be classed either as work or play according as you choose to regard them" (George Orwell, The Road to Wigan Pier, 1937).

INTRODUCTION

Online recreation and play are becoming new "contested terrains" in organizations as managers and employees both seek to understand and control them, often at cross-purposes. Advances in computer and network technology have brought new dimensions to recreation in workplace settings, from frolicking online agents and assistants to sophisticated Internet games with thousands of participants. Online shopping, stock trading, and gambling are adding to the already formidable roster of recreational opportunities. The problems organizations are facing that are linked to these technological applications have gained the attention of the popular media. Consider the following *Newsweek* commentary describing the average workplace: "With the Internet morphing into the virtual Mall of America, day trading, Quake playing, vacation planning and hard-core porn (not to mention gateways to exciting new careers) are all just a click away" (Naughton, Raymond, Shulman, and Struzzi, 1999).

This chapter analyzes the emerging forms of online recreation and play in the workplace and addresses how their benefits and drawbacks are being defined. It discusses how online work and play are often becoming seamlessly melded and sometimes confused, as predicted by Orwell in the epigraph. Managers are responding to online recreation in a wide spectrum of ways, from restricting all "personal" uses of computing to openly encouraging them (often as a means of keeping employees at their desks for long hours). In turn, many employees are devising sophisticated ways of countering managerial restrictions and of utilizing online recreation and play for their own purposes. New terms are being coined to characterize these phenomena, including "cyberloafing" and "cyber-slacking" (Oravec, 1999). A growing number of organizations have embraced a variety of forms of recreation, food and beverage services, as well as other perks as ways of affording individuals who are rooted to their workstations the opportunity to take a break without leaving the confines of their workplaces. Some guidance as to how to make workplaces more appealing to those who occupy them have emerged, such as *Managing to Have Fun* (Weinstein, 1996) and *The Art of Napping at Work* (Anthony and Anthony, 1999). However, in many organizations the computer network has been transformed into a virtual battleground, with managers and employees at odds as to whether or when computers should be used for "personal" (and presumably non-work) purposes. There have already been many battlefield casualties: some employees have lost their jobs because of non-sanctioned recreational uses of computers, and the issues involved have consumed valuable managerial and personnel resources.

WHY IS ONLINE WORKPLACE PLAY SUCH A CONCERN?

With the Internet, a wide variety of online recreation can take place in the interstitial periods between various workplace activities— and without the direct face-to-face interaction of individuals. The shop floor was identified as a contested terrain in past decades (Edwards, 1978), with blue collar workers opposing their bosses on a variety of matters relating to everyday workplace conditions. Today in high-tech settings many managers and employees are wrestling with issues of whether or when online recreation and play are appropriate and as to how these activities are to be characterized and framed (which is in itself a kind of game). What nonwork uses of computers and the Internet are to be condoned, and which should be restricted? Which uses of computing are indeed aptly labeled as "nonwork" in an era when computers are generally advertised as being fun to use? These questions are being addressed via technology (the use of monitoring devices) and with policies and social sanctions, along with reasoned discourse.

Managerial policies and activities concerning online recreation are just some of the many forms of control that organizations institute over what goes on in the workplace, but they are important ones. Managers' stances toward online recreation signal their approaches toward larger issues of how work is to be constituted within the organization. The hard-line positions of some managers against some forms of online recreation may be required in some instances and directly related to important organizational goals. For example, air traffic controllers should be expected to keep focused on landing real airplanes rather than escape into fantasy video games during their assigned working times. However, many managers who place heavy restrictions on online recreation are often signaling to their subordinates that what is more highly valued within the organization is not productive work itself but the superficial appearance that people are indeed being "busy" and that work activity of some kind is going on. For example, managers who stop workers from checking their horoscopes or playing solitaire in idle moments on the job— who would rather that they do unnecessary tasks or just sit still— are reflecting their perspectives toward work and the roles of employees. Some may prefer that employees engage in a kind of charade, remaining at seemingly high attention levels so as to appear as if they are working (even if no work is immediately available). Others may believe that allowing workers to use computers in ways that are recreational will send them down a slippery slope to complete hedonism on the job. The chapter discusses some means through which organizations can look beyond the surface concerns about online work and play in the workplace and implement "constructive recreation" strategies, ways of opening the dialogue between managers and employees about online recreation. Constructive recreation strategies can help to integrate a wide assortment of "personal" uses of the Internet into the workplace, including computer-supported leisure and play opportunities, so as to increase levels of productivity while enhancing individuals' well being.

Issues concerning online recreation have long roots. Workplaces have served as platforms not only for managerially labeled "productive" effort but also for recreation, whether impromptu or organized, sanctioned or unsanctioned. However, recreation in uncontrolled, spontaneous forms can be frightening to managers who associate the notion of "management" with the immediate control of worker activity. Frederick Taylor included forms of "managed recreation" as part of his *Scientific Management* strategies. He sought ways to harness the needs of workers for breaks and refreshment to serve the ends of management (Taylor, 1913/1947). Through the twentieth century, many organizations have sponsored parties, picnics, and newsletters, often designed with the help of human relations experts with the aim of increasing employee morale as well as loyalty to the organization.

In an effort to obtain some of the benefits of recreation, many organizations sponsor various forms of after-work activities, such as golf and football outings or community volunteer initiatives; informal business discussions are often held during these gatherings. In general, the overlap or interaction between an employee's sanctioned work activity and other activities has been a major focus of attention for managers and researchers for the past several decades, with "the recognition that a person' s work and personal lives are not separate entities but, instead, interrelated and intertwined domains having reciprocal effects on each other" (Danna and Griffin 1999, p. 357). For example, Siemens Corporation provided workers with on-site recreation facilities in the 1970s and has continued its linkage between health and workplace performance with the institution of an online health program that employees can access while at their desks. Many kinds of recreational or "personal" uses of computing are not sanctioned, however, or are sanctioned only within limited contexts. Construction of acceptable limits for such uses is a continuous process within organizations that takes many forms, from the individual supervisor talking with a subordinate to the monitoring of the computer-based interaction of everyone in an organization.

Many programs to provide employees with recreational opportunities have afforded considerable benefits. However, for many individuals a good share of everyday recreation— the leisure activities that are needed for them to function normally— has to be obtained during breaks and in idle moments rather than in after work initiatives, and often in ways that are not yet sanctioned by management. In *Ten Thousand Working Days*, Schrank (1978) labeled the use of work time for nonscheduled breaks and socializing with others on the job as "schmoozing" (from "schmooze," a Yiddish word). Despite the higher levels of productivity associated with modern machinery, in most Western countries the overall workloads of households are increasing (as described in Schor, 1991). Life after working hours can be even more stressful and chaotic than time on the job— filled with housework, commuting, care for children or aging parents, as well as community obligations. Many individuals are also "on call" after their formal working day ends or take work home with them at nights. This arrangement leaves very little time for the kinds of activities traditionally associated with recreation— such as day-long golfing or boating events that take people away from their workplaces and homes— or even for watching television or relaxing at home.

Compounding the pressures of increasing workloads are those involved in an increasingly-competitive society. The books *Netslaves* (Lessard and Baldwin, 1999) and *Nudist on the Late Shift: And Other True Tales of Silicon Valley* (Bronson, 1999) provide narratives of long hours and intense business rivalries. Other accounts relate how a number of high tech employees are simply afraid to take vacations, believing that they will be replaced or will become less valuable to the organization if they do (Bole ,1998). Even in less hectic business arenas, there are many pressures to stay current and connected by spending many hours on the job. Online diversions are ready-at-hand in these environments; they can help provide a means for individuals to express themselves in ways that differ from their demanding organizational and family roles and activities, as well as obtain a sense of control even in otherwise chaotic workplace circumstances. Individuals who play computer games at their desks take on different roles— if only for a short while— and have successes and failures based on their gaming abilities, not solely on their prowess in dealing with the exigencies of organizational life. They construct new identities (that of the person who scored the lowest in a golf match against a "virtual" Jack Nicklaus, for example), identities that differ from their normal organizational roles. These identities can play powerful roles in individuals' lives, serving as a counterpoint to institutionally-assigned identities that are less rich and varied.

Some social scientists who have studied time and leisure issues have projected that individuals in our society attempt to "increase the yield" of their recreational hours by consuming more goods and services (Godbey, Lifset, and Robinson, 1999), in much the same way that providing the proper resources can raise levels of workplace productivity. For example, individuals purchase better golf clubs or fishing gear in order to make the limited recreational times that they have more fun and the stories they tell about these times more interesting. In similar ways, online recreation is part of many individuals' efforts to increase the yield of their working hours by more tightly coupling (if not fusing) work and recreation. The idle moments at the office spent waiting for someone or for resources to arrive can be filled in a way that refreshes the worker and makes it possible to work longer periods on the job (although this in itself can cause problems, as related in an upcoming section). Online recreation allows many individuals to "multi-task" their work and recreation, making their working lives increasingly complex and multidimensional.

ONLINE RECREATION
AND KNOWLEDGE WORKERS

Issues concerning online recreation and play in the workplace are especially complex concerning knowledge workers since they often work irregular schedules and labor long periods of time without supervision. "Knowledge workers" are individuals who handle streams of complex ideas in their day-to-day efforts. Runge (1994, p. 10) describes these workers in the following fashion:

> They are highly skilled, well educated, and work with complex and intellectual tasks. Instead of iron and steel, they work with electronics, biotechnologies, communications, and information systems. They must deal with multiple causes and effects. Regardless of the company organizational charts, there is substantial overlap between worker and manager...

Many dimensions of online recreation and play can apparently serve to increase organizational productivity and enhance employee well-being, especially among knowledge workers. Online recreation is immediately at hand and can often be engaged in without directly disrupting work schedules. The ability to access such recreation at will can provide a useful safety-valve for individuals who are facing tough and often unyielding situations on the job. However, there is much about recreation and play that is not understood so any analysis of this sort soon becomes highly speculative. Play is often considered a "necessity" for children in today's society, supporting their intellectual and social development; the role of play in adult lives is less clear, however.

Drawing an analogy to physical sport and exercise, online recreation and play can equip individuals with the means to challenge their intellects in ways that vary from their everyday workplace activity (a kind of intellectual "cross-training"). For example, many forms of online play can teach the skills of simulation, strategy, and war gaming that are particularly useful in knowledge-work contexts. Perhaps more importantly, online recreation (as well as non-computer-based forms of recreation) can enable organizational participants to compose other sorts of narratives about themselves than the kinds that are related to their organizational activities. In a manner similar to the carnivals of the Middle Ages, recreation can provide a venue for reversing social roles and exploring new ones (Bakhtin, 1984), of providing counterbalances to the often regimented worlds of the workplace. Adults who are not afforded such venues can lose perspective on workplace and other everyday activity and become less flexible in terms of their social roles.

The benefits of recreation for adults have been explored by a number of researchers in the social sciences and industrial engineering. For instance, Coleman and Iso-Ahola (1993) show that participation in physically and socially active leisure can buffer the stresses associated with the challenges of everyday life. "Leisure-generated self-determination disposition and leisure-generated social support are the two main properties of leisure that presumably buffer against increased life stress," (p. 114). The active choice that people make of engaging in online recreation (and the related self-determination) is thus a part of its benefits, along with its positive and supportive social aspects, both of which may be lacking in hectic or overly competitive working environments. Labeling the few minutes that it takes to check online sports scores or horoscopes at one's desk as "recreation" may seem a stretch, but such recaptured moments allow individuals to have some control over their activities in situations that are otherwise stressful and constraining.

However, there are less rosy aspects to online recreation. Most of us have heard anecdotal accounts of computer addicts for whom the pursuit of online recreation has taken an unfortunate turn. According to some medical specialists, some individuals can become "addicted" to computer games and other kinds of online pursuits, and the benefits of such recreation to the individual and organization can thus be decreased. An Internet Addiction Syndrome (IAS) has been specifically identified by some psychologists (Young, 1998) with characteristics that include (1) access of the Internet for progressively longer periods of time, (2) ineffective attempts to decrease Internet use, (3) expenditure of considerable amounts of time on Internet-related activities, (4) letting social and occupational responsibilities suffer, (5) withdrawal symptoms, and (6) persistence of behavior even though the sufferer acknowledges its negative personal and social impact. Online gambling can provide particularly difficult dimensions of this problem. Many kinds of social behavior have been labeled as "addictive," and including online addictions into this mix may be excessive. However, there is a great potential for some individuals to exceed reasonable limitations in their pursuit of recreation, a problem that will be difficult for managers to confront. However, eliminating all online recreation because of the problematic behavior of some individuals would be an unfortunate response to this situation.

THE EVOLUTION OF ONLINE RECREATION IN THE WORKPLACE

In past decades, computer-supported recreation and play had often been tightly controlled (even during work breaks) because of the drain they placed on limited organizational computing resources. Individuals who wanted to indulge in such classic computer games as Zork (which was originally a text-based adventure game) had to use their organization's mainframes during late night or early morning hours. Since many computer programmers did their work at odd hours anyway this was not taken to be an extraordinary inconvenience. Today, PCs, workstations, and laptops with substantial computational power are readily available to employees, providing a ready outlet for intellectual and social escapism. The gaming industry has used the power of these new computing tools in ways that are designed to capture the attention of adults as well as children. For example, in the early 1990s imaginative adventure and puzzle-style games such as Myst by Broderbund rekindled interest in gaming among adults who may have tired of the classic arcade games. Today, gaming portals such as gamers.com link players with thousands of online gaming opportunities as well as business news about the gaming industry. There are still some concerns about the drains on organizational network resources that certain Internet games can engender, especially in smaller organizations with limited network bandwidth, but the primary focus of attention of managers to online recreation issues has been related to their social and economic dimensions.

In online settings, recreational opportunities are seldom far away from more "productive" workplace activities. Learning online games has been frequently used as a way to decrease individuals' computer anxiety levels and introduce them to computing skills (Bloom, 1985). Microsoft Corporation has long had a practice of bundling games (including solitaire and mine-sweeper) with its operating systems, so it is easy for employees to locate sources of entertainment. Reportedly, Bill Gates had minesweeper removed from his own system because he found it to be personally addictive (Allerton, 1997). Many of the computer games available today have high quality graphics and sound capabilities and thus can help individuals understand and explore new forms of interactivity— especially the kinds that pertain to role playing and character construction. Game designers often "push the limits" of technology and explore technological features (especially in the arena of 3-D graphics) that later emerge in everyday commercial products.

The computer technologies that support such recreation (especially graphical and networking capabilities) have greatly expanded in quality and availability over the past decade. Modes of computer-based play include single-player games on PCs along with multi-player games on organizational intranets or the Internet. Multiplayer gaming does not require individuals to locate their own partners: Playsite, for example, offers hundreds of games and matches players with willing partners worldwide (www.playsite.com). Online games can be complex and demanding, such as role-playing games that involve numerous characters and complicated rules. Some of these games can be especially addictive, such as EverQuest, which has been banned in a number of organizations. Many less involving games (such as popular board games) are also available online, and some have been reproduced in 3-D or otherwise enhanced. Those who believe that online recreation can be easily resolved by monitoring computer network activity will be dismayed by the increasing sophistication of hand-held devices such as the Nintendo *Gameboy* and virtual pets; many of these can be concealed in desk drawers or jacket pockets. The *Palm Pilot* that holds one's business receipts and contact list can also hold *Tiger Woods' PGA Tour Golf.*

Many recreational activities are intended to hook individuals into regular participation, including chat rooms, online gambling, and shopping malls. There are soap operas on the Web as well as a number of horoscope services. It is often difficult to tell which uses of the Internet are related to business needs and which are recreational; many sites have dual purposes, combining games or sports scores with more serious pursuits. Workplace network connections are generally faster than those available in homes, so the temptation to access sites that require substantial bandwidth at work can be strong.

Microsoft Corporation developed a number of products that integrate opportunities for entertainment and forms of social engagement with user assistance in its "social computing" initiatives. Social computing is the design of user interfaces to provide some of the dimensions of human-like interaction. In *Office 97* and *2000*, users have a choice of clever "office assistants" that can aid them in solving problems (including an Einstein-like character and a dancing paper clip). One of Microsoft's pioneering social computing initiatives, *Bob*, was designed to introduce novice users to computer applications through the use of wise-cracking cartoon birds and animals and other kinds of clever animation. *Bob* was not commercially successful; however, many of its features have become integrated into more mainstream computing applications. Intelligent "agents" are being designed that appear in the form of characters that are entertaining but also have powerful computing functions. Online virtual pets are also becoming popular: "Dogz" (from PF Magic Corporation) can be prancing around spreadsheets and word processing programs while employees perform their everyday tasks. The Dogz are "digital puppies" that can reside on a screen along with more serious application programs. Dogz demand attention at random intervals, and respond with tail wags when they are given their virtual puppy treats. An assortment of new interactive toys (some of which connect with the Internet in some way) are also providing workplace diversions (Oravec, forthcoming).

Other kinds of online diversions and distractions are emerging in workplaces that may eventually have even more extensive ramifications for what goes on in routine organizational activity. For example, some parents can observe their children over the Internet as they play in day care centers; they have access to frequently updated snapshots of their children's activities through software such as SpyCam. The parents are provided codes to enter on a particular web site that give them access to these snapshots, thus allowing them to ascertain what their children are doing without leaving work. Other Internet sites allow individuals to manage their personal investments and perform other activities online; the growing acceptance of online brokerages (such as eTrade) has added a new category of personal use of computers in the workplace, one that is popular even among the more serious-minded. Soon, many people will also use the Internet to verify that their home security systems are working. Checking on children and financial holdings can serve to reduce stress and ultimately make individuals more productive. However, in some circumstances, these efforts at stress reduction can be dysfunctional as they increase in extent (though perhaps not in effectiveness); they have the potential to draw people away from what is happening in the workplace and into their own personal realms.

Some "serious" computer applications blur the line between work and recreation, which can provide related difficulties for organizations. Often surfing the Internet or fiddling with various computer applications in regular workplace efforts can interfere with productivity, as individuals focus more on the application of the technology than on demonstrably productive effort. The search for certain materials on the Internet or the perfecting of a desktop publishing creation can involve employees to such an extent that they lose a sense of proportion as to the value of the item or the business relevance of the endeavor. Simple efforts to obtain a quote for the epigraph of a report or locate a special font can become worldwide scavenger hunts as individuals enlist others in their quests. John Kemeny, the developer of the Basic programming language, once remarked that the everyday notices produced by his academic department at Dartmouth were beginning to look like "illuminated manuscripts" as faculty and students showed off their desktop publishing skills. The savings in time associated with the computer were drastically being reduced as a consequence (Kemeny 1990). Managers can find this kind of playful and exploratory approach to everyday tasks frustrating to control; the standards for the visual quality of everyday posters and other print items have risen dramatically, for example, and many individuals counter the suggestion that they settle for a less-than-perfect item with moral outrage. However, the benefits of having a company picnic or softball game announced with a graphically-stunning document are dubious.

MANAGERIAL RESTRICTIONS AGAINST ONLINE RECREATION ... AND EMPLOYEE RESISTANCE

Organizations are socially constructed entities, with various aspects of organizational life being negotiated through organizational policies and through everyday interaction among individuals (Oravec, 1996). Time on the job has often been considered as properly belonging to the employer, and when employees directed their energies to nonwork activities they were construed as akin to thieves, except for management-sanctioned recreational opportunities and breaks. However, in practice many kinds of nonwork activity have been deemed acceptable in workplace contexts. The kinds of nonwork activities that are allowed if not supported in organizations reflect the organizations' culture and values, from softball teams to holiday parties. Restrictions of online recreation and the monitoring of workstations to implement these restrictions have symbolic value in organizations, signaling to organizational participants the "proper" way to view worktime and computing resources. They show that management believes that the realm of cyberspace is one that can and should be controlled, sending out a challenge to employees who may feel (because of their levels of expertise or interest) that cyberspace is indeed rightfully theirs.

Managers do have some reason to be concerned about online recreation, however. In widely-disseminated survey results, the monitoring software firm SurfWatch estimates that businesses lose more than a billion dollars per year because of online recreation, a figure that can be expected to grow in coming years (Naughton et al., 1999). There are also less tangible side effects. For example, many forms of computer-based play can serve to isolate individuals from others in the workplace. Friendly sports betting pools in an office can serve to bring people together; however, a comparable activity on the Internet may draw individuals away from their co-workers (unless the co-workers are frequenting that particular Internet site). Computer-based play can also encourage sedentary behavior; people taking a break from their normal work routines through computer games or recreational surfing lose the opportunity to vary their postures and move around their work areas. In the near term future, computer games and virtual reality (VR) adventures that are integrated into exercise routines may be more common (as they are in some gyms), but currently most individuals engage in online recreation in much the same physical posture as their other workplace activities. Online recreation thus can compound the physical problems triggered by long days on the job. Another concern is the new varieties of "horseplay" that have emerged in online realms; some individuals who are more proficient technically tend to tease or harass novices online (Fox, 1993), resulting in the loss of productivity of both parties.

The complexity of organizational recreation issues is compounded by influences from the media and from new or returning entrants to the workforce. Young people can easily acquire images and expectations from the popular media of how recreation and play will be coupled with work. Television sitcoms generally portray organizations that are filled with levity and amusement, with hapless bosses incapable of creating order— which does not provide a useful model of how to couple recreation and work. The average age of regular players of computer-based games in the office is reportedly 31 (SBT Corporation, 1997), which shows that the online recreation problem is not merely associated with young people. Few schools are preparing students to use online recreation in constructive ways. In preparation for their future careers, students beyond the early years have often been educated that time spent in play is "wasted" time, with the exception of various structured sport activities (which are associated with increases in physical health).

With expanding levels of online play activity and other managerial concerns has come an increased emphasis on workplace monitoring, which has evolved in power and complexity. Managers have an assortment of new means for monitoring employee activities in minute detail, from systems that list every Web site employees visit within a certain period of time to those that display what is currently being projected on employees' screens. Kinds of software for monitoring computer and Internet usage are expanding in variety and availability, including *GameWarden* by Wards Creek Software as well as NNPRO (a program from NetNanny Software International, whose main product is designed to monitor children's computer usage and filter out inappropriate websites). Monitoring of everyday computer usage may cause stress and trigger resentment in employees, whether or not it serves its primary purposes. The *Wall Street Journal* reports that the technical people who are involved in monitoring are gaining considerable power in organizations, generally with lack of laws to restrict their actions or solid legal precedents (McCarthy, 2000). Social solutions to online recreation concerns should thus be explored before introducing monitoring, such as enlisting project team members to keep each other's workplace recreation within reasonable levels; peer pressure is a powerful device within workgroups and there can be considerable peer opposition to abuse of computer-based recreation and other organizational perquisites.

In its efforts to control online recreation, some organizations (such as Mellon Bank) have banned the personal use of the Internet while at work ("Mellon Outlaws," 1998). Websites included under Mellon's restrictions include entertainment, games, humor, gambling, drugs, job searches, lifestyle, sports, opinion, politics, and religion. Other organizations have taken severe stands toward computer-assisted recreation by periodically removing all games from organizational computers. Governor George Allen of Virginia issued a directive that banned all games from state offices, and the US Senate voted in 1997 to ban games from federal computer systems (although the measure did not pass both houses of Congress). Senator Lauch Faircloth (R-N.C.) declared that, "It's ludicrous that taxpayers are paying people to play computer games. They do nothing but decrease productivity" (Allerton 1997). A number of writers on management topics have also supported such hard-line approaches toward online workplace recreation; O'Connor (1996), for example, declares that if employers were not currently focusing on other important workplace issues more of them would seek to eliminate such activities. Hard-line policies against the recreational use of computers may indeed serve the short-term goal of restricting some forms of access to online play opportunities. However, they do not resolve the larger issues of creating a workplace that is optimally productive and supportive of its participants' well-being. Thus managers and employees need to work together to harness the positive dimensions of recreation and minimize its dysfunctional aspects.

Employees have not been passive onlookers in the struggle to control this virtual terrain, however. Employees develop various kinds of resistance to managerial policies and practices that they find constraining or unreasonable (de Certeau, 1984), and opposition to policies against online recreation is no exception. In many organizational contexts, workers must appear to be working for long hours, whether or not productive work is actually being done or in fact can be accomplished. However, by using their workstations, they can take short "fantasy breaks" and in other ways gain some distance from their work (and possibly some perspective as well). Some technological forms of resistance to managerial sanctions against online recreation have thus been fashioned. For example, a large variety of forms of computer-based recreation are emerging that are nearly impossible to control, including those provided by hand-held systems. The "boss button" was invented for web pages and computer games as a means for disguising employees' activities:

> Boss buttons allow Web surfers to instantly erase the screen they're
> looking at — for instance, the Web page dealing with Chicago's best

taverns — and instantly replace it with a sham spreadsheet, just in case a manager walks by Daumeyer (1996, p. 1B).

Along with boss buttons are "spreadsheet blackjack" games that enable employees to appear to be working on a "serious" spreadsheet application while they are really playing a form of blackjack. A variety of levels of "gaming" are thus transpiring here, including the organizational games between managers and employees as well as the computer game itself (although if computer monitoring is involved, most boss buttons and spreadsheet blackjack ploys can be foiled). Thus unfortunately, rather than challenging inappropriate or confining norms about the appearance of workplace activity, online recreation can support them, continuing the workplace games that many employees and managers engage in everyday. Employees can siphon energies into computer games that are possibly better spent in striving for better working conditions. There are no simple ways to eliminate these presentation games, but open discussion between managers and employees about the constructive uses of online recreation can help to increase the potential for it to be used in ways that benefit both individuals and the organization as a whole.

The kinds of problems that organizations are facing as managers and employees counter each other on the virtual contested terrain are literally moving to the home court. As teleworking and the "virtual office" become more common, more individuals are tackling comparable issues of self-discipline and personal control in their own home offices (Apgar, 1998), and managers are trying to figure out how to retain their positions as "managers" in these realms. Organizations will have to deal increasingly with matters of trust on a number of fronts as workers perform many of their activities away from direct supervision. Individuals working from home are learning to counter such disturbances as friendly next-door neighbors while performing adequately at their virtual workplaces, though some are apparently not very successful at balancing work and nonwork realms. Teleworkers who have used games to decrease their stress levels when at home will certainly want to engage in comparable activities while they spend time in traditional workplaces. The skills that the managers of telecommuters and virtual office participants learn include enhanced communication and time management abilities as well as ways to establish and maintain trust. These skills will be of great assistance in resolving the virtual contested terrain battles described in this chapter.

SOME CONCLUSIONS AND REFLECTIONS: TOWARD AN END TO THE VIRTUAL BATTLES OVER ONLINE RECREATION

Online recreation provides yet another contested terrain in the workplace— where managers and employees work out roles and relationships often through confrontation, conflict and subterfuge as well as reasoned discourse. Knowledge workers (along with many of their white-collar counterparts) are generally only a keystroke away from online recreational ventures. Such online activities are often part of the process through which individuals construct an identity in workplace contexts in a way that extends beyond the traditional organization chart. Online recreation can also be part of individuals' strategies to "increase the yield" of their waking hours, helping them to extend the limits of their working days by providing an extra dimension to the time spent in the workplace. Rather than going through the effort of "looking busy," a set of performances that was very common in generations past, today's employees can utilize their spare moments on the job in doing something that will refresh themselves and possibly recharge their mental batteries. Such constructive uses of recreation require a number of organizational changes, such as shifts in management styles and increases in the empowerment and self-direction of employees.

Organizations can work to integrate opportunities for recreation into more "productive" computing functions; managers and employees together can attempt to construct workplace environments in which trust and mutual respect increase the potentials both for productive work and constructive recreation. In their efforts to integrate online recreation into workplaces, organizations can benefit from the approaches that are being developed to manage individuals who spend their working hours outside the confines of the traditional workplace, including those who telecommute. Education and training initiatives can be useful for organizations in these efforts as well: New employees and students can be aided toward understanding how to couple work and recreation in ways that increase their effectiveness. Integrating recreation into the workplace can be hard work in itself, however; recreational uses of computers can encounter "glitches" as well as more serious uses, and eliminating these glitches can consume organizational time and effort. Online recreation and play will thus present persisting concerns as well as alluring potentials for organizations in the decades to come.

It is nearly inevitable that online recreation will become an integral element of day-to-day workplace activity in many organizations, despite the effort of many managers to contain it. Online recreation in the workplace can indeed have considerable advantages, both for the individuals involved and for the organization as a whole.   These activities can serve to relieve stress as well as open previously blocked creative channels.   Such recreations as computer games can give individuals much-needed diversions and increase their senses of control while providing some specific educational benefits, in particular the ability to understand and work within the confines of simulated worlds. Surfing the Internet can expose employees to useful online resources. Elements of recreation can also be infused into various mundane computing activities: For example, entertainment in the form of computer agents and assistants is already being integrated into commonplace tasks such as word processing, and computer games are provided along with operating systems. Some individuals can indeed take these recreational aspects too far, investing extraordinary amounts of time and effort into everyday computing tasks, fine-tuning their computer-based creations or otherwise displaying their newly acquired expertise.   Advances in computing technology are thus serving to blur the distinctions between work and play, and the "contested terrain" between managers and employees is likely to expand dramatically.

REFERENCES

Allerton, H.(1997). "Working life," *Training & Development,* 51(11), 103-6.

Anthony, B., and Anthony, C.(1999). *The Art of Napping at Work*, Larson Publications, Burdett, NY.

Apgar, M. (1998). "The Alternative Workplace: Changing Where and How People Work," *Harvard Business Review*, 76(3), 121-137.

Bakhtin, M.(1984). *Rabelais and his World*, Indiana University Press, Bloomington, IN.

Bloom, A.(1985). "An Anxiety Management Approach to Computerphobia," *Training and Development Journal*, 39(1), 90-92.

Bole, K.(1998). "Workers tell what they didn't do on their summer vacation," *Business Journal Serving San Jose & Silicon Valley*, 16(5), 55.

Bronson, P.(1999). *Nudist on the Late Shift: And Other True Tales of Silicon Valley,* Random House, New York.

de Certeau, M.(1984). *The practice of everyday life*, University of California Press, Berkeley, CA.

Coleman, D. and Iso-Ahola, S. (1993). "Leisure and health: The role of social support and self-determination," *Journal of Leisure Research*, 25(2), 111-128.

Daumeyer, R.(1996). "Net surfers not doing bosses any favors," *Cincinnati Business Courier*, 13(26), 1B-2B.

Edwards, R.(1978). *Contested Terrain: The Transformation of the Workplace in the Twentieth Century,* Heineman, New York.

Fox, R.(1993). "Cyberbashing," *Communications of the ACM*, 36(11), 11-12.

Godbey, G., Lifset, R., and Robinson, J. (1999). "No time to waste: An exploration of time use, attitudes toward time, and the generation of municipal solid waste," *Social Research,* 65(1), 101-141.

Kemeny, J.(1990). "Computers in education: Progress at a snail's pace," *EDUCOM Review,* 25(3), 44-47.

Lessard, B. and Baldwin, S.(1999). *NetSlaves: True Tales of Working the Web*, McGraw-Hill, New York.

McCarthy, M. (2000)."Web surfers beware: The company tech may be a secret agent," *Wall Street Journal — Eastern Edition,* 235(7), A1.

"Mellon outlaws online loafing with strict policy on nonwork uses,"(1998). *American Banker*, 163(179), 5.

O'Connor, R.(1996). "Correct use of resources," *CA Magazine*, 100(1081), 16-19.

Oravec, J. (1996). *Virtual Individuals, Virtual Groups: Human Dimensions of Groupware and Computer Networking,* Cambridge University Press, New York.

Oravec, J.(1999). "Working hard and playing hard: Constructive uses of online recreation," *Journal of General Management*, 24(3), 77-89.

Oravec, J.(forthcoming). "Interactive toys and children's education: Strategies for educators and parents," *Childhood Education*.

Orwell, J. (1937/1958). *The Road to Wigan Pier*, Harcourt Brace Jovanovich, San Diego.

Naughton, K., Raymond, J., Shulman, K., and Struzzi, D.(1999). "Cyberslacking," *Newsweek*, 134(22), 62-66.

Runge, L.(1994). "The manager and the information worker of the 1990s," *Information Strategy: The Executive's Journal*, 10(4), 7-15.

SBT Corporation (1997). Survey of office workers (reported in www.smartbiz.com/sbs/arts/swp11.htm). SBT Corporation, Sausalito, CA.

Schor, J.(1991). *The Overworked American*, HarperCollins, New York.

Schrank, R. (1978). *Ten Thousand Working Days*, MIT Press, Cambridge, MA.

Taylor, F.(1913/1947). *Scientific Management*, Harper, New York.

Weinstein, M.(1996). *Managing to Have Fun,* Simon & Schuster, New York.

Young, K.(1998). *Caught in the Net*, John Wiley & Sons, New York.

Chapter 9

Play's the Thing
... on the Web!

Laku Chidambaram
University of Oklahoma, USA

Ilze Zigurs
University of Colorado at Boulder, USA

While the original architects of the Net developed it to withstand a nuclear attack, today's pioneers have adapted the medium to include a variety of leisure activities. Leisure and computers. Not long ago, those words would have been viewed as being contradictory—not even spoken in the same sentence. Today, we eagerly ask when's the next version of Doom coming out? Is the Sony PlayStation II all it's cracked up to be? Have you seen the new voyeur-cam of Survivor? As these kinds of questions become ubiquitous, what are the impacts of virtual play on society? Should we be concerned about social issues such as Internet addiction, reduced physical activity and decreased social interaction? These are some of the questions this chapter addresses.

Tragedies abound in the media of today. The aftermaths of school shootings highlight the role of computer games that depict graphic scenes of violence. Arguments about computer games and video arcades that seem to promote violence on-screen have taken on a new seriousness. Movies and television have pervasive effects, yet no one is sure of what those effects are or how to control their impact. One key question that has been debated in the public arena is the following: Are violent cyber-games merely reflecting the reality of living in a violent world, or are they helping to create that world?

Analysts agree that cyber-media have the ability to disconnect people from reality and thereby desensitize them to violence and graphic imagery. These media can offer a cloak of anonymity that can disguise people and personas. As children become increasingly exposed to such media, will society become a collection of desensitized, isolated individuals connected to a virtual world that they play in but disconnected from the real world they live in?

A contrasting viewpoint suggests that cyber media can leverage social services and enhance some traditional leisure time activities. For instance, volunteerism has been a traditional leisure time activity, and many areas of society are organized around a network of people willing to become involved in the hands-on work of such things as elder care, pet adoption, homeless shelters, battered women's counseling, and so on. Nonprofit organizations such as Red Cross and Second Harvest have proven that the Web is a unique and effective mechanism to enhance such volunteer activities.

Thus, when we indulge in virtual leisure, the two ends of the spectrum—unwanted social influences and desirable social outcomes—are evident from the scenarios outlined above. A goal for society would be to promote the latter and reduce the former. However, no clear or easy answers exist for this and related dilemmas, but the issues they raise have been and continue to be examined via public discourse. Our goal in this chapter is to continue this discourse and provide an analysis of how our virtual world has affected and is likely to affect leisure at a societal level.

PLAYING IN THE PHYSICAL AND VIRTUAL WORLDS

Leisure is an important and changing part of our culture. It is an area of study that has increasingly garnered academic attention over the last three decades and a large body of research literature has developed around it. As early as 1960, the term "new leisure" was used to describe a new awareness of leisure time and its growing role in overall fulfillment of people's lives (Brightbill, 1960). Clearly, leisure has different meanings in different cultures, but in the Western world, we typically think of it as time and activities that are outside of work and other responsibilities.

Consider the differences between traditional places and things for leisure versus the virtual equivalents of those places and things. Infrastructure for traditional leisure means parks, libraries, and other public places *where* people can play. A massive system for development, management, and public dialogue about these physical resources exists at the national, state, and local levels. Concerns for discussion might include environmental impacts, overcrowding, upkeep, accessibility, and so on.

In the virtual world, infrastructure usually means computer and communications networks. In many instances, to take advantage of virtual play, one has to connect to the vast network of the Internet. Accessibility to that infrastructure takes on a whole new meaning, and public policies along with free market forces play a large role in determining accessibility. Although the demographics of those connected to the Internet are changing, one thing that remains constant is the so-called digital divide (McConnaughey & Lader, 1999). Higher-income, white males are still more likely to be connected to the Internet than other demographic groups. Clearly, accessibility to the new infrastructure for leisure remains uneven.

Devices for accessing the Internet vary widely and new ones are being developed every day. One might be connecting through a "traditional" desktop computer, a WebTV, a Web phone, a pager, a palm device, and so on. The device will define the extent to which we are mobile or stationary, and mobility is increasingly expected. Although the price of devices inevitably declines, enhanced functionality of new generations means that costs overall do not really decrease very steeply. The consumer culture in the United States certainly assures a high level of continued spending for the latest technologies.

The infrastructure also defines payment mechanisms for delivery of goods and services through it. Payment is a particularly thorny issue for the Internet, with new mechanisms being tested and deployed constantly (Seitz & Stickel, 1998). An important barrier to the delivery of leisure-related products has been the problem of micro-payments, i.e., a cost-efficient way of dealing with very small transactions. In a physical store, it is a simple matter to pay cash for a 25-cent baseball card, but processing that small a transaction on the Web is still problematic. Once the problem of micro-payments is resolved effectively, a plethora of "small" items and services will likely become more widely available on the Web.

Trust in the virtual world's infrastructure remains an issue. A solution to a technical problem may be found, but whether consumers of leisure products and activities will place their trust in that solution is another matter entirely. For instance, attitudes toward privacy on the Net vary widely. There is no question that people are concerned about privacy, but the kinds of things that concern them are quite different (Cranor, Reagle and Ackerman, 1999). You may not care that your on-line bookstore knows what kinds of books you buy to pass the time, but your neighbor will. There are interesting implications for the design of delivery and tracking mechanisms for such leisure products as books, music, and so on.

Below we have examined four scenarios related to play and leisure activities on the Web. Each scenario examines changes in how the Web affords new opportunities for play while at the same time imposing new challenges for players. In addition, the scenarios also attempt to evaluate some of the impacts of these changes on individuals and society.

SCENARIO ONE: ON-LINE GAMES

Computer games have always been popular, starting with the card games that came with early personal computers. Sega and Sony established an entire category of entertainment with their console games played by single individuals or a small group huddled together over their control devices. Now, a whole new world of games is emerging on the Internet. These games create communities of people who are playing together in a virtual world. Chapter 7 describes one such kind of community of individuals playing on-line poker. But the stakes for on-line games go beyond poker.

The big companies that dominate the console-player market are searching for ways to be a part of this market. Sega's web site (www.sega.com) advertises its DreamCast player as "the most immersive and compelling gaming experience available ... This ultimate game machine hooks you up to the world via a built-in 56K modem ... Surf the web and battle it out in an online showdown." Sega's concept derives directly from the success of their stand-alone consoles and also illustrates some of the difficulties of trying such a direct transfer. The cost of hardware and software along with the bandwidth of the Internet connection are key intermediaries in the success of these direct link efforts. Haar (2000) points out the detrimental effects of slow connections on these "twitch games" that rely so heavily on quick hand movements. It's hard to twitch on the Internet!

Pogo.com is one example of an on-line gaming company that has shifted its business model in an effort to take advantage of the unique capabilities of the Internet. Rather than just trying to transfer console-type games to an online, Internet-connected environment, pogo.com began to emphasize family games and personal online relationships. The company also moved from relying on usage fees to developing advertising partnerships with Internet portals such as Excite. Their strategy has been quite successful so far—as of April 2000, the pogo.com site had more than 4.5 million users a month (Haar, 2000). The CEO and president says they have learned two key lessons—to keep the content simple to use, and to create an interactive, many-to-many environment rather than just imitating what can be done on television or radio (Caulfield, 2000).

Another kind of game is Ultima Online (www.uo.com), a role-playing game on the Internet where subscribers become part of the medieval world of Brittania. Players choose their own roles and live out their virtual lives; they can "build a house, craft a sword, tame animals, run a shop, delve deep into perilous dungeons or just chat over a goblet of virtual ale." Ultima Online was launched in 1997 and runs on 21 server sets located on four continents. The average player is logged on more than 21 hours a week, and more than half the players log on every day (VGF, 2000). Recently, a new "land mass" was added to provide a place where players who did not want to engage in war could develop their virtual lives in peace.

These examples illustrate different business models for on-line gaming and the different ways in which these models play out from a consumer perspective. Revenues come from hardware, software, subscription services, advertising partnerships, etc., and all these choices have an impact on how people interact as well as who is interacting. It is not surprising that the demographics of users vary widely across the different types of games. One thing is certain—this market will continue to grow, as will new ideas for taking advantage of the Web's unique nature for playing games and paying for them.

SCENARIO TWO: ONLINE MUSIC

In a *Newsweek* (June 5, 2000) article, the band Metallica's lead drummer, Lars Ulrich wrote,

"My band was recording a song called 'I Disappear' for the 'Mission: Impossible 2' soundtrack when we heard that six different versions of the song—works in progress—had been made available on Napster. We don't know how the music got out, but somewhere in the chain of things it was leaked. But when we found out that people were trading these songs on this thing called Napster, which we hadn't even heard of, we felt a line had been crossed."

There is no doubt a line has been crossed in the music industry. Until recently, the one-to-many distribution system was the only way of distributing music recordings. Such strict control of the distribution channel made it easy to control access and sell music as a product. However—perhaps unwittingly—Napster's founder, Shawn Fanning, a teenage music buff and a college-dropout, may have launched the first salvo against this business model when he created a way to index MP3 files on his hard drive so they could be shared with others.

This new model of sharing content without the intervention of the traditional "seller" has a number of people worried, including recording artists (such as Metallica's Ulrich), music companies and retail outlets. With the threat of legal action looming, many universities shut down access to the Napster.com site. In another sign of the brewing trouble, recording artists even downloaded the names of people logged on to Napster.com as a possible prelude to legal action.

Increasingly, students and others are downloading music from the Napster Web site without having to pay anyone for the intellectual property embodied in the songs. Levy (2000) provides anecdotal evidence that some teenagers have stopped buying CDs from record stores; they sample new songs at the local record store and then download them for free from the Net. "Napsterization" of music can spread to other digital media such as movies. If big budget Hollywood movies become available on the web (perhaps even before they are released in theaters or on video), the hue and cry over copyright protection will rise to a fever pitch. The slew of lawsuits filed by recording artists and others against Napster will undoubtedly influence the growth of online music in the future.

SCENARIO THREE: E-BOOKS

Even the print media, long the linchpin for delivering new content from authors, has begun to face challenges from the Web. Early in the year 2000, bestselling author Stephen King penned a short 66-page horror story, "Riding the Bullet," during his stay in the hospital while recovering from an automobile accident (Offman, 2000). Interestingly, King eschewed his time-tested delivery mechanism of print media in favor of the Net. The novella, "published" by Simon & Schuster, could be downloaded from select websites for a nominal fee of $2.50. ETailers such as Amazon.com were deluged with King fans clamoring to download the e-novel. While works of fiction and nonfiction abound on the Web, authors of King's stature have generally avoided the new medium to deliver content. While King's novel represents a small step in the erosion of traditional monopolies, it highlights the potential for the web to serve as an alternative *and* effective mechanism for delivering a variety of leisure-related content—from music to books to movies.

New ways of publishing require new ways of paying as well. Consider one model for how authors who choose the new media are paid. MightyWords.com, the publishing arm of FatBrain.com, an Internet startup, pays an author 50 percent of the revenue from the sale of a book (Offman, 2000). While MightyWords offers thousands of titles, which reduces the ability to showcase individual books, the royalties offered far exceed the usual 5 to 15 percent offered by traditional publishers. New or unproven authors are most likely to find such payment packages attractive. The lure of higher royalties on the Web may tempt some better-known authors to consider cyber-publishing more seriously—a nightmare scenario for traditional publishers.

SCENARIO FOUR: ACCESS TO VIRTUAL PLAY

Leisure practices have always differed among people, based on personality, culture, economics, and a whole host of other factors (Rojek, 2000).

Traditionally, family income often determined the types of leisure activities people had access to, as well as the amount of time they had available to spend on those activities. In the new digital economy, money still matters but the availability and type, and hence cost structure, of leisure have changed enormously. Consider the following examples of what can be accessed virtually.

An enormous amount of information about options for leisure is available on the Web. A quick visit to a Web search engine, using the keyword "leisure," produced 276,000 entries. The search took a tenth of a second. For most of us, that outcome represents both good news and bad news, i.e., a vast array of information is available to us almost instantaneously, but we now have to search through that information for the most relevant entries. Many of the entries were sites that compiled links to other sites, customized for a particular audience. For example, the city of Sacramento lists pages of activities for people with disabilities (http://www.cityofsacramento.org/ohs/access.htm). Other sites included those of universities, libraries, public offices, and individuals, along with links for boating, art, movies, theater, books, sports, tourism, and so on.

Access to that information has various costs, depending on where one is accessing the Web. For families who cannot afford their own Internet service at home, kiosks in libraries, city centers, and schools are available. But the technology itself is not the only cost of access. Awareness of the *possibility* of access comes first, followed by a perception that one will be able to do it. The nature of the access issue changes and, for some who are still uncomfortable with technology, rises to a whole new level.

In addition to just providing information, the Web also provides the actual *venue* for leisure, as discussed elsewhere in this chapter and in other chapters of the book. Museums are an excellent example of how virtuality changes access. Directories of on-line museums around the world are easy to find with that same tenth-of-a-second search engine (see, for example, http://www.icom.org/vlmp/). A Web site visit is an order of magnitude cheaper than airfare to Barcelona to see a Joan Miro exhibition. Ultimately, the Web becomes one's personal museum or one's own library that combines all the libraries of the world.

Another change in the nature of access is based on the attributes of individual personality. Extroverts and introverts choose different leisure activities, as do people with different physical skills. In the physical world, personality and physical attributes are quite visible. Not so in the virtual world. The role that one might choose to play in Brittania, on Ultima Online, is not restricted by anything other than one's own imagination. Similarly, the development of relationships on-line, as brought to popular consciousness in the movie "You've Got Mail," can occur with anyone.

These examples show how access to leisure resources and activities has increased dramatically via the Web. People who were previously denied access due to economic, cultural, personality, or other reasons are no longer denied. What about the reverse? Are there ways that our virtual world denies access that was possible in the physical world? The most significant issue is comfort with technology, and that chasm often runs along lines of gender, age, and socioeconomic categories. Traditional chasms have the potential to reassert themselves in the digital divide, and it is here that public policy-making can have an enormous impact on ensuring training and, ultimately, universal access to virtual play.

THE CONTEXT AND CONSEQUENCES OF CYBER PLAY

As people and play increasingly migrate to the Web, three key changes have occurred in: (a) the context of play; (b) the content delivery mechanisms; and, (c) the commercial models of play. Each of these "c" changes is examined below.

The context of play: Generation D is the moniker used to describe the "digital generation," one that has grown up with computers *and* connectivity. This generation is one that uses computers not just for work, but also for play. This generation is the one that online game developers are targeting in droves. Forrester Research estimates that online gaming will account for nearly a fourth of all interactive entertainment revenues—currently estimated at $7 billion—by the year 2004 (Li, 2000). Corporate response to such potentially high growth has been predictably eager: Sega International has created a new company called Sega.com to take advantage of this rapidly growing market while Sony Online Entertainment has entered into a partnership with LucasArts to create online games based on the Star Wars characters.

One of the earliest online games—Ultima Online—has also proved to be the most long-lived. As discussed earlier in this chapter, the game is a medieval adventure played around-the-clock by a group of players each of whom pays $9.95 a month to participate. The original Ultima was developed back in 1979 and has a strong offline following; the company expanded on this loyal user base by launching Ultima Online two decades later. Electronic Arts, the game's publisher, estimates the number of subscribers at around 150,000. Other "persistent" online games have also enjoyed modest success, including Microsoft's Asheron's Call and Sony's Everquest.

Factors that have contributed to the success of online play include a worldwide community of players (as with Ultima), a viable business model (usually a monthly subscriber fee), minimal bandwidth requirements (such as integrating a game disc in the user console/PC with online transmission of play information) and an imaginative and dynamic play environment (as with Everquest).

Content delivery mechanisms: Traditional modes of leisure, particularly entertainment and mass media, are controlled by a few organizations, often with tremendous power over what gets produced and how it gets delivered. Companies such as Time-Warner, Disney and Sony control the entire entertainment chain—from the artists, to the studios, to the channels of distribution and the channels of redistribution. In essence, they are the gatekeepers to the music that we listen to, the movies that we see and the TV shows that come into our homes.

The Web challenges the preeminence of these gatekeepers by offering alternative delivery mechanisms, and thereby alternative content. Consider for example the case of two independent film producers—Atom Films (of Seattle) and iFilm (of Los Angeles). Films made by these producers can be seen on the Web, providing an alternate medium for viewing movies. Even more remarkable is the fact that changes in delivery mechanisms wrought by the Web have, in some instances, begun to transcend the Web itself. Anderson (2000) reports that iFilm has partnered with TiVO, a San Jose-based personal TV service, to provide some of its best short films to TiVO's subscribers. Thus, after the TiVO box is hooked on to viewers' TVs, they can click on their film of choice to view it. New films can be uploaded via cable modems or phone lines as needed. This case highlights the far-reaching impact of changes in delivery mechanisms of leisure content, first seen on the web and now evident in other media.

The commercial models of play: Clearly, the traditional models of payment will not work in the Internet era. Digital forms of leisure content— music, movies, books, software and games to name a few—will need new models of payment. Micro-payment, which involves the user making small, digital payments as digital content is consumed, has been proposed as one option for a new commercial model. Another payment option that has worked well in other settings such as with services provided by ISPs and cellular phone companies is a combination of recurring payments and pay-as-you-use plans. Regardless of which option is chosen, payment models in the digital age will need to closely track actual usage of services compared to payment models with traditional media.

CONCLUSION

Numerous opportunities for leisure and play—such as listening to music, watching movies, reading books and playing games—exist on the Web. All indications are that these opportunities are being sought after eagerly by a growing and diverse range of users. On the other side, the competition to fulfill the opportunities for play and leisure is also growing rapidly. Numerous contenders exist and even more contenders are emerging. As the world becomes more wired and the Web becomes more accessible, more leisure activities will migrate to the Web drawing in even more people. The drive to entertain the growing masses of consumers is likely to generate even more competition among the content providers. While consumers will have more leisure content to choose from, they will also face difficult choices in terms of regulating some of the content available online.

REFERENCES

Brightbill, C.K. (1960). *The Challenge of Leisure*, Englewood Cliffs, NJ: Prentice-Hall, Inc.

Caulfield, B. (2000). Playing for keeps, *Internet World,* April 01, 2000, http://www.internetworld.com/print/2000/04/01/business/20000401-playing.html

Cranor, L.F., Reagle, J., & Ackerman, M.S. (1999). Beyond concern: Understanding net users' attitudes about online privacy, AT&T Labs-Research Technical Report TR 99.4.3, http://www.research.att.com/library/trs/TRs/99/99.4/99.4.3/report.htm.

Haar, S.V. (2000). The Internet don't play that, *ZDNet Interactive Week Online*, April 3, 2000, http://www.zdnet.com/intweek/stories/news/0,4164,2504417,00.html

Levy, S. (2000). "The Noisy War over Napster," *Newsweek,* June 5.

Li, K. (2000). Looking for a winner, *The Standard: Intelligence for the Internet Economy*, April 17, 2000, http://www.thestandard.com/article/display/0,1151,14051,00.html

McConnaughey, J.W., & Lader, W. (1999). Falling through the net II: New data on the digital divide, http://www.ntia.doc.gov/ntiahome/net2/falling.html.

Rojek, C. (2000). *Leisure and Culture*, New York, NY: St. Martin's Press, Inc.

Seitz, J., & Stickel, E. (1998). Internet banking: An overview, *Journal of Internet Banking and Commerce*, 3(1), http://www.arraydev.com/commerce/JIBC/9801-8.htm.

Ulrich, L. (2000). "It's Our Property," *Newsweek,* June 5, 2000.

VGF (2000). Ultima Online reaches 150,000, *VGF.COM: Video Gamers First Network*, February 24, 2000, http://www.vgf.net/genres/online/0200/uo150000.htm

Life
in the
Virtual World

Chapter 10

Citizens and Spokesmen: Politics and Personal Expression on the Web

Jennifer Petersen
University of Texas, Austin, USA

In a 1996 article in *The New Yorker*, Adam Gopnik (1996) recounted a story about how France got online. Gopnik argued that French interest in the Internet had hinged upon the migration of politics to web pages. In particular, the story revolved around a religious conflict between the Vatican and a French bishop who devoted much of his time advocating for the "excluded" (the homeless, who in France also are nationless), in part via frequent appeals to and appearances in the media. Not surprisingly, the Vatican did not appreciate the bishop's unorthodox (and somewhat leftist) views. As punishment, the Vatican came up with the rather ingenious plan of reassigning the bishop to the diocese of Partenia, which, while vaguely locatable in Saharan North Africa, has not had any particular geographical location nor bounds since it was abandoned to the Saharan sand sometime around the 4th century. Without any solid geography, the bishop would be left with no subjects, no pulpit, and — conveniently — no more media spotlight.

However, the bishop reversed the logic of his "virtual" appointment, "relocating" his geographically indeterminate diocese to the abstract space of the Internet, creating a sort of trans-national diocese of heterodoxy. Of course, no one can go to confession or receive communion within the virtual diocese, but the domain of Partenia (www.partenia.fr) carved out a legitimate place within the Church for any left-of-the-Vatican Catholic with a computer. Much to the Vatican's chagrin, Catholics looking for more inclusive (and more socialist) gospels now had an official place of worship within the Church, and an ordained bishop to oversee that space, technically accessible around the globe.

According to the author, the media coverage of the dispute over Partenia was instrumental in bolstering the Internet into the French cultural spotlight. Gopnik went on to quote the bishop hailing the political promise of the Internet to create horizontal networks. To underscore the potential of such networks, the bishop compared them to the structure of early Christian church, which he noted had circumnavigated the highly vertical Roman Empire.

The story recounted in *The New Yorker* is exemplary of the political expectations and hopes many of us place upon the Internet. It is popularly represented as a tool by which the small (the lone activist... or the lone hacker) can defeat institutions, if not governments. We are told that horizontal networks similar to those of the bishop will revitalize political debate and democracy in America. Whether it is due to the horizontal aspect of computer networks or the interactivity of the Internet as a medium, a wide range of people are looking to the Internet for a way to improve democracy — or even for a road to increased personal freedom. Many of these hopes are focused upon the assumption that the Internet will increase direct personal interaction with and participation in the decision-making process, or that the greater availability of information from divergent sources will enable greater freedom in forming the opinions which motivate political action. These hopes of a citizenry moved to action have so far seen little fruition. The Internet has not drastically changed the way we interact with political institutions, nor has it changed voting habits, nor is there compelling evidence of major switches in patterns of information consumption among the mass voting populace. It should come as no surprise that the Internet alone is not changing the political behavior of the majority or bringing about a politicization of mass culture. By restricting the discussion to looking for participation in legislative politics on the part of an envisioned mass public, any action in the sphere of cultural politics is automatically beyond the scope of discussion.

In this chapter, I suggest that rather than focusing the discussion of the socio-political impact of new communications technologies solely within the realm of electoral politics, the scope of analysis should be broadened to take into consideration how individuals are using the Internet and how those practices relate to social and political life. I argue against the equation of technology with increases in individual political agency and suggest an approach that is based in Internet use patterns. Research that does focus on individual web use suggests patterns and strategies of use that do not fall under the purview of these discussions but are nevertheless germane to U.S. democratic politics and public discussion.

THE DISCOURSE ON DIGITALLY-ENHANCED DEMOCRACY

Celebrants of the Internet's social potential often predict the technology will inaugurate a more active and powerful citizenry. By and large, this process is conceptualized in two ways: It is either seen as the result of increased free time (the dividends of automation), or that greater communicative abilities and choices (of where and when to communicate) will lead to more informed citizens and greater political participation.

The first claim — that technology will increase personal freedom through taking over trivial tasks — is checked by the fact that currently computers are being used to monitor ever more closely the productivity of workers, especially low-rung, low-power workers, and that employers are enlisting communications technology to move the workplace into the home, as in the burgeoning "homework" industry (Millar, 1998). It is the second claim — that greater communicative ability will increase political participation — that is most often present in popular predictions of the Internet's emancipatory potential, and in political rhetoric and policy decisions. As the more influential one, it is this second claim that I will focus on here.

The Internet is credited with decreasing distances between people and places, or decreasing geographic barriers to communication. This brings us back to the story of the bishop and his virtual diocese. The increased ability to communicate across distance — in particular, to communicate in an asynchronous, relatively impersonal way — is the particular aspect of new communications technologies at stake when the Internet is described as enabling horizontal communication and organization. These communication patterns and the relatively low entry barriers for would-be information providers have been the basis of assertions that the medium is, in and of itself, a democratizing force.

Many have argued that the horizontal communication enabled by the Internet will increase individual access to democratic institutions and enhance participation in governmental decision-making processes. This argument is based upon the assumption that the Internet will allow average citizens greater access to politicians and decision-making institutions, decreasing institutional as well as geographical barriers. Following this logic, these decreased barriers will then allow individuals greater impact upon the political system. Similarly, decreasing barriers between individuals is seen as an important move toward revitalizing civic engagement and the democratic process. These arguments run into problems both theoretically and in practice.

First, the above line of reasoning relies on the presumption of a direct relationship between communicative networks and political freedom. The ability to send a message directly to one's senator does not necessarily equal the ability to have agency in the decision-making process in question. Nor do more channels of communication necessarily translate into higher quality communication or even the availability of more information. The idea that an increased communication infrastructure would lead to greater democratic social organization is an old one that informed many development programs in the "Third World," often with less than democratic outcomes. The relationship between technology and democracy is not a simple or direct one. Technologies do not exist in a void but are caught up in cultural definitions, drives and applications; discussing technologies as independent variables can make complex relationships seem simple or direct. Assuming that increased chains of communication translate into an expansion of democracy (and an increase in individual agency) is roughly equal to assuming that networks are inherently democratic, if not emancipatory. However, the meaning and use of networks is as culturally embedded as any technology. The connection of networks, or horizontal organization, with freedom is cultural; in China, for example, networks connote surveillance and horizontal structures of domination (Menser and Aronowitz, 1996).

Secondly, asserting that communications technologies allow individuals to overcome institutional barriers to participate equally with elites is to say that the medium, or access, provides equity. It also ignores the imbalances of power and status that are inherent in such exchanges. Stating that the mere fact of being able to communicate one-on-one with decision-makers ensures or equals greater individual involvement in the democratic system is to assume that the decision-makers are listening and engaging in return — an assumption which has little supporting evidence in any other arena of social life.

Conceptions of the Internet as a space which allows for any individuals to converse on equal footing, no matter their "real-world" social stations is epitomized in the now-infamous MCI commercial that described the Internet as a (utopian) place *without* difference, in which there were no such distinctions as gender, race or age. Such formulations of the Internet as a space of equal access and discursive democracy are seductive in the way they facilely sweep under the carpet connections between online speech, the status afforded by institutional affiliation, and the effect of "real world" social status and discrimination on online speech. Even divorced from tags of institutional affiliation (as in domain names and signature files), social status does not disappear the instant one logs in to a computer.

In addition, such formulations do not address the fact that Internet access is primarily afforded to a very small and homogeneous demographic group. While the initial gender gap for Internet use (and web site production) appears to be diminishing (Wakeford, 1997; "Women Take the Lead," 1999), there are significant differences in computer use across educational and income levels and along lines of race. Census data indicate that, as of 1997, Caucasian households were more likely to have personal computers and Internet access than were Hispanic or African-American households, across all income levels. The study also showed that holders of university degrees were four times more likely to have a computer at home than those with high school degrees (U.S. Department of Commerce, 1998). Clearly, the increasing numbers of people conducting business and pleasure online daily cannot be assumed to be representative of the general public of the United States. In addition to the fact that simple physical access to computers is not evenly distributed, ethnographic research conducted in library and community center computer stations in Austin, Texas, suggests that users from different socio-economic and racial backgrounds often have different expectations in terms of what to use computers for, and different strategies of computer use (Lentz, Straubhaar, LaPastina, Main and Taylor, 2000). These factors complicate any deductive assumptions about the ways in which Internet use is affecting personal political engagement on a broad scale.

Citizens and Publics

Discussions of a digitally-inspired transformation of citizenship have focused on an amorphous "citizenry," or "public," assigning this aggregate actor a fairly homogeneous set of motivations, considering the diverse political interests of the population it represents. By failing to differentiate uses and motivations in its concern over how Internet use may transform democracy, the discussion has created a falsely homogeneous picture of the public of opinion formation. Predictions that new communications technology will enhance freedom have tended to focus on the technology itself and assume the opinion-forming democratic public that is being influenced by the technology is a relatively homogeneous field. At the very least, these predictions assume that there is such a thing as a general public that is representative of the more complicated demographics of the actual population.

Such conceptions of a unitary public, which assume a representative or common interest, are highly contested ones, however, and have come under attack by many as exclusionary and internally conflicted. Many suggest that political opinion formation has never been a simple matter of decisions made by one "representative" public, but a complex and competitive interrelation of the internal subgroups that make up the broader public (Fraser, 1992). In this formulation, one may hold sway over the others but never acts alone.

If, then, a homologous mass is not the only way to consider large-scale political participation, there is no reason to restrict discussion of the relationship between the Internet and political process. In fact, if it is true that in practice, the Internet largely brings people more of what they are familiar with (familiar stores and products, the largest and best publicized informational conglomerates) (Aspen Institute, 1995), then there is no reason to expect the Internet to play any role in creating or activating a "representative" mass public. This view is supported by the research on political participation, which suggests that Internet use does not transform media use patterns. If a large portion of people tend to look for more of what they are familiar with in terms of informational sources online, then we have to wonder just how broadly useful all the alternative sources of information available online are. While many people have taken advantage of the relatively low cost of production and horizontal distribution to offer high-quality alternative sources of information (and personal articulations of experience), if a large portion of people are not looking for these sources of information and interaction, most people are unlikely to come across these information sources and less likely to use them.

However, there are significant numbers of people who are not happy with the information typically available in normal broadcast media or who are not happy with the articulations of group identity expressed through local community and/or large media. These people, then, are more likely to be looking for — or to create — something different. And it is worth looking to see what citizens are utilizing the medium in an effort to make their particular interests public and how. If we discard the notion of a unitary public as that which makes democratic decisions, and consider various publics participating in any democratic exchange (or any social exchange), there are other potential sites for examination of the interrelations between new communications technologies and the political sphere. In order to get an idea of what these sites and potentials are, it is necessary to turn to empirical research on actual use patterns.

INTERNET USE, POLITICS AND IDENTITY

In empirical terms, studies of Internet use also cast doubt on the medium's promise as either a tool for more direct democracy or as a revitalized realm of equal access and political engagement in the general sense. Findings from a Rutgers survey (Barber, Matteson and Peterson, 1997) of the contents and discussions on political web sites suggest that most political institutions offer more information and advertisement than interaction. Similarly, a University of California at Santa Barbara study (Bimber, 1999) indicates that as few as half those with Internet access use that access to get information on politics, and that far fewer use that access to contact the government or political organizations. Studies on Internet community have yet to show that online communities are in fact revitalizing either offline community ties or political debate (Bimber, 1999; Downing, 1999). Grassroots political movements in Germany and in Sri Lanka that have attempted to harness the potential of new communication technologies have met with little success in trying to impress their agendas on national politics and policy (Tehranian, 1990). In a brief survey of various online political "communities" around the world, the networks which contain the greatest promise were all marginal groups (mainly diasporic ethnic groups), and the promise these communities afforded appeared mainly to be outside the immediate sphere of legislative politics (Downing, 1999). One positive site noted in the study was America Online's broad-based anonymous discussions on race, which the author argued provided an important venue for exchanges that are often very difficult face-to-face. This broad discussion, however, is the exception. And while it is a discussion that engages many people from different backgrounds and communities, and with different interests, it still is not aimed at political action in the traditional sense of legislative or judicial politics.

That the Internet may not be the great social and institutional leveler it is sometimes cracked up to be does not necessarily mean it has no political potential. It does mean use of the medium is unlikely to change the face of representative democracy, overcome social inequities, or even provide an open and democratic space of dialogue and consensus building. Current use patterns suggest that this potential is more likely to be found in the realm of cultural politics than in that of "representative" democracy.

Any claims on the political promise of the Internet are based in assumptions that the medium is fundamentally different than other communicative venues. There are three primary ways the Internet differs from other media: 1) it allows for increasing control over the time and place of communications 2) it erodes the distinction between center/production and periphery/audience 3) it challenges people to new modes of expression and organization, by virtue of its very perceived newness. These three mutually re-enforcing particulars provide the basis of arguments on the effects of the new medium.

As noted earlier in this chapter, the first two distinctions are the most commonly cited particularities of the Internet, especially when the discussion is focused on politics. The shift in perceptions of proximity — in which information brings individuals "close" to one another — means that similarities such as social position and taste define the distance between individuals more than do geographical distance or daily life. This affiliational proximity, of course, creates other separations (Menser and Aronowitz, 1996), most often cultural and socio-economic, just as much as it erases geographical ones. And differences in culture and technology can separate groups of people more than does geography.

Affiliational proximity relies not only on greater control over other forms of distance but also on the interactive aspect of new communications technology. In particular, the Internet allows individuals to produce "material" communications and interactions, such as messages preserved on bulletin boards and personal web pages. The static "sites" produced by individuals are then sorted by theme, interest or informational content with other similar sites by search directories. For the person searching for information, sites appear organized by information rather than by geography. In constructing web sites as well, authors "locate" themselves through the sites to which they are hyperlinked, or made proximate (Turkle, 1995). Personal web sites, in particular, establish identity (and encounter their audiences) in large part through establishing proximities to other sites (Turkle, 1995; Wakeford, 1997). This organizational logic has been used to facilitate the formation of social networks along lines of affiliation — whether those affiliations are along lines of politics, consumption, or identity.

Affiliational networking is one of the ways in which the Internet is being put to use, and one of the uses around which it is developing. As of 1993, the most active newsgroups were those centering around soap operas, homosexuality, ethnic cultures, and computers (Baym, 1995). All of these topics center around issues of social identity or cultures of consumption (or taste cultures). The popularity of identity-centered networks has not gone unnoticed by commercial interests: The *New York Times* reported that the initial public offering of iVillage, a company professing to build specialized "communities" of women, was of the most successful initial public offerings of an Internet company as of spring, 1999.

Identity and Affiliation: Two Uses

In order to look more closely at just how individuals are creating these distances online and why — as well as what this means in terms of political and social change — I'll look more closely at two sets of Internet use: popular newsgroups and personal Web sites. Topic-oriented newsgroups attract individuals through levels of interest in and identification with the topic of discussion. Research shows the most attractive topics as largely dealing with issues of identity: homosexuality and ethnicity are primary social markings of identity, and computer programmers have their own subcultural status. Research that focused on a newsgroup of soap opera fans suggested that newsgroups offered an alternative social field in which users discussed personal issues, and sought and gave emotional support (Baym, 1995). Research into the psychology of newsgroup use has similarly found strong affective impacts. A study of marginalized groups and newsgroup use found that the affiliational networks provided by newsgroups had a strong impact on social identities. The study further found that newsgroup participation strengthened identities of socially marginalized individuals by offering peer groups and peer reinforcement of those identities (McKenna and Bargh, 1998).

The popularity of newsgroups is likely tied to the fact that they are based upon relationships of interest rather than obligation (Baym, 1995). The fact that the discussions and networks in which large numbers of people are voluntarily joining are focused on taste cultures and social identity is significant. People largely use the Internet to replicate or further indulge their interests (Aspen Institute, 1995), and it appears that taste cultures and social identities are high on that list. As in other areas of American life, civic engagement does not appear to be high online. Nor do the newsgroup interactions referenced above resemble in form the vision of a broad-based, consensus-building political public that is at the heart of many a hopeful vision of electronically-enhanced democracy. The exchanges that appeared to fuel interest and participation in these studies focused more on levels of personal trauma, identity formation, and taste (and media interpretation).

My own research has focused on a somewhat similar issue: personal web sites that are used as public diaries. The sites I have focused on use the public "space" of the Internet to elaborate experience and identity (particularly conflicted identities), through personal narrative and responses to media representations. As home page journals are not an easy subject on which to perform a conventional search, many of those engaged in online autobiographic projects host growing lists of links to similar projects. Within the loosely-knit network I studied, the affiliational themes were issues of gender and ethnicity — often both. My qualitative analysis focused primarily on three such sites: two of the authors identified as Chicana or Latina and one as a (white) woman athlete. These markers — each ways in which the women identified themselves as socially different or marginal — were central to all three of the women's online self-constructions.

Gender and ethnicity being two markers of difference within the larger social arena, I argue that these authors are using the productive aspect of the web to try to publicize aspects of experience that are not represented elsewhere. Much as newsgroups provide the only social network of peers for many people with marginal social positions, these Web sites and the discourse surrounding them represent attempts to solidify social identities currently in definitional flux. (Many of the authors that I studied thanked their online networks and/or audiences for helping them to come to better understanding of the identity issues addressed in their self-representations. In this way, the interactions have a therapeutic dimension similar to the therapeutic aspect of newsgroups described above.)

For many people representing themselves online, socially assigned difference — as an important aspect of individual identity — becomes a key aspect of self-representation. For these authors, the Internet is not providing a space in which social differences can be erased, but one in which those differences are solidified and highlighted. As illustrated by the aforementioned research on newsgroup use, issues of identity, especially marginalized identities, are some of the larger draws that motivate people to participate in online networks. Particularly for those who are socially or geographically isolated from others with similar identities, such networks can be a primary source of social recognition.

In one of the sites I looked at, the author remarks that she started her site as a way of dealing with social isolation and personal trauma. She continues to comment that the network of like-minded people she has encountered online is one of the reasons that she has continued with the project. Other online autobiographers expressed similar feelings of social recognition and reciprocity from reader interactions. Each noted the influence these interactions had upon their representational projects.

Audience plays an integral, and interesting, role in these self-representations. Whether or not the sites have many (or any) readers, the very public nature of the representation presupposes an audience; the self-representations are geared toward that (envisioned) audience. One young woman, whose site chronicled a transformation in ethnic and personal identity that took place during her first years at college, made it clear she intended her self-representation to influence that audience, saying she wanted her site to "help those who do not realize or value who they are become more aware of themselves" (Eskimo Diaries, 1998). As in the other sites I analyzed, the author here assumes a key feature of her audience: that their concerns and experiences will be similar to hers. This very focused implicit audience is a way of defining the community the author is trying to create. Each of the sites I analyzed was similar in this respect; the authors all assumed that the points with which their audiences would identify were the points of difference around which they organized their self-representations (gender, ethnicity).

In addition to the creation of affiliational networks, there is another aspect of recognition the authors often note, that of self-recognition. In mass mediated societies, representations of social distinctions and groupings are key to the development of individuals' identities and understanding of their place in the social world. One author elaborated on the import of being able to construct and control representation of her social identity: "I very much choose to be here. In this forum, I can set the terms of debate, I can decide how to represent myself, and I can choose who/what to engage" (la malinchista, 19979). Another site mocks the notion of role models for anyone who does not "fit" the narrow range of socially available gender and ethnic molds. The importance of self-recognition online, or seeing one's social position represented, for members of minority communities has been noted elsewhere as well (Wakeford, 1997).

The main themes that emerge from looking at these two areas of Internet use are the importance of difference as a motivation for community formation and the use of these communities as loci of self-recognition and normalization of marginalized identities and experience. These motivations and uses have so far been powerful and popular online practices. For those groups that do have access, the medium has provided a useful tool for strengthening group ties and community when other media resources offer no outlet for the group's voice and concerns. In terms of politics, the sense of common ground provided through the identity-based communication observed in newsgroups and personal web pages can lay the foundation for the formation of political aims and actions.

The Politics of Identity Claims

I have argued here that discussions on what potential new communications technologies have to affect social life should be based upon current practices — both on and offline — rather than on abstract and unsubstantiated equations of technology and particular forms of communication with transformations in political behavior and agency. Of course, findings spurred by these questions will be very different from those sought by investigations into the potential of technology for revitalizing participation in electoral politics.

By taking this more inductive approach, it is possible to look at Internet use as one indicator of how individuals are organizing and grouping themselves; it also allows for the inclusion of forms of politics that are often overlooked in more deductive analyses. Looking at emerging online networks and around what issues and expressions those networks are forming may give a better indication of active areas of citizenry than focusing on voter turnout and online engagement with party politics. In particular, examining networks that center on the normalization of marginalized identities and recuperating personal interpretations of experience are sites worth watching. One way in which individuals and groups who do not usually have access to media are using the Internet is for articulations and reformulations of experience and identity, even if only within those networks themselves.

This re-articulation of experience is not necessarily simply personal expression — it is an important component of emancipatory social movements. This sort of group dialogue is an important part of forming a (political) group identity. The process of formulating a group understanding of experience is key for marginalized groups in defining a common voice, political position(s) and opinions from which to engage in action (Fraser, 1992). The process of interpreting and articulating experience is a fundamental political issue: How one interprets experience determines whether or not that experience is understood as neutral or as politically charged. And understandings of individual experience are affected by other articulations of experience, particularly when those articulations take place through media channels. In this light, social formations online that are tightly focused on reformulations of experience (such as identity-specific newsgroups and self-defined political autobiographical web sites) are a form of politics in themselves.

CONCLUSIONS

While I have not argued that all Internet communication and community-building is based in shared interest or identification, I have stated that this has proved one of the most powerful draws of the Internet within the United States. While in France it took what Gopnik (in his *New Yorker* article) referred to as an eruption of "querulous metaphysics" to get people to go online, in the U.S. it has been the promise of community — but more specifically, the promise of finding someone like oneself, whether in terms of hobbies or in terms of shared social conditions — that has pulled people online.

This is evidenced in the affiliational networks examined here by the fact that the audience addressed is often assumed to be in some way similar. Newsgroup use focuses on issues of similarity in identity and interests. The points around which the authors of personal web sites expect their undefined audiences to see and respond to their self-representations coincide with how the author has defined his/herself. Within the studies cited above, these online constructions most often center on points of social difference or distinction, whether those points are particular social practices (such as hobbies and fan groups) or issues of gender, race, ethnicity and sexuality. In other words, while these networks are based in distinction, their focus (as defined by their implied audience) is within the community or network.

While it is exactly this sort of group-specific "enclaving" that is necessary in order for groups concerned with mainstreaming marginalized social positions to consolidate a group voice (and, here applicable, solidarity in group demands for justice), the political import of this "enclaving" is external. The purpose of having a group voice is to speak externally, seeking recognition from a broader audience. The effectiveness of any attempt to make any changes outside the bounds of the group in question hinges upon addressing those changes to a broad range of individuals — and, importantly, individuals that hold the power to form legal and institutional decisions. So far, there is little evidence of this sort of discourse taking place online.

While the Internet is being used to produce in-group discourse on difference and social inclusiveness, how well this will translate out of those groups remains to be seen. It is not clear whether new communication technologies, and the uses to which we put them, will be of any use in struggles to enhance the democratic process, or to introduce new, pluralist voices. As mentioned above, the Internet is not an arena of free and equal exchange. And, if patterns of Internet use continue to focus along lines of interest and habit, it may not prove an effective channel for making new or different arguments heard outside the boundaries of the groups that formulate them.

REFERENCES

Aspen Institute (1995). "The Future of Community and Personal Identity in the Coming Electronic Culture: A Report on the Third Annual Aspen Institute Roundtable on Information Technology," The Aspen Institute, Washington, D.C..

Barber, B., Matteson, K., and Peterson, J.(1997). "The State of Electronically Enhanced Democracy." http://www.wwc.rutgers.edu:80/markleproj.htm, Rutgers University, New Jersey, November .

Baym, N. K. (1995). "From practice to culture on Usenet," in *The Cultures of Computing*, Sociological Review Monograph Series, Susan Leigh Star (ed.), Blackwell Publishers, Oxford.

Bimber, B.(1999). "Notes on the Internet and Civic Engagement," Excerpts from the conclusion of "Information and Civic Engagement in America: Political Effects of Information Technology," http://www.polsci.ucsb.edu/~bimber/research/civicnotes.html, University of Santa Barbara, Santa Barbara.

Downing, J. (1999)."Global Networks Toward New Communities," in *The*

Promise of Global Networks, Institute for Information Studies.

Eskimo Diaries (1998). http://www.geocities.com/CollegePark/Quad/1784/eskimo.html, retrieved May 1998.

Fraser, N.(1992). "Rethinking the Public Sphere: A Contribution to the Critique of Actually Existing Democracy," in *Habermas and the Public Sphere*, Craig Calhoun (ed.), MIT Press, Cambridge.

Gopnik, A.(1996). "The Virtual Bishop: What does it take to get the French to turn on their computers?" in *New Yorker*, March 18, 59-63.

La malinchista (1999). http://members.tripod.com/~malinchista/index.html, retrieved July.

Lentz, B., Straubhaar, J., LaPastina, A., Main, S., and Taylor, J.(2000). "Structuring Access: The Role of Public Access Centers in the 'Digital Divide'," Paper to be delivered at the 50th Annual International Communication Association Conference, Acapulco, Mexico, June.

McKenna, K. Y. A. and Bargh, J. A.(1998). "Coming Out in the Age of the Internet: Identity 'Demarginalization' Through Virtual Group Participation," *Journal of Personality and Social Psychology*, 75(3), 681-694.

Menser, M. and Aronowitz, S.(1996). "On Cultural Studies, Science, and Technology," in *Technoscience and Cyberculture*, Stanley Aronowitz, Barbara Martinsons, and Michael Menser, with Jennifer Rich (eds.), Routledge, New York.

Millar, M. S.(1998). *Cracking the Gender Code*: *Who Rules the Wired World?* Second Story Press, Toronto.

Piel Morena (1999). http://members.theglobe.com/pielmorena/main.html.

Tehranian, M.(1990). *Technologies of Power: Information Machines and Democratic Prospects.*, Ablex Publishing Company, Norwood, New Jersey.

Turkle, S.(1995). *Life on the Screen: Identity in the Age of the Internet*, Simon & Schuster, Inc., New York.

U.S. Department of Commerce (1998). "Falling Through the Net II: New Data on the Digital Divide," National Telecommunications and Information Administration, Washington, D.C..

Wakeford, N.(1997). "Networking Women and Girls with Information/Communication Technology: surfing tales of the World Wide Web," in *Processed Lives: Gender and Technology in Everyday Life,* Jennifer Terry and Melodie Calvert (eds.), Routledge, London.

"Women Take the Lead,"(1999). *CyberAtlas*, http://cyberatlas.internet.com, November 11.

Chapter 11

The Virtual Community: Building on Social Structure, Relations and Trust to Achieve Value

Urs E. Gattiker, Stefano Perlusz,
Kristoffer Bohmann and Christian Mørck Sørensen
Aalborg University, Denmark

The growth of the Internet and its extensive use at work and in private life has offered new opportunities for communicating and staying in touch with others around the world. The Internet enables people to form virtual communities in addition to a social community such as one's local church. A social community can be distinguished based on shared experiences of members, where language and culture may be important ingredients for mutual understanding. A virtual community represents a communal experience whereby people may not necessarily know each other very well nor meet in person very frequently, if ever. Instead, communication and exchange are done through a mediator, namely the information technology and electronic networks. Another characterization distinguishes voluntary and non-voluntary communities, such as virtual task forces and, as importantly, communities that can impose controls to reduce free-riding, where members benefit from others' contributions while not contributing themselves (de Jasay, 1989).

This chapter advances our understanding about a virtual community sponsored by a not-for-profit association and including members from around the world. In particular, this chapter (1) addresses similarities and differences between social and virtual communities, (2) outlines how an inter-routine domain of virtuality and social capital theory may help explain levels of trust, structure, understanding, and free-riding in a virtual community, (3) describes a specific virtual community, its focus and the efforts undertaken to motivate its members, and (4) provides some preliminary data about how this virtual community works on a daily basis in cyberspace.

SOCIAL COMMUNITIES VERSUS VIRTUAL COMMUNITIES

Communities have been around as long as humans have been on this earth. While in the past a community may have represented a small group of settlers trying to live in harmony, today a community may be based on a neighborhood or a local church. However, 'groups of everybody' might easily become 'groups of nobody' if there is not some cohesion attained by following norms and rules of the community.

Defining a Social Community

A social community has the following components: (a) personal relationships making up a social network; (b) simple and open access to the community for interested parties; (c) personal meetings and understanding of each other; (d) dialogue, feedback, and shared experiences; and (e) a common history (Gattiker & Hedehus, 1999). Besides shared cultural experiences, e.g., having grown up in the same neighborhood, a social community member may have also been exposed to the same, or at least similar, media such as TV shows or newspapers. A social community member has to fit in to be accepted, e.g., a club of folk dancers may require an interested individual to apply for membership. Acceptance may depend upon current members' feelings that the new member will fit the group, add new talents and/or share the group's interests and values. A social community might also try to limit the number of free-riders. Hence, a theatre club may use a member roster to assure that everyone volunteers as an usher at least once during the theatre season, thereby contributing one's share to the success of an event and thus the club's mission (de Jasay, 1989). Other examples may be that one has to attend a certain percentage of monthly or weekly meetings to be a member in good standing.

Defining a Virtual Community

Some of the characteristics of a social community may also be inherent in a virtual community. However, virtual communities rarely encompass all of these characteristics and may contradict some of them. Key characteristics of a virtual community include: (a) styles of imagining the community, based on people's interests such as their jobs or hobbies (Kjaerulf, 1998); (b) blurring of identity, based on speaking about friends who one has never met in person; and (c) interaction based on information transmitted and not on appearances (Primuth, 1998).

Virtual communities may serve several purposes. Career-related virtual communities help one establish credibility in a professional field and provide pertinent information to help with career and job issues. Job-related virtual communities facilitate the acquisition of the latest information on a pertinent subject. Consumer-related virtual communities provide credible and trustworthy information about products and services, such as cars, insurance, appliances, and so on. Hobby-related virtual communities serve needs for entertainment, social interaction, and spending time with others.

The utopian ideal of an Internet community is closely related to the notion that the Internet constitutes a qualitatively distinct sphere of human life that might be called cyberspace. Here, a cultural ideal is being projected onto technology. Agre (1998) pointed out that this concept resonates with a half-forgotten ideal of days gone by: a community whose members had known each other for years. Agre suggested that both economists and Internet enthusiasts misguidedly advocate the compulsive establishment of relationships with people one hardly knows. Psychologists would call this "instant intimacy," which might not necessarily be to the advantage of the individual. Boundaries help people establish some trust between each other, before they open themselves unnecessarily to harm. Developing intimacy, personal relationships, shared experiences, and trust in other people takes time, so a person may be a long-time member of a social community. But most virtual communities come and go, and membership can change frequently.

A virtual community needs to develop intimacy, social networks, understanding, and interaction amongst its members, thereby making it a community of members who share similar values, submit to similar norms, and allow trust to develop. To accomplish these objectives, a virtual community may be made up of various groups or teams, helping to reduce the danger of a virtual community becoming a group of nobodies. The danger in a virtual community is that most members may have little if any contact with other members except for those who hold a central position (e.g., a moderator of a listserver). To reduce feelings of being alone or lacking in social interaction, sub-groups of members may evolve.

We often assume that a virtual group is a unit of a larger organization, association, or social community. The latter could be virtual, as in the case of people interested in playing cards online, or physical, such as a local church.

A virtual community may simply support the physical association's activities by providing members the additional opportunity to stay in touch or interact and work together in virtual space besides the opportunities provided by activities in a physical space.

Challenges to Virtual Communities

People with similar interests living in a limited geographical area may form cyberspace communities about a topic of shared interest such as cooking or kiting. Geographical proximity may then be maintained to some degree by limiting access to the group. In turn, this proximity makes it feasible for various "chapters" of the community to organize social events where members meet, be it parties, weddings, business openings, or receptions. While such social activities are organized via cyberspace, they happen by getting people together at the same time and geographical location. Naturally, such a virtual community supported by social events is far different in its objectives, activities, and membership than communities of customers in e-commerce.

Ownership of a virtual community might be a factor in how various stakeholders are served. A not-for-profit organization needs to offer whatever its members expect in return for their contribution in fees and time donated to the association. A for-profit virtual community must satisfy various paying and nonpaying stakeholders (e.g., advertisers and users). These factors influence the content and events, as well as services offered by a virtual community. Accordingly, while a virtual community about health issues owned by a drug manufacturer might offer great benefits, its independence and neutrality as an information source for sick patients is always in question (Gattiker and Hedehus, 1999a).

A major challenge for virtual communities reaching beyond geographical boundaries is that members often use the *lingua franca* of English, and hence, non-native speakers are unable to use the language to its full richness. Semantics and vocabulary used become narrower or more simplistic than in the usual discourse between two native speakers. Even when chatting on the Internet, native speakers can draw on a large set of humor and shared experiences which can help in further illustrating meanings or in portraying certain images to the listener. Hence, if a virtual community reaches beyond a geographical territory, the lack of shared language may further complicate communication (Rice and Gattiker, 2000).

Members of virtual communities also face other limited commonalities. Some members may have provided certain content and services but consumed little if any content from the site. Through hyperlinks, a reader may not even finish reading a document but, instead, connect to another site and start reading other information. Because of intrinsic characteristics of the technology, people who visit a Web site do not necessarily share the same experiences by proceeding and reading the same content as other persons (Gattiker, Perlusz, Bohmann, Seiferheld, and Ulhøi, 1999).

DOMAINS OF VIRTUALITY

The previous section illustrated that a cyber community may have some similarities to a social community such as a sport's club, but differences do exist (Gattiker and Hedehus, 1999b). We can further assess the domain of a virtual community through the concepts of intra-routine and inter-routine domains of virtuality.

Intra-Routine Domain of Virtuality

An intra-routine domain of virtuality describes the use of technology for traditional activities, such as using the Internet to telephone a friend. This activity may be supported by an on-line video camera that sends pictures of oneself sitting in front of the terminal to the other person, while speaking through a microphone and/or sharing documents and files on the screen. These traditional activities are routinely conducted over network structures. To illustrate, people switch from traditional means of communication such as surface mail to using electronic networks by sending an e-mail. Such activities as communication with colleagues and friends, shopping for clothes, ordering flowers, and getting entertainment can be done and enjoyed in one's home using a computer. Paraphrasing literature on virtual organizations (Palmer and Speier, 1997; Quinn, Anderson, and Finkelstein, 1996), we name this the *intra-routine domain of virtuality* because it occurs within routine and well-established activities.

As mentioned earlier, a social community may use the Web to further support activities that occur in a physical setting. For instance, electronic networks might be used to send out a moderated weekly newsletter with headlines to members. Members may discuss or post comments about the newsletter's content on an electronic bulletin board or use a virtual chat room during a pre-arranged time to exchange comments and ideas about the newsletter's content. Here, the traditional way of distributing a newsletter has been replaced by electronic means, while getting 'letters to the editor' through the bulletin board, the virtual chat room and/or e-mail. An intra-routine domain of virtuality is at the heart of these activities. The primary reason for sending out a newsletter is still to share and exchange information with members, and the only thing that changes is how the community goes about it.

Inter-Routine Domain of Virtuality

The *inter-routine domain of virtuality* represents the expansion of dimensions in people's habits and customs, where technology is used for entirely new activities. The lack of physicality in networked activities not only characterizes the new means for daily routines, but also provides an opportunity for new experiences and changes in beliefs, attitudes, and behaviors. This domain may include such things as anonymous discussions about frivolous subjects, learning the etiquette for participating in groups of interest, or improving the knowledge needed in our studies and careers by finding information not accessible elsewhere. A person's habits may change entirely, from no longer attending physical get-togethers and instead substituting a virtual equivalent. How this may affect people's behaviors toward and communication between each other is still unknown (e.g., Rice and Gattiker, 2000).

Another example of an inter-routine domain of virtuality is how people manage their wealth. An individual may have previously invested in mutual funds or a savings account, but that behavior might change to using brokerage facilities offered via the Internet or the mobile phone. The individual may become an active investor doing frequent stock trades and making his or her own investment decisions. In the past, a more passive investor would have left decisions to a broker and rarely sold or purchased stocks.

Both intra- and inter-routine domains of virtuality exploit electronic networks. The difference between the two is that for the inter-routine domain of virtuality, *the novelty is not limited to the means*, such as using e-mail or a listserver. Instead, *it also represents the creative variation of personal traits or characteristics and behaviors*. This broader concept of people's virtuality does not reduce to temporary tasks performed incidentally on electronic networks. Instead, this domain of virtuality becomes embedded and a stable element of life. Its stability is, therefore, found in the constancy of its presence in behaviors, instead of in its specifications. Accordingly, we can change areas of interest, friends, ways of harvesting information, but still we engage in networked activities that broaden our traditional thinking and experiences.

For a virtual community, people may use an intra-routine domain of virtuality to stay in touch with each other. An inter-routine domain comes into play for a virtual community when members start to change or vary their traits or behaviors. For instance, instead of walking down the corridor to chat with each other or attend a coffee break in the nearby employee lounge, the individual prefers e-mailing a few short messages back and forth with one or two people. Some people prefer e-mailing versus face-to-face meetings or phone calls.

Individuals may also interact differently on-line than when using a telephone or face-to-face communication, by being more direct and less inhibited by rules and norms (Rice et al., 2000). For a church community, inter–routine domain issues may come into play when some members start preferring virtual services to attending the local church each Sunday. Inter-routine virtuality may also be affected by the social capital inherent in a virtual community. For instance, the structure, relations between members, and their cognition may all influence how we use new technology and, as importantly, how this may alter our personal characteristics and behaviors.

SOCIAL CAPITAL IN VIRTUAL COMMUNITIES

Social capital in virtual communities is grounded in social capital theory (Belliveau, O'Reilly, and Wade, 1996). According to Tsai and Ghoshal (1998, p. 464), social capital was initially used in relation to human interactions which help develop individuals in social organizations (e.g., Jacobs, 1961; Loury, 1977). Recently it has been applied to a broad spectrum of social relations, including the family (Coleman, 1988), the firm (Burt, 1992), and the public life in modern society (Putnam, 1993). In the context of firms, social capital is a productive resource that helps the creation of value, like physical and human capital (Nahapiet and Ghoshal, 1997). In more general terms, it is a set of social resources included in human interactions, norms, and values (Portes and Sensenbrenner, 1993) and is formed by three elements: *structure, relations,* and *cognition.*

Structure, Relations, and Cognition

Structure is formed by social interactions: Group members experience a "mediated" personal contact to obtain information, access resources, and participate in various activities. Each member has a different positioning in the group and this provides advantages and disadvantages in terms of contacts. For instance, in a virtual community where social relations are highly structured, regular communication through listservers or meetings held in virtual chat rooms could ensure that people are kept abreast of new developments and in touch with each other. People with certain positions, such as the moderator of a newsgroup or news bulletin board are, of course, better connected to others in the community. They are also likely to communicate and exchange e-mails with more people than the average community member due to their position in the communication network. Naturally, they also have to contribute more, especially if the community is a voluntary type of organization where time and work committed depend on the member.

Relations are the characteristics or attributes of interactions. One of these attributes is trust, and trust is of paramount importance in virtual groups. Trust governs relationships (Uzzi, 1996), induces joint efforts (e.g., Gambetta, 1988; Ring and Van de Ven, 1994), and lets trustworthy members get other members' support. Trusting other members also enables a person to feel comfortable sharing ideas and private matters with others and asking them for advice, input or comments.

Cognition is the common understanding and sharing of the group's mission, objectives and purpose. It creates ways of behaving in a community and represents part of its resources. It also includes ideological beliefs by members of a virtual community, such as religion or understanding of ethics or family life, and its sharing and acceptance of the community's mission and objectives (Gattiker and Hedehus, 1999b).

A Schema for Social Capital in Virtual Groups

Figure 1 shows the three dimensions of structure, social relations, and cognition. The ideal situation is the *Religious Cell*. Here not only is trust among community members high but, just as importantly, structure is well-defined and social relations are highly developed. By combining a high level of understanding and sharing of the group's mission, objectives and purpose, such a virtual community should have high output. In such a community, members may self-select to active positions and encourage others to become equally active. Trust ultimately has a positive effect upon the level of interaction, exchange, and output coming from members and the community.

In the *Club Cell*, trust and sharing of the mission are high, but structure and social relations are low. The moderator of a newsgroup or news bulletin board may have regular contact with members by posting news or distributing messages from members. But this type of star communication network, whereby most communication goes through the center, may limit contact among members.

Groups can move from one cell to the next as they develop. An extended family (cell D) might be able to increase the level of understanding and sharing of its mission and objectives, thus becoming more like a club. A community might invoke a greater structure to improve communication among members and become more like a religious group. The cells in Figure 1 are not meant to suggest that there is a dichotomy of low vs. high, but instead a set of continua along which groups may move. Hence, a virtual community's social capital is in continuous flux and necessitates active contribution, participation, and support by members in order to develop more trust,

Figure 1. Social Relations, Trust, and Structure in a Virtual Community.

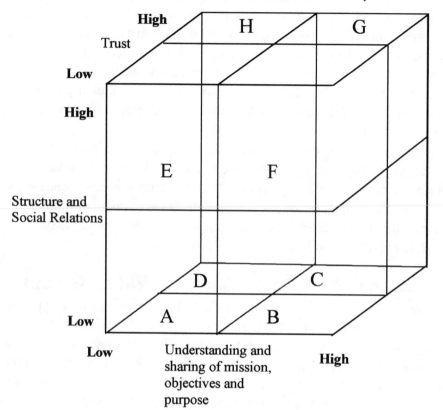

Quadrant A: Nobody's Pet, e.g., a group of clients in a consumer community on a vendor's webpage

Quadrant B: Anarchist Cell, we share a philosophy but hate rules, structure, and distrust everybody

Quadrant C: Club Cell, members of a philately club who have known each other for a long time, share the same interest and trust each other, but structure of group is low

Quadrant D: Extended Family Cell, includes aunts, cousins and others beyond immediate family

Quadrant E: Newsgroup/Bulletin Board Cell, structure is high on how to communicate or post to group, but sharing of mission and trust are low

Quadrant F: Terrorist Cell, highly structured, shared mission, with low level of trust

Quadrant G: Religious Cell, high on all dimensions

Quadrant H: Pal Cell, group of school pals meeting virtually, no particular mission except keeping in touch structure, and sharing of objectives, which in turn makes the community more valuable to all.

Managing a Virtual Community

The three elements of social capital are reciprocally linked. For instance, the more interactions and social relations an individual has within the group, the more this person will share its mission and be perceived as trustworthy. Identifying and recognizing the importance of these three elements in the individuals participating in a group's life, however, is not straightforward. It is difficult to assess the level of trust attributed by members to each other, and the structure of personal interactions is not visible by people not directly involved in the contacts. However, investment in the social capital of a virtual group is essential, since it enables the creation of value for its members (Tsai and Ghoshal, 1998).

The concepts of social capital are linked to the ideas of inter- and intra-routine domains of virtuality. For instance, unless trust levels are high in a virtual community, one could assume that people may be unwilling to change their beliefs, attitudes, and behaviors. Members may use technology such as e-mail or on-line chat to exchange ideas, but without trust they will not be willing to take the risk to explore other possibilities.

FREE-RIDING AND SOCIAL CONTRACTS IN VIRTUAL COMMUNITIES

Because virtual communities may find it difficult to develop personal relationships, familiarity, and social networks, free-riding may be a real challenge for them. Access to a virtual community can be like access to a *nonexclusive good*, where users can increase their share of resources from the virtual community without contributing much, if anything, to it. Hacker 'communities' have tried to deal with this problem by using a bartering system. To illustrate, one hacker may post a message on a board asking for new code or interesting images, while offering interesting material in return. If the offered material is of equal value, the deal may go forward; otherwise, no deal may ever be consummated. In this example, free-riding opportunities are limited and the less one contributes, the less one will receive from the hacker community (de Jasay, 1989). In social psychology, this is considered a social exchange process, where people keep track mentally of what they have contributed and received. For example, a person is not willing to always be the one to initiate contact with a friend, but expects the friend to also sometimes initiate contact (Studd & Gattiker, 1991).

A shared mission in a virtual group can help create a productive atmosphere and avoid opportunism and free-riding (Ouchi, 1980). The challenge, however, is to enforce social contracts between community members in an anonymous society where most goods are intangible (e.g., service and information). How can a social contract be enforced in a virtual community where participation is voluntary? Social contract theory looks at our ancestral past, all the way back to the Pleistocene era (Cosmides and Tooby, 1994). Human beings have formed mechanisms of thought to solve behavioral problems that increase our chance of survival—when we were hunters, creating and abiding by social rules was essential for survival (Cosmides, 1989). Ancient hominids had a tacit contract with their groups: to sacrifice something of their resources in exchange for a higher chance to survive (Cosmides et al., 1994). The cheaters who broke these rules had less chances to reproduce.

The idea of exchanging sacrifices and benefits is almost lost in circumstances where cheating on one side of the exchange does not provoke a loss on the other side. This is the case in a society where the source of wealth has been the production of services and is now becoming the possession of information. Social rules are often violated, without the person feeling dishonest (Gattiker and Kelley, 1999). People install the same software on their computer at home and on the laptop without purchasing two licenses. Frequent flyer miles and other fringe benefits gained at work can be monetarily quantified, but seldom do people include these benefits in their tax form.

The social contracts that we maintain on the Internet fall in unfamiliar territory. Some problems, such as bartering one's privacy for free services, are difficult to solve because we have not elaborated the reasoning behind them (Cosmides and Tooby, 1994). Making the cheater-detection algorithm the decisive concept for perceiving a rule as a social contract renders the Internet a subtle environment. Here some intimate parts of our lives are at the mercy of the social contracts to which we subscribe. For instance, one's privacy or how personal information is being used by an e-commerce site may be at the mercy of the Internet service provider or a commercial Web site.

On the Internet, maintaining social contracts loses importance. For instance, obtaining free e-mail service usually requires the user to submit information to the provider, such as name, address, age, gender, income, and shopping habits. The provider can then try to provide the user with advertising such as banners or e-mail messages with targeted advertising. Here we have an implicit social contract that says by providing information about oneself, one receives a free service in return. But the user can provide incorrect information or block out banner advertising, and the implicit social contract is broken. The user's failure to pay the cost of this social contract may be impossible to assess or enforce.

EXAMPLE OF A VIRTUAL COMMUNITY

A specific example of a virtual community helps to illustrate these ideas. The virtual community that we use for illustration is part of EICAR (*http://www.EICAR.org*), a European association of information security professionals. EICAR has always had working groups, but the board felt that these groups should become more focused and produce deliverables for the membership. Working groups are usually established to share interests and increase knowledge. The board of EICAR supported an ad hoc approach where groups could easily form, reform, and dissolve as needed.

Here, we focus on the Trust in E-Commerce working group, which is part of the larger EICAR community. When the community was being established in 1997, the EICAR board had just decided that the association had to undertake efforts to improve its reach into the research community. At the same time EICAR was striving for maintaining its close link to vendors and industry experts. It was hoped that these efforts would help the organization to expand its focus beyond anti-malware and computer viruses to information security, e-commerce, and use of the Internet at large.

Development of the Community

The EICAR task force on Trust in E-Commerce was started in the summer of 1997 to focus on information security. At that time it had a listserver through which the moderator provided members with information (primarily one-way communication). Three of the members wrote a white paper together and continued these activities in 1998, while other members provided limited feedback and input.

During the annual meeting in 1999, interest by EICAR members mushroomed, somewhat to the surprise of the core members of the group. One reason given by an attendee was that "this group seems to be the most active and looking at this year's EICAR Best Paper Proceedings, several of its reports, ideas and deliverables are available for members to read or use. This is in contrast to other groups where far less seems to be happening." This new interest was positive and encouraging, but did not automatically lead to action. Change in the group's leadership also caused some restarting. However, instead of waiting for people to come through with contributions, an inner core of the group started developing a modus operandi, including a Web page for the group. About half of the core group was employed at the same organization and thus could interact informally several times during the week. This core group reached out to several individuals, canvassing them via e-mail, meeting them personally at conferences, or talking to them over the phone, and individuals were asked to commit to specific tasks.

Developing and Maintaining the Mission

The group's current mission is to focus on e-commerce. Deliverables to be developed include white papers, code, and reports, as well as discussion meetings and presentations at the annual conference. Getting people in this virtual community to become involved and productive was difficult. People volunteered for specific tasks, but follow-through was uneven. Encouragement via e-mail did not always help. Structured events like conference deadlines encouraged motivation. It took from March 1999 until October 1999 for the group to develop a list of activities and objectives, including a dictionary of urban legends, a bibliography of white papers and research reports, a research program on e-commerce, and symposia for the next year's conference.

The group also wanted to develop news material to reach a larger audience beyond EICAR membership. *TIM-Security News* was developed as a collaborative effort between the task force, other EICAR members, and individuals from the information security community. A paid editorial assistant ensures that deadlines by contributors are kept and that the electronic newsletter is e-mailed and available on the Web. The newsletter now has over 500 subscribers around the world (*http://Security.WebUrb.net* look under Newsletters, ISSN: 1399-3860).

A semiautomatic news bulletin board was developed to post newsworthy material related to e-commerce, information security, and the Internet in general. It took from October 1999 through June 2000 to implement the bulletin board. Not only was it necessary to agree on what it would cover, but several programming efforts were needed to create the necessary databases to allow searches, while permitting the secure upload of information by various individuals. The number of posting members has expanded to six individuals, each of whom is expected to contribute at least two items per week.

Finally, the *Information Security This Week* evolved out of the Newsboard. Top stories are selected and mailed out with a hyperlink to subscribers every week. One of the members produces the newsletter each week with limited help. The first issue appeared in June 2000 (*http://Security.WebUrb.net*, ISSN 1600-1869).

Once the group had its new mission and tasks developed by October 1999, several additional ideas came up on how the group might be able to better leverage its activities and output. Again, the core group located at one organization with the chair of the group was instrumental in getting the ball rolling. At another association's annual meeting in the U.S., the chair and another affiliated group member had discussed whether a research papers database on the Web might be helpful for task force members and others (*http://Papers.WebUrb.net*). Another idea that took shape was a jobs search database for IT professionals, intended to enable people to list jobs easily and for free, with a search facility offered on-site (*http://Jobs.WebUrb.net*). The Project Information Networking Tool (PINT) was an idea to help cope with managing the many tasks of the group but, as importantly, help EICAR members who were part of the program committee for the annual conference to schedule and manage their deadlines effectively. PINT is set up to help virtual teams keep track of who is doing what tasks by what time and where (*http://Pint.WebUrb.net*).

Motivation to Maintain and Build the Community

The ad-hoc working group has approximately 20 members, and people can join or leave at any time. Members are professionals in the field of network security (e.g., antivirus software producers), researchers, and a few students. The community's intention is to have a few competent and dedicated individuals as core members, while being open to any person to join if he or she feels able to contribute something to the community's objectives and mission.

All core members actively contribute to two or more of the activities described earlier. In most cases they coordinate one activity and are also likely to be involved in two more projects. Besides the core group membership, the more peripheral group is being split into two. The first group is members who contribute in some form or another at least once every two months, e.g. sending in a news item to the news bulletin moderator or commenting on a draft report. The other peripheral group (about 30 percent of the members) takes advantage of the community's output but, unfortunately, does not actively contribute in any way, shape or form. These free-riders are approached each year during the group's meeting at the annual conference of the association to give them the opportunity to commit to a project. If such communication does not ultimately result in action, the person is asked to leave the community.

While members may share the mission and objectives of the community, active participation does not always come easily. To reduce free-riding and the necessity for sanctioning, we have devised simple rewards designed to motivate contributors. For instance, people who have placed the most news items a week or a month are prominently mentioned on the news bulletin board. For every contribution provided, the member's name, e-mail, and affiliation are published.

In Spring 2000, the community established a Code of Conduct for its members that follows the association's overall code (see *http://www.eicar.org*), but more specifically outlines the expectations, behaviors, and input that are being expected from each member (*http://Security.WebUrb.net/gototrust*). The group counts on each member spending at least 10 minutes per week doing some tasks that will benefit the virtual community. Because we assume that a member's work or research overlaps with the community's interests, this time investment should, in turn, result in synergies either feeding back into one's current job and career interests and plans or from there to the community. Accordingly, by sharing one's knowledge, understanding and insights on various issues concerning Trust in E-Commerce for EICAR, community members benefit from each other's efforts that will in turn be transferred back into their jobs.

The code was developed in January 2000 and discussed with members during the annual meeting in Brussels. Members agreed that it was a good idea to phase the code in by the end of the year. So far more than half of the group has submitted to the code, which we hope will further encourage people's participation and help with the activities.

CHALLENGES OF REMAINING EFFECTIVE WHILE BEING VIRTUAL

Our group has no physical offices, which is certainly not unusual for virtual groups that live on the Internet. The issue today is not "Should we operate through the Internet?" but rather "To what extent should we use the Internet?" or perhaps "How can we exploit the Internet better while avoiding its perils?" Most companies have a virtual dimension such as a Web page or e-mail address, and many individuals have a "virtual area" of their existence, such as personal Web pages. We live in a society where children find their boyfriends and girlfriends online, people chat with persons that they will never meet, buy books, look for a new car, and find a job on the Internet (Gattiker, 1998).

Most individuals join and leave various not-for-profit organizations during their lifetime. While information technologies have opened new opportunities, virtual space may also result in challenges for participants. In the U.S. about half of the adult population engages in some form of volunteering, but half of those people has no involvement at all and very few exhibit high levels of involvement (Independent Sector, 1996). Hence, even in a local church, volunteering may represent a small percentage of membership. Additionally, Europe shows lower levels of volunteering, in part due to many social functions being administered by government agencies or nongovernmental organizations.

During the last twelve months of the existence of the task force on Trust in E-Commerce, it has sometimes been difficult to "feel" the group. Members were left to interact with each other on their own, while subgroups formed and the rest of the community remained inactive. We asked ourselves why we decided to start this activity and why we continue it.

We can use a functional approach (Clary and Snyder, 1999) to understand personal and social processes for initiating and maintaining action. Within this approach, we see several functions that have been potentially served by participation in the group, as discussed in previous sections. The group had to respond to the motivations of its members. Personal and social processes play a crucial role even when it seems that persons are pragmatically focused on outcomes. Not only do different individuals pursue different goals, but also the same individual may be motivated by more than one goal. This is an interesting departure from the altruism-egoism debate in volunteering, where people motivated by a pure selfless helpfulness are opposed to people looking for some forms of selfish benefits. More than a dichotomy between benefit-seekers and help-givers, we have experienced and benefited from a system of complex motivations, which in turn we needed to generate and maintain.

Table 1 shows the functions that might be met by virtual communities, with examples from our specific community.

Data About the Community

In the eight months for which statistics were available, monthly visits to the site rose from 27 for the first month to the current 350 (see Figure 2). Most of the time dedicated to Trust in E-Commerce is in the middle of the week, it comes mostly in early and late afternoon (i.e., GMT + 1 hour), and most users are from Europe. The community is launching a new research project to study its own communication patterns, measuring uploads made per week per member, and number of activities the member contributes to per period (e.g., acting as coordinator vs. providing inputs and contributing in form of giving feedback, resources, links, etc.).

The data in Figure 2 indicate that contributions and closeness within the

Table 1. Functions Served by Volunteer Participation in a Virtual Organization (adapted from Clary and Snyder, 1999).

Function	Examples from Task Force on Trust in E-Commerce
Career Development & Networking	Network with other experts in the field to advance career prospects and improve one's social network
Personal Development	Person feels it is important for him or her to actively get involved in specific activities
Protective or Pro-active	A corporate manager wishes to keep informed about new ways to improve data security and privacy at one's workplace
Responsibility	Member takes responsibility for activity, with milestones to be accomplished listed on group's Web page
Reward	Member's name is associated with output, e.g., presenting results at annual meeting or in electronic newsletters
Social	Community member desires to communicate and exchange ideas/information with others who share interests
Understanding	A student in computer science learns through direct experience with professional computer programmers
Values	A cryptographer feels an important social goal is to proactively defend privacy on the Internet

community are beginning to produce a greater amount of hits, downloads, and visits to the community's Web site. What is important to see in such analyses is that, as long as we sent persuasive messages that included the broadest spectrum of potential motivations in the functions presented, individuals found stimuli to initiate new activities. As importantly, it encouraged some of them to contribute actively in various ways to the life of the community by becoming active members instead of passive ones or free-riders.

IMPLICATIONS AND CONCLUSIONS

The social capital, trust, sharing of mission, and the structure of a community all affect individual members' commitment to a virtual community, but creating that commitment is a challenge. In this chapter, we have: (1) investigated similarities and differences between social and virtual communities, (2) outlined how an inter-routine domain of virtuality and social capital theory may help explain levels of trust, structure, understanding, and free-riding in a virtual community, (3) described a specific virtual community, including its focus and efforts undertaken to motivate members, and (4) provided preliminary data about how this virtual community works on a daily

Figure 2. Usage Statistics for the Virtual Community's Web Site.

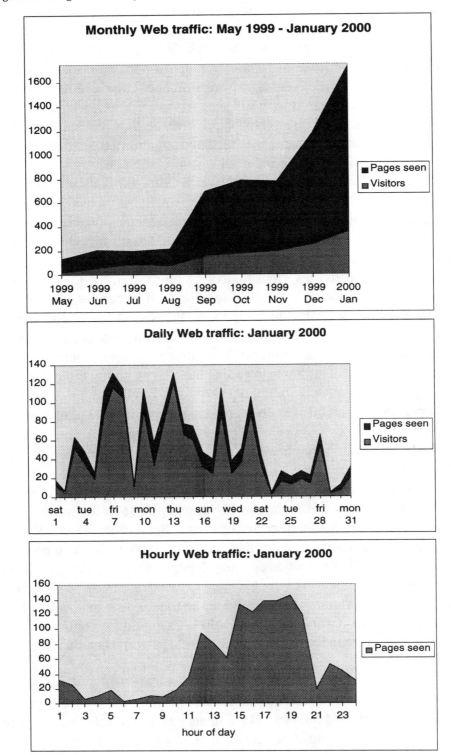

basis in cyberspace.

The biggest challenge for a virtual community may be communication (Borenstein et al., 1997). The ease of interacting with other people is usually seen as an enabling element of teamwork. But in a virtual community, communication is mediated by technology such as e-mail and it is possible to get drawn into a flood of messages. For instance, Hara and Kling (1999) reported that in Web-based long-distance education, students often do not keep up with discussions on bulletin boards because they feel inundated with information and lack the time to read all data. The ability to send appropriate messages to other individuals and to filter information becomes a precondition for being effective. There is no universal recipe for these problems, but it is our belief that the decision to remain small has helped this virtual community to avoid information overload that might cause people to tune out.

Keeping virtual community members motivated is as much of a problem as getting them to contribute to the vitality of the community. Our task force is trying to keep activities alive by asking moderators of the activity to produce progress reports, prototypes and/or drafts that then get distributed to all members or are available on the group's Web site. Activities are usually initiated by a group member whose interest is based on his or her current work or research. The individual may then approach a few others from the community and ask them to help in getting the activity going. But much if not most depends upon an activity's moderator, who has to be able to get other members interested and feeling they are being served by investing their time and effort.

Due to the voluntary character of the community, members need to understand how their values or personal development are being helped by being active in the group. In academic associations, most elected officers gain visibility in their academic community by holding these positions, as well as successfully discharging their service functions. Because most EICAR members are not employed in academia, their situation is somewhat different. How EICAR is perceived as an association may depend on many factors, including a supervisor or employer who could change more than once a year. Accordingly, unless the community served desirable functions from the member's perspective, active participation and help with producing deliverables is unlikely because the individual may fail to see a personal benefit emanating from doing so.

Table 2 summarizes these and other issues by comparing and contrasting three different types of virtual communities, related to employment, professional associations, and hobbies. The dimensions in the table exemplify the issues that need to be considered for success in virtual communities.

Table 3 outlines structural, procedural, and social characteristics that should be immanent in a successful virtual community. The table also shows how our two example communities fare on these characteristics. Certain activities are likely to increase trust, structure, and cognition within a

Table 2. Dimensions of Three Types of Virtual Communities

Dimension	Job Community	Professional Association	Hobby Community
Size of Community (approximate range)	3 to 15	10 to over 100	100 to thousands
Time Frame	Specific, dissolved once tasks are accomplished	Limited, group may extend its life by re-focusing	No time limit
Object and Purpose	Clearly defined with milestones—time, costs	Clearly defined with milestones, tentative deadlines	Not necessarily clearly defined
Performance	Meeting objectives as agreed	Producing output as agreed	Loosely defined
Structure and Responsibilities	Highly structured, few people in charge, members responsible for tasks	Limited structure, voluntary chair who encourages others to participate	Loosely defined
Time Commitment	Varies by stage of task	Varies by interest level	Varies by individual decision
Rewards	Performance-related, primarily extrinsic	Intrinsic and professional recognition; may count for service evaluation	Personal rewards and enjoyment, primarily intrinsic
Career Focus	Immediate or one to two years	Mid to long-range effect on professional credibility and status.	None
Quality Level	Determined by supervisor	Determined by professional field and member's expectations	Depends on group and member's expectations
Intra-routine Domain	E-mail, chat-facilitated virtual meetings, etc.	E-mail, news bulletin board, electronic newsletter	E-mail, chat, telephone (on Internet or other wise)
Inter-routine Domain	Meetings in far-away places may be reduced and replaced by virtual ones	Ask for advice or help on certain work-related matters using e-mail or chat forums	Spend time interacting socially via computer, while being at home
Managing of Conflict	Mediation by leader, compromise	Mediation by members or person withdraws from virtual community	Participation decreases, dropout or avoiding certain members in cyberspace

cyberspace community, may it be career or fun-focused. If cyberspace activity is supposed to mediate or facilitate other activities that support the community, such as task-related or fun-related get-togethers, trust, structure, and cognition are important dimensions when building a virtual community.

In hobby communities, arousal, relaxation, companionship, and escape from the normal routine may be important. In contrast, a virtual task force has a purpose, and gratification should go beyond relaxation or passing of time (e.g., Greenberg, 1974). A successful virtual community can be characterized by certain social characteristics. So while shared experiences, face-to-face meetings, friendships, and an active core group help a community's vibrancy, differences between a virtual community of a professional association versus a hobby-related community must be considered. The latter will probably

Table 3. Structural, Social, and Process Factors for Success in Virtual Communities.

STRUCTURAL FACTORS	Professional Association http://Security.WebUrb.net	Hobby Community http://Gisp.WebUrb.dk
Size that permits communication	Possible with community having 10-20 members	Not possible since community has about 500 members
Reason to exist	Increased knowledge about issues relevant to members	Entertainment, fun
Geographical proximity	Limited to core group	Limited to subsections living in same area of the country
Rewards	Winner of the month circle, most contributions made this month	Winner of the month circle, most contributions made this month
Personalized entry	Planned for Fall 2000	Planned for Spring 2001
Membership tenure	Average years = 2.5	Average years = 1
Stability of membership	Average = 1.5 years 50% are inactive members	Average = 1-year membership 90% are inactive members
SOCIAL FACTORS		
Shared experiences	Yes, possible	Yes
Face-to-face meeting to reinforce proximity	Once or twice annually, due to diversity in geography	Members primarily in Denmark, but no meetings held
Interaction beyond community issues	Possible	Occasional
Core group that spearheads initiatives	Coordinators of News Bulletin Board and other tasks	Webmaster spearheads most activities
Members spend time visiting community	Yes, but primarily during working hours	Yes
PROCESS FACTORS		
Quality content on Web site	News bulletin board updated frequently each day	Updated once a day
Content moderated to assure quality	Moderated before being posted	Moderated before being posted
Regular news distribution	Weekly news stories	Monthly news from the site

register most activity during spare time. Nonexclusivity of the goods and services offered by a hobby-related community may also reduce active participation and contributions (e.g., information and valuable content) to a very small percentage of membership. Cohesiveness may, therefore, also be relatively low. But, if quality content is provided regularly, while being moderated to assure certain standards and news are added frequently, members have a reason for revisiting a Web site or community space frequently.

Although we have increased our knowledge about virtual communities serving interested members of a professional association, a great deal remains to be discovered and synthesized. To guide future research and policy development for virtual communities, we must develop a better understanding of the functions served by them. We especially need to understand how interaction and output can be maintained at high levels of quality, especially with respect to not-for-profit associations beyond academia and people's hobbies. Uncovering the subtler aspects of the virtual community and the processes associated with its vibrancy and productivity, while serving its members effectively, requires additional investigation.

An early study of television (Greenberg, 1974) reported that typical gratification sought from television, in order of importance, was arousal, relaxation, habit or pass time, escape, companionship, and learning. It would be interesting to know if participating in a virtual community related to a person's hobby is also undertaken to obtain gratifications as offered by watching TV. It would also be very interesting to know whether these types of need gratification can be attained by participating in a virtual task force or quasi communities sponsored by firms e.g., medical community sponsored by drug manufacturer (Gattiker et al., 1999).

This chapter has provided some important information about what makes a virtual community work, as well as showing the utility of social capital theory in explaining some of the phenomena addressed here. The development of virtual communities and their functioning beyond the virtual organization or project team is needed to facilitate the Internet becoming an inter-routine domain of our lives. In turn, this will permit us to be more successful in our use of the many communication-mediated technologies being offered today and the near future.

REFERENCES

Agre, P. E. (1998). The market and the net: personal boundaries and the future of market institutions, *Paper presented at the Telecommunications Policy Research Conference Alexandria, Virginia, October.*

Belliveau, M. A., O'Reilly, C. A., and Wade, J. B. (1996). "Social capital at the top: Effects of social similarity and status on CEO compensation," *Academy of Management Journal* (39), 1568-1593.

Bettenhausen, K.(1998). "Group size and group structure," in Blackwell Publishers Inc., Malden, Massachusetts, 206-207.

Borenstein, N. S., Ferguson, J., Hall, G., Lowery, C., Mintz, R., New, D., Parenti, B., Rose, M. T., Stefferud, E., Stein, L., Storm, C., Vielmetti, E., Weiser, M., and Wolff, P.-R. (1997). Perils and pitfalls of practical Internet commerce: The lessons of first Virtual's first year. In R. Kalakota and A. B. Whinston (Eds.), *Readings in Electronic Commerce* (pp. 179-195). Reading, Massachusetts: Addison Wesley.

Burt, R. S. (1992). "Structural holes: The social structure of competition," in Harvard University Press, Cambridge, MA.

Clary, E. G., and Snyder, M. (1999). "The motivations to volunteer: Theoretical and practical considerations," *Current Directions in Psychological Science,* 8(5), 156-159.

Coleman, J. S.(1988). "Social capital in the creation of human capital," *American Journal of Sociology*, 94, 95-120.

Cosmides, L.(1989). "The logic of social exchange: Has natural selection shaped how humans reason?," *Cognition*, 31, 197.

Cosmides, L., and Tooby, J.(1994). "Beyond intuition and instinct blindness: Toward an evolutionarily rigorous cognitive science," *Cognition*, 50, 41-77.

de Jasay, A. (1989). "Social contract, free ride: A study of the public goods problem," in Claredon Press, Oxford, UK.

Gambetta, D. (1988). Can we trust trust? In D. Gambetta (Ed.), *Trust: Making and breaking cooperative relations* (pp. 213-238). New York: Basil Blackwell.

Gattiker, U. E. (1998). Benchmarking, innovation and re-engineering: Should we pull the plug on the Internet or make it serve us better? *Unternehmen im Wandel (Firms and Organization Change)* (pp. 351-378). Berlin & New York: Springer-Verlag.

Gattiker, U. E., and Hedehus, D. (1999a). Managing virtual communities: Challenges and opportunities. In R. Berndt (Ed.), *Management strategies beyond 2000* (pp. 309-334). Berlin & New York: Springer-Verlag.

Gattiker, U. E., and Hedehus, D.(1999b). Virtual communities: dream, nightmare or phantom for providers and users ISBN: 87-987271-0-9, *EICAR 1999 Best Paper Proceedings,*(Available on CD-Rom)

Gattiker, U. E., and Kelley, H.(1999). "Morality and computers: Attitudes and differences in moral judgements across populations," *Information*

Systems Research, 10, 223-254.

Gattiker, U. E., Perlusz, S., Bohmann, K., Seiferheld, I., and Ulhøi, J. P. (1999). How corporate clients and consumers surf the Internet: A review and future directions for research. In J. Pries-Heje, C. Ciborra, K. Kautz, J. Valor, E. Christiaanse, and C. Heje (Eds.), *Proceedings of the 7th European Conference on Information Systems* (pp. 212-234). Copenhagen: Copenhagen Business School.

Greenberg, B. (1974). Gratifications of television viewing and their correlates for British children. In J. G. Blumler and E. Katz (Eds.), *The uses of mass communications: Current perspectives on gratifications research* (pp. 71-92). Beverly Hills: Sage.

Hara, N. and Kling, R. (1999). Students' Frustrations with a Web-Based Distance Education Course. *First Monday*. [On-line]. Available: http://firstmonday.org/issues/issue4_12/hara/. Last access: 1999, December 9.

Independent Sector (1996). Giving and volunteering in the United Sates: Findings from a national survey.

Jacobs, J. (1961). *The death and life of great American cities,* in Random House, New York.

Katz, E., Blumler, J. G., and Gurevitch, M. (1974). "Users and gratifications research.," *Public Opinion Quarterly*, 37), 509-523.

Kjaerulf, J. (1998). Scope of the study, motivation and prior research in the field. Proposal for Ph.D. study,(unpublished).

Loury, G. (1977). A dynamic theory of racial income differences. In P. A. Wallace and A. M. LaMonde (Eds.), *Women, minorities, and employment discrimination* (pp. 153-186). Lexington, MA: Lexington Books.

Nahapiet, J., and Ghoshal, S.(1997). "Social capital, intellectual capital and the creation of value in firms," *Academy of Management Best Paper Proceedings*, 35-39.

Ouchi, W. G. (1980). "Markets, bureaucracies, and clans," *Administrative Science Quarterly*, 25, 129-141.

Palmer, J., and Speier, C. (1997). A typology of virtual organizations: An empirical study. *Paper presented at the Americas Conference of the Association for Information Systems, Indianapolis, Indiana.*

Portes, A., and Sensenbrenner, J.(1993). "Embeddedness and immigration: Notes on the social determinants of economic action," *American Journal of Sociology,* 98, 1320-1350.

Primuth, J.(1998). *Cyberspace: A Consensual Hallucination,* Lawrence Erlbaum Associates, Publishers, Mahwah, New Jersey, 61-66.

Putnam, R. D. "The prosperous community: Social capital and public life," *American Prospect*, 13, 35-42.

Quinn, J. B., Anderson, O., and Finkelstein, S. (1996). In H. Mintzberg and J. B. Quinn (Eds.), *The strategy process* (pp. 350-362). Upper Saddle River, NJ: Prentice Hall.

Rice, R., and Gattiker, U. E. (2000). Computer-mediated organizational communication and structure. In F. Jablin and L. Putman (Eds.), *New handbook of organisation comminication* (). Newbury Park: Sage Publications.

Ring, P. S., and Van de Ven, A. H. (1994). "Developmental processes of cooperative interorganizational relationships," *Academy of Management Review*, 19, 90-118.

Studd, M. V., and Gattiker, U. E. (1991). "The evolutionary psychology of sexual harassment in organizations," *Ethology and Sociobiology,* 12, 249-290.

Tsai, W., and Ghoshal, S.(1998). "Social capital and value creation: the role of intrafirm networks," Academy of Management Journal, 41(4), 464-476.

Uzzi, B.(1996). "The sources and consequences of embeddedness for the economic performance of organizations: The network effect," *Academy of Management Best Paper Proceedings,* 61, 674-698.

ACKNOWLEDGMENTS

The authors would like to thank Christina Sommerfeldt for her editorial assistance, and Ilze Zigurs for her support with finalizing the manuscript. We also would like to thank members of EICAR's Task Force for Trust in E-Commerce who helped us develop some of the issues addressed in this chapter. The usual disclaimers apply.

Chapter 12

Sloan 2001:
A Virtual Odyssey

Wanda J. Orlikowski, JoAnne Yates and Nils Olaya Fonstad
Massachusetts Institute of Technology, USA

INTRODUCTION

The "virtual phenomenon," as it has been labeled is eliciting considerable interest these days. The literature on this topic is currently quite broad, representing a diversity of views and definitions, and differing by unit of analysis (individual, group, project, organization, network) as well as orientation of commentator (strategy, organization design, human resource, team development, technology management) (Boudreau, Loch, Robey and Straub, 1998; Castells, 1996; Davenport and Pearlson, 1998; Lipnack and Stamps, 1997; Mowshowitz, 1997; Nohria and Berkley, 1994; Townsend, DeMarie and Hendrickson, 1998). While much speculation about the kinds of changes likely to be associated with shifts to virtual ways of working and organizing has been widespread, there is also a great shortage of empirical data about what changes are actually occurring, how, when, why, and with what consequences.

In this chapter, we provide an account of the emergence of a virtual community following a shift in institutional work practice from a traditional process to one that was primarily electronic. In the 1998/99 MBA Admissions season, the Sloan School of Management moved from a primarily paper-based application process to an entirely Web-based application process. From the Admissions Office point of view, this shift to on-line admissions was intended to be a relatively contained and simple change in medium to reduce costs in one part of the process (in order to allow greater spending on another part) and to simplify work processes in the office, as well as to reinforce Sloan's image of technological innovativeness. However, this shift was anything but contained, and we will describe how it set in motion a whole series of further changes, both in the work of the Admissions staff, and in the lives of the students applying to and admitted by the school. In a matter of months, an extensive virtual community emerged, with many members of the newly admitted Class of 2001 creating and contributing to an on-line community which took on a life of its own. While many of these changes were interdependent, building on and influencing each other, most were also unplanned, emerging spontaneously from participants' action in the moment.

This emergent process of change has been identified in the literature as an alternative to the more dominant model that portrays change as planned, episodic, and discontinuous (Mintzberg, 1987; Weick and Quinn, 1999). It has also been used to characterize a series of ongoing and situated improvisations observed by Orlikowski (1996) in her study of organizational change enabled by the use of a groupware technology. We believe that the notions of emergence and situated improvisation can help us make sense not only of the changes we observed in the shift to an on-line application process but it can help us more generally make sense of the kinds of changes likely to be associated with shifts to virtual modes of organizing. Because the phenomenon of virtuality is so new and unprecedented, there is considerable ambiguity in what it means in practice to be working or operating virtually. Given this, we might expect organizations to experiment with and learn from a variety of virtual experiences. An analytic framework of emergence and improvisation would more easily account for such diversity and experimentation in practice than alternative models of change that rely more on assumptions of inertia, intentionality, and intervention (Weick and Quinn, 1999).

Our account of the changes associated with the shift in medium by the Sloan School's Admissions Office is drawn from multiple sources: open-ended interviews, texts (paper and electronic), and a survey. We interviewed the five key members of the Sloan School's Admissions Office, working at various levels and with various functional responsibilities. In addition, we interviewed ten members of the Sloan Class of 2001, some during on-campus orientation and before the start of the academic year (August 1999), some during the first semester (September – October 1999), and some (including two interviewed earlier) at the beginning of the second semester (February 2000). These interviews were examined for key activities, events, and outcomes. We examined two primary types of textual data: the process documentation of the Sloan School's Admissions Office (both paper-based and electronic), and the electronic archive of the Sloan Class of 2001 Yahoo! Club and newsletter, representing the asynchronous electronic communication of the Sloan Class of 2001 virtual community from March 31, 1999 to

November 30, 1999. Texts of the electronic media were content-analyzed to identify patterns of usage and common categories of interest. Finally, we administered a brief Web-based survey in February 2000 to the entire 305-member Sloan Class of 2001 (response rate of 31 percent or 94 responses). This survey data gave us descriptive statistics and allowed us to take into account the experiences and outcomes of a broader set of the Class of 2001.

In the following, we provide a chronological account of the changes initiated by the institutional decision to implement an on-line application process for admission to the Sloan School—following these to the emergence of the virtual community of the Class of 2001. We offer some glimpses into the actual world of the virtual community, discussing the kinds of activities and conversations engaged in by the participants, as well as the implications of these changes for both the staff in the Admissions Office and the students who interacted with this process. We then interpret these changes in terms of an improvisational model of change, showing how a series of planned, emergent, and opportunistic changes wove together as the Admissions staff and the students responded to, modified, and improvised around the situated changes they were collectively enacting over time. We conclude by suggesting some implications of virtual organizing for changes in process and community, and suggest some unintended consequences of such changes.

HISTORY OF THE EMERGENCE OF THE CLASS OF 2001 VIRTUAL COMMUNITY

The story began with a decision late in 1997 by the Sloan School's Admissions Office to move to an entirely on-line admissions process for the MBA Class of 2001 (the members of which would be admitted during the spring of 1999). Several factors encouraged this decision, including factors related to cost and to simplified work processes. The primary driver for this shift was the high cost of the current, paper-based process. The school annually mailed out application brochures to tens of thousands of inquirers, only around 10 percent of whom actually applied to the school. Because these brochures included time-sensitive application information, they had to be redesigned and reprinted each year, a process seen as a waste of resources, but, until this time, necessary. Moreover, Alex, at that time in charge of the department which included the Admissions Office, saw an opportunity to use the savings generated by going online and create—within the existing budget—an additional Sloan brochure highlighting the school's graduates. This decision would allow the Admissions Office to print larger numbers of two very high quality paper brochures with less time-critical information and a two-year shelf life, all for the same price as printing a single new, one-year brochure two years in a row. Such an approach was possible because the Web-based version of the application brochure, with frequently updated information including critical time lines, became the official source of information for all applicants to consult when completing their Web-based applications. A secondary driver was the anticipated simplification of some work processes. In particular, the Admissions Office would receive data such as e-mail addresses and test scores already in electronic and manipulable form, rather than having to enter this information for each applicant as each paper form was received.

In addition to these drivers, issues around image and readiness encouraged the shift. As part of MIT and in its own right, Sloan embraced and cultivated a high-tech, innovation-oriented image that would only be enhanced by such a move, especially if it were the first of the MBA programs to do so. Moreover, the time seemed right for this move. Sloan's administration already knew from previous years' admissions that all applicants had e-mail addresses and were computer savvy, and many of them were using an off-the-shelf application package for generating applications to major business schools, including Sloan. Some students were also already applying via an optional on-line system, which had allowed Mark and Michael, the key players in managing the admissions process, to become comfortable with it. Thus the Admissions Office felt that they were ready for such a shift.

Given the cost and process incentives, along with the image and timing factors, the Sloan Admissions Office decided to move the 1999 MBA application process entirely to the Web. The move was accomplished in partnership with a firm, GradAdvantage, with which the Sloan Admissions Office had already collaborated experimentally. This firm ran the Web site for the application process itself. As applications were completed, they were downloaded in batches to the computer in the Sloan Admissions Office for processing. Thus no one at Sloan had to enter all the data into a database—it was in electronic form from the beginning, and was transformed from GradAdvantage's format to Sloan's format as soon as it was downloaded. This transformation initially encountered some formatting glitches, but they were quickly solved and did not affect the availability of the data. From the start, then, the Sloan Admissions staff had the advantage of having e-mail addresses, test scores, and other kinds of manipulable data. This on-line process also enabled the staff to communicate with the applicants quickly and easily via e-mail, for example, to acknowledge the arrival of an application, to request missing items such as transcripts and recommendations, and to acknowledge completion of the application. Finally, it allowed the Admissions staff to send out information to all applicants on what they should expect next, thereby reducing applicant anxieties and anticipating common questions that would normally have been handled by telephone for many individual applicants. For the Admissions Office, this change in process had many benefits, both expected (more brochures for a lower cost, access to data without data entry, reinforcement of desired image) and unexpected (ability to manage applicant questions promptly and in many cases proactively).

To complement this new Web-based application process and the e-mail communication it facilitated, the Admissions Office decided to set up a Web site that would serve as a source of information for students once they were admitted. The decision to set up this Web site for admitted students was made well after the original decision to use the GradAdvantage site for on-line applications, but before the admissions process really got underway. The decision to create this complementary Web site—which came to be known as the AddMIT Sloan site—was taken largely to be consistent with the earlier part of the admissions process. The Admissions Office staff felt that as the application process had been handled electronically up to that point, admitted students would expect this electronic means of communication to continue.

According to Alex, the AddMIT Sloan site was designed to achieve three general goals: to market Sloan to the admitted students and encourage them to accept their offers of admission, to manage the matriculation process by facilitating the processing of required forms quickly and accurately, and to connect admitted students with one another. The Web site was designed around the first two goals, with the idea that the Admissions staff would add information and features related to the third goal (connecting admitted students) in the summer before students arrived on campus.

The Admissions staff believed that the site was reasonably successful in achieving their first two goals. As soon as students were offered admission (which occurred in two waves to match the School's two application deadlines), they were sent (via e-mail) the URL of the AddMIT Sloan site and told that they should use this Web site as their primary source of information about the next stages in the process. This Web site replaced what had previously been several mailings to admitted applicants which included forms to be sent to various offices and information on a range of issues related to attending Sloan. The Web site also provided time lines and extensive information aimed at persuading potential students to accept the School's offer, including news stories aimed particularly at this audience, electronic chat sessions with faculty and staff, and access to alumni/ae mentors. In addition, this Web site was the only place where applicants could accept their offers of admission to the school. So, this Web site served as a central hub for all admitted students.

The last goal for the AddMIT Sloan site—to connect students—was rendered moot by the emergence of the student-driven virtual community of the class of 2001, which facilitated student connections more rapidly, more effectively, and in a different form than had been expected by the Admissions staff. This virtual community also indirectly advanced the first goal, as we will see in what follows. To achieve the goal of connecting students, members of the Admissions Office had intended to add information and features to the AddMIT Sloan site during the pre-matriculation period, posting e-mail addresses and facilitating communication of admitted students before they entered. Well before they took this step, however, students had initiated the virtual community, with the AddMIT Sloan Web site as a critical but unplanned element in the initiation. One of the features of the AddMIT Sloan site was a "chat room," set up to host virtual discussions between admitted applicants and specific faculty and staff members. It was the site of a key interaction that initiated a powerful snowballing effect. The first scheduled virtual chat with a faculty member was held on March 31, 1999. After it ended, and the professor and the Admissions staff had signed off from the chat room, several admitted applicants stayed on and continued to chat among themselves. Out of this interaction came the idea of establishing an electronic message board and chat Web site for students admitted to the Sloan Class of 2001.

Before getting to the outcome of that meeting, however, we must understand how the predispositions of these admitted students to communicate electronically had already contributed to what occurred at that chat session. Prior to the faculty chat session, one of the attendees, Megan, had already electronically met two of the other attendees, Karina and Luis. Karina and Megan had met through the MIT Sloan club hosted on the Yahoo! Web site (in Yahoo!'s MBA-Central area). Most members of that club were Sloan graduates, with only a few current students participating. Karina had discovered this site while surfing the Web, shortly after being admitted to Sloan. Excited about her new affiliation, she posted a message saying that she had been accepted at Sloan. Megan, who also happened to browse this Web site, saw Karina's message and contacted her via e-mail. Thus began an on-going e-mail interaction. Megan had also (electronically) met a third attendee at the faculty chat session, Luis, this time through the community Web site, PlanetAll. In her PlanetAll profile, Megan had indicated her status as an admitted Sloan student. Luis noticed this and contacted her directly via e-mail to report his similar status. Thus at least three of the newly admitted Class of 2001 members participating in the first faculty chat session had already had electronic contact with one or more of their future classmates also attending the chat.

Excited about attending Sloan, the eight or ten students who stayed on after the March 31 faculty chat session exchanged e-mail addresses and continued "talking." During this conversation, they came up with the idea of starting an electronic message board and chat room for admitted Sloan applicants. They considered both Yahoo! and PlanetAll as possible hosting Web sites, and ultimately decided to try both and "let the market decide." By later that evening, the Yahoo! club had been established and the opening message announced: "Welcome, This is the Yahoo! Message Board for MIT Sloan class of 2001 community." This Yahoo! site quickly won out over the PlanetAll alternative, also established immediately, primarily because it was more familiar to the early members of the community. One early member noted that "The most ingenious idea [of the founders] was to leverage what already existed"—the ubiquitousness of the Yahoo! platform. In commenting on the adoption of the Yahoo! site, he noted that while other websites might have had more features or been better in various ways, the simplest solution to their goal of communicating with each other was the one that won out.

At the start, only a handful of admitted students participated in the Yahoo! club. These included the group of students at the original faculty chat session, as well as a few other admitted Class of 2001 students known to the founding members. The second posting to the message board, however, reflected the founders' interest in using this electronic medium to establish connections among themselves:

> Let's make this work... it's up to us. When could we chat? Let's invite more people to join that we know got accepted!!!

As indicated in this message, the Web site had both a chat room for synchronous, transitory communication and a message board for asynchronous posting and archiving of messages. The first chat session on the Yahoo! club was scheduled for the next Monday night. Because these chat sessions were transitory, we have no direct access to their content. However, our interviews with participants as well as our reading of the comments posted to the message board right after the sessions suggest both their freewheeling character and their popularity among a small core membership in the club (including the initial members). Indeed, one participant noted that they were "addictive," while another commented:

> It was much more fun to be in the same "room." These chats were ephemeral and so we were more free and open as a result. The sessions were scheduled for Mondays from 9pm to 11pm but they would go on till at least 1am or 1:30am.

The initial Yahoo! Club members appear to have been highly committed, but in the first few weeks of April, membership in the club grew slowly, and participation on the message board not at all. A couple of members attended various local Sloan events for admitted students and announced the existence of the club, gaining a few more members. One of the founders, Karina, engaged in what she called "guerilla marketing," that is, marketing the club directly to others. Karina was living in California at the time, and she asked the Admissions Office for the e-mail addresses of other admitted students living on the West Coast. She then e-mailed each of them an invitation to join the club, in particular telling them about an upcoming Monday chat session they could join. The founding members estimate that this direct marketing effort brought in some 60 to 90 new members, some of whom undoubtedly participated in the chat, but postings to the message board were still few and primarily by the same small set of individuals.

The largest impact on both club membership and use of the message board came when the AddMIT Sloan site added a link to the Yahoo! club. As early as a week after the club was started, the idea of the link had been proposed to the Sloan Admissions Office and reported on the message board: "We may be getting linked to the MIT Sloan official site. Keep checking...." Behind the scenes, Michael (a member of the Admissions staff) passed the request for a link to the Sloan 2001 Yahoo! club up to Alex (his boss). When Alex accessed the Yahoo! club's message board to see what was going on there, he was impressed to see the energy and variety of the people posting to it. He saw that this club was indirectly contributing to one of the major goals of his marketing efforts in general: to highlight the diversity and well-roundedness of Sloan students. While Sloan already had an image of technological innovation which the move to electronic admissions enhanced, Alex felt that Sloan did not have the image of student well-roundedness that he felt it deserved to have. This club demonstrated that well-roundedness in a direct and compelling way. As one participant noted in a comment posted to the message board during this early period:

> *One thing that amazed me is how many different professions were represented at yesterday's chat. The stereotype about Sloan being dominated by engineers just doesn't seem valid. There was a international trade consultant (Karina), a venture capitalist (John), an I-Banker (Jason), a student of Public Policy (Ricardo)—the list goes on.*

Given the positive image projected by the Yahoo! club, the Admissions Office readily agreed to include a link to it on the AddMIT Sloan site. The link was actually launched with significant fanfare in an item in the "New and Noteworthy" section of the site on April 28, 1999. The item was titled "Meet and Greet Your New Classmates on the Internet," and included a general invitation to join the Club, the link to the club, a brief history of the founding of the club recounted by Karina, a brief article by Megan entitled "Random Thoughts in Cyberspace," and a final section on FAQs (Frequently Asked Questions) labeled "How to Use the Club: Questions and Answers." The AddMIT Sloan site thus provided not only a link to the club, but details on its content, context, history, and usage norms. In addition, and perhaps more importantly, the inclusion of club information on the official Sloan Web site gave the club immediate legitimacy. As one founding member put it, the AddMIT Sloan site "got it [the club] branded, and gave it credibility."

This Sloan link was the beginning of a new phase in the club's life. It was key to making the club known and accessible to far more than the initial small group, or even that group plus those reached by the guerilla marketing. From this time on, the asynchronous message board became increasingly used by admitted students as a vehicle for sharing information helpful in preparing for life at Sloan, as well as for getting to know each other (described in more detail in the next section). An additional and interesting use of the message board was the posting of photographs taken at face-to-face functions so that others could vicariously share in the local events.[1] The growth in club membership was also manifested in the expansion of the synchronous chat sessions. These had been originally scheduled for once a week on Monday evenings (Eastern time), but as membership grew these were quickly expanded to three times a week at various times to accommodate participants living on the West Coast and in other parts of the world. After the club took off, its activities thus represented both increased participation and increased diversity of participation by the students in their efforts to connect with each other.

The Class of 2001 virtual community involved more than expanded membership and participation in the Yahoo! club itself. The next development was the creation of an electronic newsletter. Again, a serendipitous interaction played a key role. At a Boston "C-function" (this term—referring to a "Consumption Function"—is used in the broader Sloan community to designate social events involving the consumption of food and drink), the idea to hatch such a newsletter emerged from a conversation between a few attending admitted students and Mark, a member of the Admissions Office. All of the participants in this discussion agreed that this was a good idea. From the students' point of view, it would provide another outlet for creative energy and visibility within the new Class of 2001 community. From the Admissions Office point of view, it would provide another means of disseminating useful information and offering a student-generated picture of the diversity and well-roundedness of the incoming class. Within a week, the first issue of the electronic newsletter was made available on a student-maintained Web site and a link to it was soon set up on the AddMIT Sloan page to allow for easy access[2]. The newsletter was labeled "2001: A Sloan Odyssey," and the homepage for the newsletter described it as created:

> *By, of, and for the Sloanies of '01, their SOs, families and other hangers-on, during our collective transition between "Life As We Knew It" and "Life At Sloan"!*

Notification of the newsletter and its Web site was made via a broadcast e-mail message sent by the Admissions staff to all admitted students. The newsletter also included a brief description of the Yahoo! club and a link to the club Web site. This brought in a number of new participants into the club, particularly international students.

The foreword to the first newsletter reflects the growing enthusiasm of club members for their virtual community:

> *Sloan 2001 is the first class to apply online. It was only appropriate that we would meet each other electronically first.*
>
> *There was a perceived need for a newsletter to go along with the regional C-functions and Yahoo! club activity. So some energetic admits decided to get cracking.*
>
> *This and following newsletters will serve as a countdown to our final convergence to Boston in August.*
>
> *Sloan 2001 is on a voyage of discovery together. Now that Julie, Pat, Joyce, Anita, Edgar, Frank, Millie, and Megan have gotten the ball rolling, we want your help to keep it going. Submit articles, ideas, calendar events and anything else which you would like to share.*

After providing e-mail addresses to use in submitting items, the description ended, "Let the journey begin ..."

While membership numbers weren't logged over time, the club eventually reached a size of over 300 (including a few members of the Class of 2000 and staff in the Admissions Office) during the summer before the students started pre-term activities in mid-August.

ENACTING THE VIRTUAL COMMUNITY

As we saw above, admitted students had a variety of electronic means to connect with their classmates: the message board, their regularly scheduled chat sessions, and the newsletter. In addition to these interactions, some admitted students met face to face in a variety of events organized by themselves or Sloan, some had personal telephone conversations, and some exchanged person-to-person e-mail. Thus, interactions were diverse: one-to one, one-to-many, and many-to-many, and these interactions used both synchronous and asynchronous media.

Our primary sources of data on students' interactions are the archived messages posted on the Yahoo! Club Message Board and the electronic newsletters. In this section, we will focus on these two sources, and especially on the interactions on the message board. While the postings to the message board do not completely capture all the interactions of the Class of 2001, they do reflect the general rhythm and timing of concerns and interests that were occupying the minds of the incoming class as they prepared to become full-time students. We first examine the general pattern of postings throughout the life of the message board, and then consider the general content of messages posted. In the following section, we will complement this discussion with interview data from participants and admissions staff.

During the period between March 31 and November 30, 1148 messages were posted to the message board. As illustrated in Figure 1, the majority of these messages (1068, or 93 percent of the messages) were posted during the four months between April 28 and August 31. April 28 is when the Admissions staff added a link from the AddMIT Sloan site to the Yahoo! club, and announced that link in their "What's New" section. As a result of the sudden

Figure 1: Number of Messages Posted to Yahoo! Class 2001 Message Board per Day

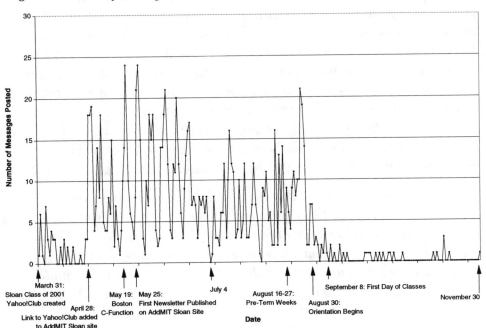

increased visibility of the club and its message board, the number of postings surged from an average of one a day to ten a day. After August 31, with Orientation Week underway, the number of messages dropped significantly (almost down to zero). By this time, members of the Class of 2001 had all moved to the Boston area, and had completed most of their preparations for school. More importantly, they were meeting and developing connections face to face. The message board, as a common place where admitted students still dispersed all over the world could interact, was no longer necessary.

The postings to the message board also had a general weekly pattern: few messages were posted on weekends (7 and 9 percent of total messages were posted on a Saturday or Sunday, respectively), while the majority of the messages were posted between Monday and Thursday (about 72 percent). Wednesday was the most popular day for posting (22 percent of the messages). This pattern suggests that most members of the Class of 2001 were participating during regular work hours.

Our analysis of the content of the messages posted on the message board indicates that the participants engaged a wide range of subjects. Initially, we categorized these messages into 20 broad subject categories (see Table 1). Subsequently, we grouped these 20 categories into two general clusters: messages which include participants' activities and efforts to connect with and learn about their peers ("Getting to Know Each Other"); and messages which describe participants' activities and concerns in preparing to become students at Sloan and residents of the greater Boston area ("Getting Ready For Sloan").

The subjects within the cluster "Getting to Know Each Other" represent a variety of ways through which participants became familiar with their future colleagues, including self introductions, coordinating and reporting on real-time interactions (both in electronic "chats" and face-to-face functions), commenting on the community or peers met during the real-time interactions, discussing common personal interests, and sharing photos of each other on the Web. Messages typically included multiple subjects. For example, one participant posted the following message on June 6 with the subject line "San Francisco Mates." In it she briefly introduced herself, described a personal interest (water rafting), and offered to coordinate a group water-rafting trip:

> *Hi to anyone joining the class of 2001 who lives in the San Francisco Bay Area! I've only just joined the "club" (sounds so elite!) and missed a number of functions y'all put together. I'd love to know who you are and if anything else is upcoming. I'd also love to organize something myself if there's interest! I'm a rafting guide and would love to do a river trip for us on the American River if*

Table 1: Subject Categories of Messages Posted on Yahoo! Class 2001 Message Board

Getting to Know Each Other

chat
refers to the Yahoo chat sessions (scheduled for three times a week on the club web site)

f2f meeting
refers to events when members met each other face to face or visited Sloan

group
refers to the group participating on-line, such as commenting on the diversity of participants

index
refers to an index that was created of messages posted to the board

medium
refers to the web medium for the Yahoo club discussions and chats, e.g., the Yahoo site, Yahoo versus PlanetAll, archiving messages, accessing the site

newsletter
refers to newsletters that were put together by participants for the Class of 2001

peers
refers to characteristics of the Class of 2001, fellow Sloan MBAs, how others perceive Sloan MBAs, and need to enrol more women into Sloan

personal interest
refers to members' interests along professional (e.g., VCs, business) and leisure lines (e.g., dancing, traveling, movies, etc.)

photos
refers to any photos of the members posted on the Web

pybk
refers to the "pre-yearbook" picture book and on-line database (both of the incoming Class of 2001) developed by some of the members

self
refers to personal characteristics, e.g., nationality, ethnicity, educational qualifications

Getting Ready for Sloan

academics at Sloan
refers to course or track options in the curriculum, e.g., ITBT Track

accepting offer
refers to the decision to accept the Sloan offer

auto
refers to owning an automobile in Boston, whether or not to have one, and where to get insurance

books
refers to course books, e.g., what books to get and where to purchase them (on- and off-line)

hardware
refers to discussions about the kind of computer to buy (including computer bags, cell phones, financial calculators, palm pilots)

housing
refers to various housing options, e.g., apartment hunting, off- versus on-campus housing, lottery, temporary housing, selling furniture, insurance

life at Sloan
refers to aspects of life as a Sloan student, e.g., logistics, rankings, GMS dues, financial aid

life in Boston
refers to general life issues, e.g., what bank to join, local travel option

there's interest..... any takers? Willing to trust me to get you down the river?! (not to worry - it's how I financed my undergraduate education!). It would need to be before August 1 most likely, and if midweek works for anyone, it's the most enjoyable (but not a prerequisite).

Anyways, if someone has a list of addresses and wouldn't mind sending me an email offline so I can get in touch, I'd really appreciate it!

Harriet

harriet@Web.com

As this message illustrates, the message board became a medium used by participants to get to know each other, electronically and face-to-face.

The second general cluster of subjects on the message board concerned "Getting Ready For Sloan," and these dealt with the practical issues associated with preparing for attending Sloan and living in Boston. For example, on June 10, one participant posted a message soliciting advice and sharing information regarding the MIT on-campus housing lottery:

[Subject line:] Lottery is In : Seeking Housing Advice !

Hi there,

My number has come and I have been offered Tang Hall. Does anyone know the pros and cons regarding Tang vs. Edgerton?

For all those in a state of housing anxiety, I heard yesterday (June 9) via email and my number was 253.

Thanks,

Sam

Postings in these "Getting Ready For Sloan" categories included discussing housing options, finding roommates, comparing types of laptops, reporting good deals on books, and seeking advice on financial issues such as insurance and financial aid. As suggested in the example above, and discussed in the following section, the exchange of information was both practical and anxiety-reducing.

Of the 1,148 messages that were posted on the message board, about 72 percent (842 messages) dealt with subjects in the "Getting to Know Each Other" cluster, while about 40 percent (442 messages) focused on subjects related to "Getting Ready For Sloan." Only a few messages—about 10 percent (118 messages)—had content in both clusters of subjects.

Similarly, the largest percentage of articles posted in the newsletter dealt with subjects regarding "Getting to Know Each Other." The newsletter published a total of 77 articles in 7 issues between May 25 and September 8. Of these, 68 percent (52 articles) contributed to "Getting to Know Each

Other," including items on personal interests (e.g., in one issue there was a series of articles dedicated to the musical interests of class members), an author's travel experiences, a calendar of events listing get-togethers, and an "Announcements" section describing personal accomplishments of participating class members. Articles covering issues related to "Getting Ready For Sloan" (either by themselves or in addition to subjects classified as "Getting to Know Each Other") made up about 52 percent (40 articles) of those posted. These articles included interviews with faculty members describing various academic tracks at Sloan, personal experiences with the area housing market, and an international participant's observations of cultural particularities of the United States. Table 2 compares the percentage of items posted in both the message board and newsletter that covered issues in either or both of the "Getting Ready For Sloan" and "Getting to Know Each Other" subject clusters.

Table 3 summarizes the eight most popular subjects covered in the message board and the newsletter. Examining specific subjects within the "Getting Ready for Sloan" cluster, we see that the message board dealt more with obtaining a house or apartment ("housing") and choosing computer equipment ("hardware") while the newsletter addressed such matters as immunization shots and loans ("life at Sloan") and academic life at Sloan ("academics at Sloan").

Finally, while we do not have direct access to the interactions students engaged in during the weekly chat sessions, it is reasonable to assume that a range of subjects similar to that represented in the message board and newsletter was covered in these informal, synchronous conversations. Indeed, one message posted on the message board and referring to recent experience in a chat session, suggests this as well:

What an invigorating chat! I spent something like four hours

Table 2: Percentage of Postings in Message Board and Newsletter

	Message Board (percentage)*	**Newsletter (percentage)***
Getting Ready For Sloan	38.50	51.95
Getting to Know Each Other	71.78	67.53
Getting Ready For Sloan and *Getting to Know Each Other*	10.28	19.48

* Please note: Because several postings covered two or more subjects, the total adds up to over 100 percent.

Table 3: Most Popular Subjects Covered in the Message Board and Newsletter

Message Board subject (percentage)*	Newsletter subject (percentage)*
chat (7.14)	f2f meeting (9.09)
life at Sloan (8.01)	academics at Sloan (10.39)
hardware (9.76)	group (12.99)
self (14.72)	life in Boston (18.18)
housing (15.42)	self (20.78)
group (15.59)	peers (20.78)
personal interest (19.34)	personal interest (23.38)
f2f meeting (19.60)	life at Sloan (29.87)

* Please note: Because several postings covered two or more subjects, the total adds up to over 100 percent.

chatting with various people as they wandered into the chat room from ... San Francisco, Tijuana, Bogota, New York, Oslo, the Basque region of Spain ... forgive me if I've forgotten anyone who was there!

We talked about so many interesting subjects: - Housing (of course!) - Roommates - Religion - Music - Travelling - The logistics involved in moving to Cambridge - Work/Quitting Work/Getting Ready to Quit Work - Motivation (or the lack thereof) at Work - Back injuries and surgery - C-functions - Playing around with the "Emotions" function! - Sloan and HBS - Rankings - Financial Aid and Scholarships - Camaraderie and Teamwork at Sloan Hmmm....maybe I should have written this right after the chat. Or taken notes. My head is swimming...

Julie—I kept wondering if you were going to be there, you party girl, you!

Well, have a great week, everyone! Feel free to join in on any of the scheduled chats, or get together with others and schedule your own!

Enjoy life! Millie

The virtual community clearly had plenty to discuss in all its media.

MAKING SENSE OF THE VIRTUAL COMMUNITY

One important way to understand the emergence of this virtual community is to understand how the participants made sense of it and what value they obtained from it. Our survey and interview data suggest that the students experienced a number of outcomes through their participation in the virtual community, most—but not all—of which were positive.

During the period between their admission to Sloan and their arrival in Boston, students indicated that their participation in the virtual community had made them less anxious about their capabilities and preparedness for Sloan and helped them with the practical details of preparing to attend Sloan:

> It was exciting to get a sense of who my classmates were – their concerns, opinions, etc.

> I started feeling a part of the school before I got here.

> I got a sense of community, a better feel for my classmates, a better understanding of the Sloan experience and forthcoming opportunities.

> It was social interaction, and it was a lot of comfort that you know, … probably most of the people that come into such a, you know, demanding program, are really worried, "am I good enough?" … So, it was a lot of comfort because you could see other people had the same worry. … It was such a relaxed environment, and everybody was so open that really, you know, it was very comfortable to bring up any issues we had.

> A great chance to "meet" people before coming to Sloan. Found out about people's work experiences, interests, cultures. It was also a good resource for finding answers to the many questions we all had during our transition (moving, housing, cars, etc.)

> The club was fantastic. It eliminated a lot of concerns I had about things like housing, laptops, bags, … Being in [a foreign country], I had no idea what I was getting into in Boston and Sloan. And I got a lot of good information from the club.

> [I] learned about housing opportunities. Arranged temporary housing with people I "met" in the club.

> Information about computers, what were the good choices others were buying, prices they were paying, etc.

Useful information on a number of very relevant topics, such as housing, books, classes, matriculation process (e.g., health examination) plus the social aspect of getting to know future classmates.

In the interviews, the founders of the club and a small group of other admitted applicants have suggested that the weekly chat sessions were the most "fun" part of the club, but the chats were only a small part of the whole community. Attendance at these chats only ranged from 10 to 30 individuals, according to estimates from a few of the participants. For those active in them, the chats enabled them to get to know others on a more personal basis. For example, one student noted:

On the chat, it was, you know, it was fun, and I actually had a couple very good electronic friends that we kind of made, made chats a routine. And we said we'd chat every Monday, and Wednesday. We knew that 9:00 in the evening we had, you know, a couple of hours, so we had, like the regulars of the chat, and then people would come in and join in the discussion.

Still, the survey (which is likely to overstate, rather than understate, actual participation in all aspects of the club) indicated that only 44 out of 94 respondents read and/or contributed to the chat sessions, while 81 of the 94 read and/or contributed to the message board and 62 read and/or contributed to the newsletter. One survey respondent noted that the chats were: "fun at first, but became tiresome because the same 5 or 6 people dominated the room." Participation in the chat sessions was more difficult for international students who could only join the chats for short periods of time or not at all to avoid tying up telephone lines and running up phone bills.

Students' experiences in the virtual community particularly affected their experience in orientation activities—the face-to-face events organized by the Sloan School right before the term starts to welcome the new students and have them form their teams. Indeed, the virtual community seems to have played an important and positive role in paving the way for face-to-face interaction. One student who had deferred admission from the previous year and who had participated in the previous year's orientation was able to directly compare the different orientation experiences in the two years:

I mean, the first day it was like very different. When I got here to orientation last year, I almost didn't know anybody. Although I've been to those two C-functions, the luncheons, but those are so formal and so you don't get to say more than "Hi, what's your background?" So at the orientation last year, it was more like, you know, checking out the atmosphere and standing back and looking around to see what other people are doing. If someone made eye contact with you, you kind of tried to say hi. But this time, the first day of orientation there was so many hugs and yells, and laughter, and people that finally got to see you face-to-face after all those months. You know, there were people I wasn't very close to, people who only posted a couple of messages, but I got some really very big hugs from some of them.

Other students similarly noted that the virtual community had made the initial face-to-face meetings at Sloan much more enjoyable:

Orientation was not as intimidating because we had gotten to know each other on the Yahoo! Club.

First off, you could build on sort of what you had talked about earlier [on the message board]. "So, Joyce, how is this thing?" You know. Meeting people in person was easier because you already had a building block, a frame of reference for them. You already had a connection. Then you go into other things, you know. So you sort of felt that since you already talked about certain things before, you could sort of use that as a frame of reference, sort of as a building block, for other things too.

One of the most exciting parts of the beginning of orientation was discovering who each of the Yahoo personalities were in person. People would say to me, "Oh, you're [username]" and I would respond, "you're the one from Israel (or Canterbury, or Hong Kong, or Spain) I chatted with!" It was a marvelous journey of discovery.

My personal feeling is that it had a tremendous influence. I was not walking into a room with a bunch of strangers who were all competing with me. These were friends that I'd gotten to know over three months, and shared the things I loved with them. So, the rules were very clear – we were friends, here to have fun.

The survey responses and interviews both suggest that the influence of the virtual community waned once the term began. When asked about the influence of the Yahoo! Club on life at Sloan during the term, the majority of survey respondents responded "none," roughly a quarter reported a residual positive influence, and no one reported negative effects. The interviews and informal contacts with students suggested a minor negative influence, though most of it at an earlier point in time. For example, a few students who joined the club some time after it had started indicated that they were a little overwhelmed and "intimidated" to find hundreds of postings already. One student noted his anxiety at the time about being "behind" even before the term began. One participant observed in an interview that:

> Perhaps the club created a bit of a hierarchy—the more you were heard the more people knew you. It seems almost inevitable that it created something of a class structure. ...I saw some resentment towards the people who were on the club. Some people who came late to the club felt there was some exclusivity in the club, that it was a "clan," that they were left out of. Some people told me that they did not feel welcome.

These more negative understandings of the club also occasionally emerged after the term began when some students who had not been involved in the virtual community asserted themselves in the face-to-face community. In one participant's view, this process occasionally downplayed the importance and value of the virtual community and created a bit of a "backlash" against its founders.

However, both interviews and survey responses reveal an ongoing positive influence on friendships and community. A number of the students we interviewed noted that they had met and formed good friendships through the virtual community, friendships that have been sustained through the transition to face-to-face interaction:

> The friendships you make during preterm, are, you know, really strong, and they kind of carry on.

> Actually most of the people that I'm most close to are people that I had some kind of contact with over the summer. ... most of them, kind of sorted them out, themselves out over the summer. Because you had a lot of time to kind of figure out who was who from their postings on the message board and from their contributions in the chat rooms.

> There is still a sense of community today. I know a lot more people than I would have if I had not participated in the club. The community was very important during the transition to Sloan.

One student elaborated on the value of the network she had formed before the term began on her experience of and performance in the first term at Sloan. When she encountered academic or interpersonal challenges which she could not address within the boundaries of her assigned team, she was able to draw on the broader network she had formed earlier:

> So, the fact that I knew people, and I was close enough to them to afford to make a phone call in the evening when I had a problem [I] couldn't

solve, and [...] it was helpful to know who came from finance when I had a problem with finance.... [I]t's not only that I met people over the summer, but also knowing how the system works, and knowing how you can reach out, like having more knowledge before starting school, I think it helps. Because, that gave me confidence to reach out to people, second year [students], even if I didn't know them.

THE SLOAN ODYSSEY AS IMPROVISATION

As is evident from our description of the Sloan School's shift to an entirely Web-based application process, many of the changes and consequences associated with that shift were both unintended and unplanned by the Admissions staff as well as by the admitted students. This process of change resembles that referred to by a number of commentators as *emergent* change (Mintzberg 1987; Mintzberg and Waters, 1985), *continuous* change (Weick and Quinn, 1999), or *improvisational* change (Barrett, 1998; Orlikowski, 1996; Orlikowski and Hofman, 1997). Mintzberg and Waters (1985) suggest that because emergent changes are realized solely in action, they can be differentiated from deliberate changes which are planned ahead of time. Weick and Quinn (1999, p.375) note that continuous changes are "ongoing, evolving, and cumulative" and that they are "situated and grounded in continuing updates of work processes and social practices."

In the context of new technology, Orlikowski and Hofman (1997) suggest that improvisational change is the iterative series of often-unpredictable changes that evolve out of the situated experiences, evolving capabilities, emerging practices, and unplanned outcomes typically accompanying the ongoing use of new technologies. Because the shift to on-line admissions and the emergent virtual community both depended substantially on the use of new technology, we have adopted the analytic framework of improvisational change here.

Building on Mintzberg's (1987) distinction between deliberate and emergent strategies, Orlikowski and Hofman (1997) distinguish between three kinds of interdependent and situated changes that weave together over time: anticipated (or planned) changes, emergent changes, and opportunistic changes. *Planned* changes are designed ahead of time and occur as intended. *Emergent* changes develop spontaneously out of local innovations and are not originally anticipated, designed, or intended. *Opportunistic* changes are not planned or designed substantially ahead of time but are introduced purposefully and intentionally in response to an unexpected opportunity, event, or breakdown. Where both planned and opportunistic changes involve deliberate action, emergent changes arise tacitly out of people's situated practices.

Where both emergent and opportunistic changes are situated, developing from particular action, planned changes are planned ahead of time and then implemented subsequently. The order in which these types of changes occur is not predetermined.

In contrast to the deliberate or episodic models of change, an improvisational model recognizes that change is an ongoing process made up of opportunities and challenges which are not necessarily predictable at the start. As Weick and Quinn (1999, p. 381) evocatively put it: "change never starts because it never stops." Improvisational change recognizes that in attempting to make sense of and respond to new situations, technologies, and events, people engage in a series of interdependent and ongoing adaptations — planned, emergent and opportunistic — which result in a series of organizational adaptations, experiments, and outcomes, some intended and some unintended, some positive and some negative. In the process of change associated with the Sloan School's move to on-line applications, we see instances of all three types of change: planned, opportunistic, and emergent. We will consider these changes from the perspectives of the two different key groups involved in the changes – Admissions staff and admitted students.

Admissions Staff

The Admissions staff had intended and planned for the shift to a Web-based application process, and they expected this change to make better use of the budget for printing brochures, simplify the work process, and increase the visibility of the school. In addition to, and complementing this shift in the medium of applications, the Admissions staff saw an opportunity to implement a new Web site, the AddMIT Sloan Web site, which they then planned to use to market the school to admitted students, to manage the matriculation process, and to connect the students. The first of these was greatly and unexpectedly enhanced by the emergence of the virtual community, while the last of these was essentially supplanted by the virtual community.

While moving to an on-line application process and implementing the AddMIT Sloan site were both deliberate changes made by the Admissions staff, though with differing amounts of advanced planning and opportunism, they had not expected or planned for the extent of student interest in connecting electronically prior to arriving at the school. The Admissions staff became aware of this interest as they witnessed students' spontaneous interactions following the faculty chat sessions on the AddMIT Sloan site and the students' subsequent creation and expansion of the Yahoo! Class of 2001 club. Having observed this student interest in and enthusiasm for connecting electronically, the Admissions staff recognized its potential value to the school and consequently initiated a number of opportunistic changes to reinforce and legitimate the students' efforts. In particular, they advertised the Yahoo! club in their various face-to-face and telephone contacts with admitted students, they established a link to the club from their official AddMIT Sloan site, they encouraged the idea of the newsletter and then disseminated information about it to the whole class once the first issue had been completed, and they occasionally provided informational support to the club by participating directly on the Yahoo! message board.

The Admissions staff involvement in these subsequent unplanned changes initiated by the students' activities resulted in a number of unintended consequences. The Yahoo! club gave the Admissions staff an additional forum in which information about the school was disseminated and which provided answers and guidance to students deciding among schools or preparing to enroll at Sloan. In addition, the Admissions staff believed that the nature of discussion in the Yahoo! club reflected well on the school, providing an unintended but very welcome and particularly effective additional source of information about the school. As Alex, a senior staff member noted, "The club helped to show the multi-faceted nature of the school in a way that we could not have done."

This is an interesting instance of the kind of "distributed construction" that Boczkowski (2000) identifies as increasing user participation in the creation of content on news Web sites. He suggests that the increased role of users in content creation leads to a blurring of the previously tightly-controlled and tightly-defined boundaries of information production and consumption. In the case of the Sloan Class of 2001 virtual community, we can see how the students, by engaging over time in open and detailed conversations about their backgrounds, interests, experiences, and concerns, produced a rich portrayal of themselves (and hence of the school to which they had all been admitted). From the Admissions Office point of view, then, the virtual community was an instance of distributed construction of content for the new class.

Admitted Students

From the perspective of the admitted students, the changes they participated in were neither planned in advance nor intended. Rather, they engaged in both emergent and opportunistic changes. The process started with the eight to ten admitted students who stayed logged on after the first scheduled faculty chat session organized on the AddMIT Sloan site. The idea of staying in touch electronically emerged from this spontaneous chat session. Following up on this emergent idea, a few of the students created a couple of Sloan Class of 2001 Web clubs on the Web sites of Yahoo! and PlanetAll. Within a number of hours, the Yahoo! club emerged as the favorite Web site, due largely to its "simplicity and ubiquity," as one founding member told us. Use of the Yahoo! club emerged initially in two forms: synchronous chat sessions scheduled for once a week on Mondays (and later expanded to three times a week to accommodate different purposes and international participation) and asynchronous postings to the message board at any time.

Whenever and wherever possible, members of the club spread word of its existence via announcements at face-to-face events and through broadcasting e-mail messages to admitted students in particular regions such as the West Coast and New York. The impact of such opportunistic diffusion of information about the club was significantly amplified when a few of the students asked the Sloan Admissions staff to include an announcement of and link to the club on the official AddMIT Sloan Web site, and when the Admissions staff, recognizing the inadvertent contribution of this site to their marketing efforts, did so. The result of this move was dramatic. Membership in the club increased as did the active involvement of students in both synchronous and asynchronous interaction.

A further student-driven opportunistic change occurred a few weeks after the emergence of the increased participation. A few students and a member of the Admissions staff chatting at a Boston-area consumption function generated the idea of producing an electronic newsletter for the incoming Class of 2001. In this move, they were helped and encouraged by the Sloan Admissions staff, who saw this as a further marketing opportunity, notified all the students in an e-mail message about the completed first issue of the newsletter, and eventually put a link to the newsletter on the official AddMIT Sloan Web site. In the first issue of the electronic newsletter, the students include a prominent mention of the Yahoo! club and its activities. This produced a second marked and emergent increase in participation, particularly among international students, in club membership and participation on the message board. Finally, the drop-off of message board participation and of all activity in the Yahoo! club after the class assembled at MIT for Orientation and thus met each other face to face was unanticipated by the student participants and emergent in nature.

Improvisational Change

Table 4 presents the various changes experienced by both groups of players. In examining this sequence of changes over time for both groups, we can see how an initial intended and planned change implemented by one group created the conditions for a series of emergent and opportunistic changes in another group, which in turn led to additional opportunistic changes

Table 4: Types of Change Associated with Shift to Online Application and Emergence of Virtual Community

Key Players	Nature of Change	Type of Change
Admissions Staff	• shift to a Web-based, on-line application process (working with third party: GradAdvantage)	Planned
Admissions Staff	• establish a Web site for admitted students (AddMIT Sloan) which facilitates information distribution and hosting of faculty chats; subsequently edit Web site to accommodate student-led initiatives	Planned and Opportunistic
Admitted Students	• explore the idea of starting own Web site for electronic connection before arriving at Sloan, and generate the Sloan Class of 2001 Club on the Yahoo! web site	Emergent
Admitted Students	• discuss how to increase participation in Yahoo! club in the chat sessions and on the message board	Emergent
Admitted Students	• inform fellow students of Yahoo! club at face-to-face events and via regional broadcast e-mail messages	Opportunistic
Admissions Staff	• include a description of and link to the Yahoo! club on the AddMIT Sloan Web site	Opportunistic
Admitted Students	• increase participation in the Yahoo! club chats and message board	Emergent
Admitted Students & Admissions Staff	• generate the idea of and create an electronic newsletter which includes link to Yahoo! club	Opportunistic
Admissions Staff	• inform students of the newsletter and its location by sending broadcast e-mail message to the whole class	Opportunistic
Admitted Students	• increase the participation of international students in the Yahoo! club chats and message board	Emergent

by the first group, and so on. We can see how an initial planned and relatively contained shift in work process set in motion a whole series of unfolding, interdependent, and not-at-all contained changes in both the work of the Admissions staff and the lives of the students applying to and admitted by the school.

Recognizing these different types of changes associated with the shift to virtual admissions and the subsequent spawning of the virtual community allows us to represent this shift to virtuality as an ongoing series of planned, opportunistic, and emergent changes rather than a predefined program of change charted by either the Sloan admissions group or the admitted students. This model recognizes that changes – particularly those involving unprecedented phenomena such as virtual organizing and interacting – are unlikely to be fully planned and planned ahead of time. Rather, changes will emerge and evolve over time out of the practical experience of virtuality and the responses of various participants to the unplanned opportunities and unintended consequences afforded by a new way of organizing and interacting.

CONCLUSIONS

In retrospect, the virtual community described in this chapter was by most accounts a success. We have seen that the virtual community emerged around a few specific events (the conception and creation of the Yahoo! club; the linking of the club to the AddMIT Sloan site), grew to become a major communication vehicle during the few months before students arrived at Sloan, and died down once they arrived in Boston in August. Explanations— both of the community's usefulness during the months before arrival and its loss of usefulness once students arrived—focus on its role in fulfilling important social and practical purposes of the participants. Participating students appear to have found the club the most accessible and convenient forum in which to exchange information useful to their pending relocation to the Boston area (for most admitted students) and entry into the Sloan School. They also felt that the virtual community provided an opportunity to establish a network of acquaintances, even friends, before meeting them face to face. Once the participants arrived at Sloan and met each other face to face, they no longer had a compelling purpose for engaging with the virtual community. Their face-to-face community had developed and supplanted the virtual one.

Based on this case, we can draw some tentative lessons for nurturing virtual communities such as this one. The life and death of this community point to the importance of a compelling purpose to the vitality of a virtual group. Communities without a compelling purpose may never become established, while communities whose compelling purpose disappears are likely to die out. Another key element in the emergence of this virtual community was the use of a technology that was accessible and usable to the potential community. In an interview, one student noted how interesting it was that the Yahoo! message board and chat room technology, which he viewed as fairly basic, won out as the hosting site for the community. A common-denominator system, even at the cost of functionality, seems to be valuable in allowing the broadest participation in a widely-dispersed virtual community. Finally, the credibility of the virtual community with its target population was important—in this case, the fact that it was created and run by admitted students and not hosted by Sloan itself (though the Admissions Office certainly facilitated it unobtrusively in many ways) made it particularly credible to many of the students.

The lessons for the change process around the establishment of a virtual community center on the importance of emergent and opportunistic changes. Planned change in this, and undoubtedly in many other cases of community emergence accounts for only a limited part of the total change. As communities evolve, unanticipated emergent change is inevitable and potentially positive. Moreover, and perhaps more importantly for those attempting to support such communities, opportunistic change plays a critical role. In this case, the Admissions Office observed and reinforced desirable developments without trying to drive the change process. This approach was quite successful, and suggests a model for organizations attempting to encourage the development of a virtual community. By anticipating that there will be surprises, and watching for them, organizations can encourage small emergent changes, nurturing them into larger ones beneficial to the life of the virtual community. In addition, they can attempt to discourage negative changes, though this endeavor is more delicate and risks stifling the emergent changes so critical to the on-going life of a community [see, for example, Wenger, 1998, on various ways of nurturing communities of practice]. Thus we see that unanticipated changes, while inevitable, may support the emergence of a positive virtual community, especially when reinforced by strategic opportunistic changes.

ACKNOWLEDGMENTS

We would like to thank the Sloan MBA Office and Office of Admissions and the members of the Sloan Class of 2001 for their participation in this research. In addition, we appreciate the helpful comments of the editors and the attendees at research seminars at MIT and UCLA. The research support of MIT's Center for Coordination Science is gratefully acknowledged.

REFERENCES

Barrett, F.J. (1998). "Creativity and Improvisation in Jazz and Organizations: Implications for Organizational Learning," *Organization Science*, 9(5), 605-622.

Boczkowski, P.J.(2000). "Distribute and Conquer? Changing Regimes of Information Creation in Online Newspapers," Presentation at the Sloan School of Management, MIT, Cambridge, MA..

Boudreau, M-C., Loch, K.D., Robey, D., and Straub, D.(1998). "Going Global: Using Information Technology to Advance the Competitiveness of the Virtual Transnational Organization," *Academy of Management Executive*, 12(4), 120-128.

Castells, M.(1996). *The Rise of the Network Society*, Blackwell Publishers, Oxford, UK.

Davenport, T. and Pearlson, K. (1998). "Two cheers for the Virtual Office," *Sloan Management Review*, 39(4), 51-65.

Lipnack, J., and Stamps, J.(1997). *Virtual Teams: Reaching Across Space, Time, and Organizations with Technology*, John Wiley & Sons, New York..

Mintzberg, H.(1987). "Crafting Strategy," *Harvard Business Review*, 65(4), 66-75.

Mintzberg, H. and Waters, J.A.(1985). "Of Strategies: Deliberate and Emergent," *Strategic Management Journal*, 6(3), 257-272.

Mowshowitz A. (1997). "Virtual Organization," *Communications of the ACM*, 40(9), 30-37.

Nohria, N. and Berkley, J.(1994). "The Virtual Organization," in *The Post-Bureaucratic Organization: New Perspectives of Organizational Change*, C. Heckscher and A. Donnellon (eds.), Sage, Thousands Oaks, CA,, 108-128.

Orlikowski, W.J.(1996). "Improvising Organizational Transformation over Time: A Situated Change Perspective," *Information Systems Research*, 7(1), 63-92.

Orlikowski, W.J. and Hofman, J.D.(1997). "An Improvisational Model of Change Management: The Case of Groupware Technologies," *Sloan Management Review*, 38(2), 11-21.

Townsend, A., DeMarie, S.M. and Hendrickson, A.(1998). "Virtual Teams: Technology and the Workplace of the Future," *Academy of Management Executive*, 12(3), 17-29.

Weick, K.E. and Quinn, R.E.(1999). "Organizational Change and Development," *Annual Review of Psychology,* 50, 361-386.

Wenger, E. (1998). *Communities of Practice : Learning, Meaning, and Identity (Learning in Doing: Social, Cognitive and Computational Perspectives)*, Cambridge University Press, Cambridge, UK.

ENDNOTES

1 Another use of photographs was initiated by two of the club members during pre-term classes in August; these members developed a "picture book," essentially a database of photographs and profiles of the incoming class, by taking digital pictures at pre-term courses and posting them with bio descriptions to a database accessible through the Web.

2 Eventually, the newsletter—which would run to seven issues between May and August—was moved to the MIT Sloan Web site.

Chapter 13

The Search for a New Identity: Post-Organ Transplant Recipients and the Internet

Marios Koufaris
Baruch College–CUNY, USA

INTRODUCTION

The introduction of the Internet into our lives has been explosive and wide-spanning. While five years ago, few people had access to the 'information highway' and the World Wide Web (WWW) had not even been invented yet, today the first phrase is already considered "cliché" and the second has become a household word. Undeniably the Internet's impact has gone beyond the military, education, and business, which were its first users. It has changed our lives and in many cases the way we see, talk to, interact with, and confront each other.

At its core, the Internet is a communication medium. As such, it can enable social interactions between people in different parts of the world and at different times. The last technological innovation that changed the way we communicate so drastically was the telephone. Its social impact has been dramatic and the Internet is already influencing our lives just as significantly.

In this chapter I describe the use of a small part of the Internet by a specific social group. I will discuss the issues surrounding the use of an Internet-based newsgroup dedicated to organ transplantation. My observations will primarily deal with organ transplant recipients and their use of this newsgroup to define a new identity for themselves after the disorienting lifesaving procedure of a foreign organ grafted onto their bodies. Using an "anthropological" method of observation, by being a virtually unobserved observer, I examined the interactions of the newsgroup members without interrupting its natural process. I informed the participants of my activities only at the beginning and at the end of my research, providing them with ample time to forget my existence. As I promised to the newsgroup members I will keep all their contributions anonymous by using different names. In some cases, however, I received the information from the WWW which is considered more "public," so I will use the persons' real names.

THE SOCIAL CONSTRUCTION OF THE INTERNET

The Internet has invaded the lives and homes of many individuals across the world. Throughout history, technological innovations changed the social structure of the environment in which they were introduced while at the same time the technology itself was heavily influenced in its development by its social context. When a new technological artifact is introduced, various social groups are formed around this artifact. The members of these groups are often bound by common issues concerning the new technological system. Each group, in its own way, influences the development of such a system and its level of acceptance in society. This approach to technological innovation and development is called the "social construction of technology" (Bijker, Hughes and Pinch 1987).

For example, when the bicycle was first introduced, one social group that determined its evolution was that of women bicycle-riders. Given the times' appropriate clothing for women, mounting the bicycle was an issue faced by the members of this group. This influenced future designs of the bicycle into easier ones for women to ride (Bijker et al., 1987).

There is no doubt that the Internet and the technologies associated with it are an integral part of our social environment. In the past few years, the Internet has infiltrated every part of our lives: entertainment, business, education, romance, law, politics, and so on. And it promises to become an even more important part of our lives as more and more people are "wired" and "plugged in." While the Internet changes the way we work, play, and communicate, various interest groups are also influencing its evolution.

Examples of such groups are medical institutions, doctors, and patients that have been using Internet technologies for a few years now. Today, web sites like CBS Healthwatch and OnHealth.com are extremely popular and strong revenue generators for their owners.

More specifically, one of the areas in which the Internet is used is organ transplantation. Being an issue that involves a lot of people and requires a lot of communication, organ transplantation is beginning to incorporate the new technology. The social implications of the procedure are many and complex. The rules that govern organ donation are constantly changing and always under scrutiny. The many parties involved in one organ transplant (donor, donor's relatives, recipient(s), recipient(s)'s relatives, doctors, insurance companies, etc.) are in constant need of communication. The Internet is an efficient technology to achieve such interaction.

ORGAN TRANSPLANTATION RESEARCH

Since the first organ transplant procedure was performed in the mid-1950s, there has been a shortage of organ donors while the number of patients being put on the waiting list for organs has skyrocketed. After an uneasy initial period, it was finally determined by the National Organ Transplantation Act that human organs could only be used as gifts and could not be sold for money. While this did not help with the shortage, it prevented the exploitation of individuals for organ harvesting (Fox and Swazey, 1992).

While a lot has been written about organ transplantation, most social and psychological research has focused on organ donation and ways of increasing it. Issues such as reasons for signing a donor card, beliefs about organ donation, and the influence of religion, age, and gender on the propensity to donate are examined in articles describing controlled experiments with the ultimate goal of increasing organ donation (Shanteau and Harris, 1990). Little, however, has been written on the social and psychological issues faced by the post-transplant organ recipients (see, for example, Simmons, Marine and Simmons, 1987, or Youngner, Fox and O'Connell, 1996).

This chapter concentrates on organ recipients and their experiences with an Internet-based newsgroup that is dedicated to organ transplantation. During a two-month period, I observed their conversations on the newsgroup and I was able to give some possible interpretations to their actions as presented through the messages they posted daily.

THE NEWSGROUP

The newsgroup, known as TRNSPLNT (bit.listserv.transplant), is dedicated to the procedures, the people, and the issues of organ transplantation. Upon subscription to the newsgroup one receives the following message stating the group's purpose:

> *TRNSPLNT is a discussion list for organ transplant recipients and anyone else interested in the issues, experiences and realities of living with an organ transplant. It also serves as an open forum for discussing, and learning about current issues affecting the practice of transplantation and organ donation.*

Since this newsgroup is open to anyone interested in organ transplantation, the group members vary from organ recipients to recipients-to-be, live donors, deceased donors' relatives, and doctors. For two months I received hundreds of messages sent through the newsgroup which is based on a list server. Any member can send a message to the listserver which then distributes it to all the other newsgroup members. The others can then respond publicly by posting their response via the listserver or privately by sending a private e-mail message to the sender. The newsgroup is available 24 hours a day and can be accessed by anyone with a computer, a modem, and a basic e-mail account.

After reading hundreds of messages posted over two months, I undertook the task of sorting those messages out and extracting an underlying theme from this mixture of medical terminology, human tragedy and triumph, humor, activism, and everyday conversation. I realized after a while that an interesting common thread existed in a subset of the group members: the post-transplant organ recipients. After careful consideration of their newsgroup correspondence I saw that they were using the group as a way to establish their new identity as post-transplant organ recipients (called recipients from hereafter). People most often define themselves using those around them as a frame of reference. Whether they use a public class or caste system or a more personal measure of self identity, human beings determine their place in the world by comparison to the people who surround them. We found that the recipients who used the newsgroup behaved in exactly the same way. The rest of the chapter will demonstrate why and how the recipients used a simple, text based, emotionless technology to redefine themselves after a major surgical procedure that gave them "a new life," as they often called it.

THE EXPERIENCE OF ORGAN TRANSPLANTATION

An organ transplantation is a very serious, life threatening, and disorienting procedure. Due to the shortage of organs, patients are usually held back from having the operation until the last minute; right before their situations become so critical that a transplant would not benefit them at all. During this time, the patients' quality of life is usually very poor. In the chapter "Social And Psychological Rehabilitation of the Adult Transplant Patient" of their book *The Gift of Life*, Simmons et al. (1987) give a brief account of the physical and social-psychological sources of stress that patients face before the transplant. The failing function of a vital organ such as the heart, the liver, or the kidneys results in long periods of a physical sensation of illness. During this time, the patients may need to spend several hours attached to lifesaving machines, as in the case of kidney disease patients who must spend up to 30 hours a week attached to a dialysis machine.

The most common social-psychological source of stress for the pre-transplant patient, according to Simmons et al. (1987), is the constant threat of death. Also important seems to be the alteration of the patient's lifestyle and self-perception to conform to the identity of an invalid. The patients must learn to live a dependent life on the life-saving machines and medications that keep them alive while waiting for an organ.

Since the pre-transplant patients are limited in what they can do and they are constantly under tremendous stress and pressure, their feeling of control over their environment diminishes, sometimes along with their personal relationships with friends and family. Even their sense of time can be warped. As a friend of a woman waiting, with her husband, for a suitable heart wrote (*http://www.andreas.com/susan/ucla-1.html*):

> *I can only describe the waiting [Susan and her husband] Andreas [are] going through as a type of exile. Andreas, as any person in exile, is caught in a state where the present has little significance – the present is merely a way to get to the future. However, the only future that one dreams about while in exile is one's past. It is in this strange and sad "non-time" that Andreas and Susan are both in presently.*

After the transplant procedure, the physical sources of stress are not over, as Simmons et al. (1987) describe. An organ transplant is not a one-time procedure. It is a lifelong process. The recipients take a long list of medications after the surgery to suppress their immune systems so that they do not reject their new organs. Rejection is always a possibility and a new transplant may become necessary. Many members of the newsgroup have had second transplants. The medications have multiple side-effects including the change of physical characteristics such as excessive hair growth and a redistribution of body and facial fat (known as "moon face"). The quality of life, while definitely better than that before the transplant, is still not perfect.

Social-psychological sources of stress for the post-transplant recipient include the uncertainty of the long-term prognosis and the personal acceptance of a foreign organ in one's body. As pointed out in the same chapter, the recipient must now become independent again after a long time of dependency on doctors and machines. This is made harder by the uncertain definition of the recipient's status as healthy or ill. While the transplant enables one to lead a relatively normal life, an organ recipient may still be disabled in many ways and in a few cases recipients receive Social Security disability assistance. It is often hard for recipients to find new jobs since many employers are reluctant to hire them. Before the transplant, the identity of the individual is rather well defined as a "patient", a "dependent", one who is able to do "limited" things, or even an "invalid." After the transplant, however, the recipient does not always assume the identity of the "healthy," "independent," "unlimited" person. Very often the organ recipients find themselves somewhere in the middle unable to define new selves and new roles in their environments.

In a survey discussed in the same chapter by Simmons et al. (1987), they rate pre- and post-transplant patients on various psychological scales. One year after a kidney transplant only about 48% of diabetic and 50% of nondiabetic patients scored high in self esteem. While significantly higher than the scores in pre-transplant patients (27% diabetic and 28% nondiabetic), about half of post-transplant patients still fared low in self-esteem one year after their operation. When rated for self-image, stability, and feelings of a firm identity, 63% of diabetic and 61% of nondiabetic patients scored sufficiently high, which still leaves more than one third with low scores.

COLLECTIVE SENSE-MAKING

The newsgroup serves as an instrument of collective sense-making and understanding for its organ recipient members. As a newsgroup participant describes it:

The adjustment to life after transplantation is not just one of physical limitations, but also that of mental and emotional changes and adjustments. Being able to communicate with people all over the world who have experienced or about to experience transplantation is the best possible therapy anyone could hope for.

It is through that collective process that they attempt to reestablish stability in their lives and to develop a new solid identity. It is also through communication with others that recipients may be able to understand why they have gone through such an experience. As one member wrote to me:

The newsgroup has helped me answer the question "Why me Lord?"

This communal method is highly visible when a group member or a member's relative or friend enters the hospital either for an actual transplant procedure or because of complications from a previous transplant. In many cases, the patient or a representative post daily and sometimes hourly updates of their situation. The community of the newsgroup then responds by flooding them with messages of support. Some describe their experiences, others send poetry, some write prayers. All together, the participating members seem to go through the procedure with the patient, at least at an intellectual and emotional level. One example is Susan's story.

Susan Hattie Steinsapir, or "Hattie" as she was known by many, developed cardiomyopathy (congestive heart failure) in her late thirties. This was a terminal disease that could only be cured by a heart transplant. Susan was not new to the battle for her life. She fought Huntington disease in her twenties and had lost a lung to it. Now, she had to move from Sacramento, where she lived with her husband Andreas and their many cats, to UCLA in Los Angeles where she was put on the waiting list for a heart transplant. After a long wait during which she almost died many times, a heart was eventually found for a transplant. The procedure was termed "successful" by the doctors and Susan was once again fighting to accept the new heart and get a new lease on life. However, major complications, many brought on by the scars of Huntington disease, did not allow Susan to make it. She died on Monday, January 29th 1996 in the hospital with her husband by her side.

At first glance, Susan's story is yet another account of the countless problems faced by people in need of organ transplants with sometimes tragic ends. But Susan's story is different in at least one way. Her battle to live was followed by hundreds of people on the Internet. Susan's friend Mimi Hiller set up a web site (*http://www.smartlink.net/~hiller/susan/*) where one could find constant updates of Susan's health as well as pictures of her, anecdotes, poetry and prose related to her battle, and other links to sites with information on organ transplantation. The details of the last months of her life were shared with people from all over the world. At her funeral, friends from as far away as New Zealand were sending their regrets for a woman they only knew through their computers. And her story is available for anyone with a computer and a modem to see on the World Wide Web.

THE VIRTUAL SUPPORT GROUP

The newsgroup has a similar function as any other support group but the two also have some major differences. Support groups meet at specific times and specific places. The newsgroup is available 24 hours a day from any location enabling one to "log on when it is quiet and comfortable" as one member wrote. This is especially important for organ transplant recipients who are sometimes dispersed in different locations too far away from where support groups might meet, as this newsgroup member points out:

> *I would just like to say that I appreciate having this newsgroup available to me. I live in rural British Columbia, where I am not near any support group.*

The newsgroup also provides a sense of freedom that is sometimes not so prevalent in support groups. First, the participants are by definition only interested parties. In support groups, others may prove to be obstructive as one member points out:

> *I did attend some support group meetings and while they were helpful to a point, it was very difficult to be open about one's feelings with "staff" present. Also, a lot of people brought young children and that was very distracting.*

Second, the "faceless" nature of the newsgroup gives a certain sense of privacy while enabling one to speak freely and be less afraid of backlash or ridicule. Since there is no need to "chime in" in order to be heard, even the shyest member can voice their opinions. Finally, the Internet, being a new communication medium, is still undergoing a process of having its rules of conduct defined by its user population. This means that the messages written by the newsgroup members do not have to follow social rules of letter-writing or conversation speaking. The participants are able to express themselves freely by manipulating the written word in some ways specific to the Internet.

One major similarity between the newsgroup and a support group is the main process used by their members to define their new identities. In both cases, each participant uses the others as points of reference according to which he or she position themselves. As described above, the organ transplant procedure can be a very disorienting experience. Being able to ground oneself according to others in similar situations is very important and that is the major contribution of the newsgroup as a support group.

ESCAPISM VS. REALITY

In her book *Life on the Screen: Identity in the Age of the Internet*, Sherry Turkle (1995) describes a similar, but in some ways radically different, use of the Internet. Turkle spent a lot of time studying multi-user domains or MUDs as they are commonly known. These are text-based virtual worlds where users can participate. A user can assume any identity and can talk with other characters, walk through rooms, use objects. The people who participate in MUDs usually have more than one character at the same time and those characters are usually extremely different than their real-life personas. Some play as people of the opposite sex, others as animals, and yet others as fictional characters.

Interviewing the users of MUDs, Turkle shows how real the virtual world of the game is to each user. Sometimes, it is even more real than "Real Life" as the participants call their physical world. Some users expressed their preference for the MUD world over the real world and many place their MUD identities at the same or higher level of importance as their real identities.

While the TRNSPLNT newsgroup is also a text based virtual environment where people participate and where they can 'converse' in public or in private, the reasons for participating are diametrically opposite from the reasons MUD users roam their virtual worlds. The MUD experience is based on escapism. Those users need to escape their "Real Life" so they make it a window in the corner of their computer screen and immerse themselves in an imaginary identity in a virtual world.

The newsgroup participants do not use it to escape. They do not try to hide their real-life problems and situations. Newsgroup members always use their real names and talk about their real personal lives without hesitation. Just as in any support group, when a new person joins the group, they introduce themselves and they give an account of their personal story with organ transplantation.

The newsgroup members participate in order to put some order in their "Real Life" and make sense out of it, not to escape from it. Their efforts are well-focused and with a clear purpose. A young member of the newsgroup posted the following message about a TV show:

Who saw "Chicago Hope" the other night? It was one of the best episodes of the season. Even though it had nothing to do with Transplants it was still a great episode

Here are parts of a powerful response from another group member:

This group is for real people dealing with real issues and to cut through the [nonsense] I do not think any of us care about "Chicago Hope."

...

The vast majority of us are going through real life issues and I personally do not see any need to mention "Chicago Hope" ...

After a flood of messages from the other group members, the respondent asked for his response to be disregarded and attached in his message part of the newsgroup purpose statement. For this participant, the newsgroup is no place for escapism.

VIRTUAL PRESENCE

While the use of the newsgroup is much more down-to-earth than MUDs, the users must still use their imagination in order to be able to participate in its virtual community. While it is easy to talk about "participation," "conversation," and "community," in reality each user sits in front of a monitor screen and a keyboard alone in his or her house reading text. In order for these higher-level collective processes to take place, the user must first interpret the text on the screen as an extension of the person who wrote it. To make this leap of faith easier, the newsgroup members personalize their postings in different ways.

One male member, who admits in his messages that he has a tendency to ramble, writes in a way that resembles verbal rambling. His messages consist of half sentences that are separated by "…" and sometimes he ends his message with the disclaimer "Just thinking out loud …" Others have personal ways of spelling or abbreviating words that they use constantly throughout their messages such as the woman who spells "Docters" in all her messages. When a conversation started in the newsgroup about how to use the computer software necessary to participate in a chat room one woman showed her frustration by posting this simple message:

Aaaaarrrrrrrrggggggghhhhh!!!!!

Others also mimic their emotions and actions in their messages by spelling them out in words. At one point, the newsgroup members were following the battle of a little girl who was an organ transplant recipient and was fighting major complications. When the news of her tragic death finally reached the group, members poured their emotions on the screen by writing things like "I am now crying over my keyboard," "I can't see the screen because of the tears in my eyes," or "The pain in my heart is too much to bear." Also, when one group participant responded with praises to a potential living kidney donor, he ended his message with "(big hug)" indicating the equivalent of a physical hug.

The personalization of the postings can also be seen in the cases when members take the opportunity to vent their frustrations by doing what is known in the Internet community as "flaming." Flaming is when someone posts long, aggressive messages in a stream-of-thought writing style. One woman posted a two page account of everything that went wrong in her day and she wrote the entire message seemingly in one breath.

Humor is also used by many group members to personalize their messages and to lighten the seriousness of some of the issues presented. One member posted a question wondering how others were dealing with the excessive hair growth caused by the medications organ recipients need to take. This sparked a long discussion where some funny takes on the issue were presented. Some members had the idea of marketing the medications as hair replacement products and they described infomercials where they would sell it.

Finally, the newsgroup participants personalize their postings by their signatures. A signature is the text that appears with the sender's name at the end of a message. Not only do signatures make messages seem more personal but they also give us clues as to how these people perceive themselves and their situations. Almost all the organ recipients include a line stating the organ(s) they received and the date they had the lifesaving operation. In the newsgroup community, the organ transplant is proudly presented by the recipients like a badge of honor and not as a testament of disability or illness.

Others add quotes, personal or not, in their signatures. One member who has had a second kidney transplant signs off with "And still soldiering on" seeing himself as a soldier. Another uses a quote he attributes to Napoleon: "A leader is a dealer in hope." Hope is the subject of a quote used in another member's signature: "Be a Hero – Be a Donor!" This one is attributed to Mickey Mantle. In fact, war and hope are the two most pervasive themes in the language used by the newsgroup members. They often talk about their "fights," "battles," and "heroes" as well as "hope" and "prayers" in their messages.

These are just some of the ways with which the newsgroup members personalize their postings and make it easy for each other to interpret the text messages appearing on their screens as physical and emotional extensions of the people who wrote them. In that way they become meaningful and real. There is, however, a second step that the users must take in order to fully experience the benefits of the newsgroup. They must interpret all the messages as occurring within a virtual space. It is in that space that they immerse themselves and experience as a community.

This virtual space is usually defined by the newsgroup members as emotional or intellectual. In their postings, they call it a "family" or a "group of friends." When Susan, whose story I described earlier in the chapter, died one member wrote:

This is a community and we are devastated.

One other group participant expresses his feelings to his fellow members by describing the newsgroup as a positive place to be in:

I just wanted to thank you for being here… a great place to be when you're feeling scared, alone, confused or cut-off… and 'here' is a great place to BE that light for those that have been (or will be) in darker places...

In this member's words, the newsgroup is a virtual space where it is comforting to be and to share with the other members.

Of course it is not always possible for everyone to make that leap of faith from the text on the screen to the virtual room full of friendly and supportive people. While the members of the newsgroup were all capable of making those interpretations, one man wrote to us about his father who was not as lucky:

> *I signed him up to a newsgroup relating to a disease he has suffered for fifty years. He had never met another victim of the disease and expressed an interest in other people's experience. His physical disability made it very difficult for him to use the computer, so I ended up downloading and printing off the responses. He then complained that the stories of other people didn't help. I think what he really wanted was for the pain to stop. The Internet isn't going to do that for him.*

ON-LINE ACTIVISM AND EMPOWERMENT

One important role that many of the organ recipients have assumed in the newsgroup is that of activists promoting organ donation. Members post their experiences with organ donation awareness and suggestions for educating the public. One woman for example described how she added the phrase "Be an organ donor" on her checks. As one newsgroup participant puts it:

> *Bottom line folks... Its up to us... the WE of US... to educate the 'public' by word and example... get the 'T' word out into the light... where fear... rational fear will dim...*

The recipients' role as activists goes beyond the limited community of the newsgroup. On at least two occasions, in the two months that I was a member of the newsgroup, its members responded to two incidents with not just heated discussions but also letter campaigns. On one occasion, the TV show *Chicago Hope* aired an episode where a patient, thought brain-dead, was prepared for organ harvesting when it was discovered that he was still alive. The newsgroup members reacted strongly to the episode protesting that it promoted misconceptions and unfounded public fears about organ donation. Many of them took the opportunity to send letters of protest to CBS executives asking for more responsible programming.

The second event was a new liver allocation policy announced by UNOS (United Network for Organ Sharing), a national non-profit organization that is contracted by the U.S. government. The new policy, among other things, created a new status for patients waiting for a liver transplant that included created a new status for patients waiting for a liver transplant that included people who have sudden acute liver failure and who are the most likely to benefit from a liver transplant. This sparked protests from many newsgroup members, some waiting for a liver themselves. Once again many chose to write letters of protest to executives in responsible organizations.

Apart from the obvious benefits of this use of the Internet for activism by the newsgroup participants there is also an additional benefit. The group members are empowered by the common experiences shared by others. There is a feeling of strength in numbers that extends into the group members' personal lives. This is an important advantage for people who are regaining their independence after a time of complete dependence on medical machines and doctors. It is also important since after the transplant operation, the recipients are still required to take daily medications and visit with their doctors regularly. These requirements can cause a sense of loss of independence and loss of power over one's destiny.

A major complaint by organ recipients in the newsgroup is that their doctors are usually too busy to answer all their questions. The newsgroup provides a forum where questions and answers can be exchanged by people who may have the best answers possible: personal experience. One woman, for example, posted the following message:

> Hello. I am scheduled for a bladder-emptying test tomorrow, as part of an evaluation for a K/P transplant. Can someone please tell me what to expect? Reality couldn't be any worse than my imagination! Thanks.

The response by another newsgroup member was straightforward:

> You lie on the table, they fill your bladder up with liquid till you can't stand any more, then they have you void right on the table while they take x-rays of the process. It isn't so bad if you just figure "Hey, that is what they want me to do." Just do it and try not to think about it. I survived and so have many others.

Combined with the ability to use it as an activism tool the newsgroup becomes an empowering technology that extends the members' reach and ability.

CONCLUSION

Our sense of identity is one of the characteristics that make us unique as a species. And yet, many times we determine that identity by attaching ourselves to something larger. Whether it's religion, tradition, cultural heritage, economic status, or political philosophy, most of us define what makes us individuals through the norms, rules, and characteristics of a collective. It is this need to belong that has given rise and power to things like Christianity, communism, Judaism, Nazi Germany, and colonialism.

Despite its young age, the Internet has already clearly had a tremendous social impact. The communications network that started as a U.S. military project has expanded worldwide and can now provide instant rich information on any subject imaginable. The example of organ recipients described in this chapter is only one glimpse of how this new technology is and will be used by people everywhere in the world to search for their identity through a process of collective sense-making.

The implications of the ability to communicate both synchronously and asynchronously with people anywhere in the world, whether it's done using pure text, still images, or video, are tremendous. On a micro-level, we could see the rebirth of cultural, religious, and other traditions that have been diluted through immigration and globalization. For example, people from a small region of a country who now live all over the world can reestablish contact through web sites and newsgroups and start reviving their traditions that defined them as a people. In that way, the Internet can serve as a mechanism to protect and preserve customs and traditions. It can also bring people together that could not do so in the past. Various support groups that exist on-line serve just that purpose.

On a macro-level, we may see the proliferation of large-scale movements. Political activism can now happen on a worldwide level with a lot more ease and efficiency. Common interest groups can organize beyond their geographical boundaries to influence the course of history. We may even see the true birth of a "global citizen." As new generations grow with the ability to communicate, play, and eventually work with people everywhere in the world, they will inevitably exchange ideas, norms, and rules of life, possibly resulting in a common identity that spans many nations.

Finally, newsgroups, chat rooms, and virtual communities in general present wonderful opportunities for observing the creation of new and sometimes powerful social groups formed around Internet-based technologies. Researchers interested in the social aspects of information technology could benefit a lot from participating in computer-supported communities such as the organ transplantation newsgroup described in this chapter.

Studying the social and psychological aspects of the Internet and the social groups forming around it can educate us in two ways. First, we can observe and maybe sometimes predict how this new technology evolves as it is shaped by its users. Just like any other technological system, the Internet is following a nonlinear evolutionary path determined by the influential social groups that are forming around it.

Second, and perhaps more important, by studying the social use of the Internet, we can view the development of our own society as it becomes more entwined with and more dependent on technology. The Internet and other technologies that may follow are permanently changing the socio-psychological characteristics of our world as they bring us closer to the vision of a global village. Studying how we use the Internet may give a glimpse of our own future.

REFERENCES

Berghel, H. (1996)"The Client's Side of the World-Wide Web," *Communications of the ACM*, 39(1), 30-40.

Bijker, W. E., Hughes, T. P., and Pinch, T. J.(1987). *The Social Construction of Technological Systems: New Directions in the Sociology and History of Technology*, MIT Press, Cambridge, Mass.

Boeck, S., and Lynn, G. (1996). USA Sanpshots. *USA Today*, 1B.

Fox, R. C., and Swazey, J. P.(1992). *Spare Parts: Organ Replacement In American Society*, Oxford University Press, New York.

Press, L.(1996). "Seeding Networks: The Federal Role," *Communications of the ACM*, 39(10), 11-17.

Shanteau, J., and Harris, R. J. (1990). *Organ Donation and Transplantation: Psychological and Behavioral Factors*, American Psychological Association, Washington, DC.

Simmons, R. G., Marine, S. K., and Simmons, R. L. (1987). *Gift of Life: The Effect of Organ Transplantation on Individual, Family, and Societal Dynamics*, Transaction Books, New Brunswick.

Turkle, S.(1995). *Life on the Screen: Identity in the Age of the Internet*, Simon & Schuster, New York.

Youngner, S. J., Fox, R. C., and O'Connell, L. J. (1996). *Organ Transplantation: Meanings and Realities*, University of Wisconsin Press, Madison, Wisc.

Chapter 14

Conclusion

Laku Chidambaram
University of Oklahoma, USA

Ilze Zigurs
University of Colorado at Boulder, USA

Our Virtual World draws on a variety of experiences from a diverse group of authors to present an insightful account of new media and their impacts. Across the richness of material presented in this book, several common themes emerge:

- The transformation of structures underlying the way we work, live and play,
- Comparisons between the virtual and physical worlds in which we operate,
- Changes, and lack of changes, in the way the virtual world functions,
- Nature of the technologies that have enabled these changes, and
- Gains and losses resulting from the transformation to our virtual world. Each of these themes is summarized below.

TRANSFORMATION OF STRUCTURES

One universal theme about the new media that runs through many of the chapters in the book concerns the *transformation of structures* that enable work, play and life. For instance, Niederman and Rollier discuss the transformation of structures underlying education. One of the key drawbacks of distance education has been the lack of "rich" interaction between teachers and students. In many instances, the asynchronous nature of online education makes it difficult for students and teachers to interact the way they would in a traditional classroom. However, recent developments in multimedia and animation technology have started to address this problem. In fact, Niederman and Rollier offer anecdotal evidence about the Jason Project, where children can "conduct" deep-sea expeditions and ask questions of archeologists. The ability to mimic realistic interaction between teachers and students, the authors point out, has begun to transform the online education experience and provide better interaction processes.

Other chapters also address the development of new structures in our virtual world. Mark, in her description of the virtual teams at Boeing, points out some of the challenges of working apart and the structures needed to deal with these challenges. For instance, the ability of virtual team members to perform multitasking (numerous activities at the same time, some of which may not be related to the ongoing meeting) and their inability to see or hear all the participants can be detrimental to virtual team interactions. Mark suggests new structures that can help members of virtual teams interpret online speech and establish trust. In a broader context, Koufaris describes how an Internet-based newsgroup transformed the structure of an entire community—organ transplant recipients—by helping members of that community establish a new identity and empowering them in the process. Among its various benefits, the new structure facilitated collective sense making for an entire community.

While the transformation of structures is often viewed positively, some authors question the real nature and impact of the new structures. Oravec, for instance, critically examines the impact of Web-based structures that have enabled the melding of work and play in our virtual world. As a consequence of such melding, the issue of "cyber slacking," i.e., playing at work, has become a contentious phenomenon that employers have to deal with. Others including Peterson also question whether the new structures wrought by the Web are truly transformational. She argues that Web-based structures, in many instances, do not really transform anything, but simply deliver "more of the same." Thus, people in the virtual world get more of what is already familiar to them, e.g., more of the same products that they see from the same large companies that bring us our physical world. Overall, these authors provide a very healthy balance of skepticism and optimism about the transformation of structures—a balance that helps remind us that technology is never one-sided in its effects.

The transformations described above—both positive and negative—are clearly influenced by the role of time. For instance, in the case of the MIT student group, a virtual community developed for a period before students got to campus and then later dissolved, assimilating into the traditional, on-campus community based on physically proximity. Evidence of the rise and fall of this virtual community can be seen from the intensity of the back-and-forth messages on the group's electronic bulletin board over time.

Other patterns of change over time were also evident in virtual environments. With the IRC poker group, as the needs of the group increased and technological sophistication improved, "bots" capable of handling many variations of poker became available and games included greater vocabulary. Similarly, in the case of the transplant recipients, interactions served to expand the nature of their dialog and strengthen the support structure. In contrast to the above two cases, Mark illustrates how the initial patterns established by the virtual teams at Boeing became set in stone as time progressed. Thus, repeated meetings of the teams only served to reinforce the initial pattern of interaction. Thus, depending upon the context, time either expanded the nature of what was possible with the technology (in a majority of cases) or reinforced the status quo (in a minority of cases).

PHYSICAL VERSUS VIRTUAL COMMUNITIES

Another enduring theme throughout the book is the comparison between the physical and virtual communities that participants lived, worked and played in. Are these worlds complementary or contradictory? Some authors have pointed out the similarities between the two worlds. For instance, Gant argues that relationships add value on the Web just as they do in the real world; the Web just makes it easier to develop these strategic links. Other authors have pointed out the differences between the two worlds. Gattiker et al., in examining the virtual experiences of a "real" group of European professionals interested in Internet security, elaborate on a number of key distinctions between virtual and physical communities. Another chapter that examines the online interactions of a real group is the one by Orlikowski, Yates and Fonstad. In this chapter, the authors discuss the MBA entrants' electronic community at MIT and trace its growth from inception to conclusion. The "getting to know you" phase was facilitated through the online bulletin board and chat facility and when students met face-to-face these virtual bonds were strengthened. In fact, many friendships that formed in the virtual world remained strong in the physical, "real" world.

Venkataraman in his study of IRC poker groups also reported on how virtual poker buddies became a "real" poker-playing fraternity through their online interactions. Despite the inability to conduct discussions rich in meaning, the virtual poker players developed their own shorthand to communicate with each other, e.g., acronyms such as "lol" for laugh out loud. Hence, the lack of richness of the medium was not a drawback in fostering strong ties among the virtual poker players. Also, as in the MIT case, meeting face-to-face seemed to enable the online poker community to thrive and grow. In these examples, the virtual and physical worlds were complementary in a very effective way.

A key consideration in the success of a virtual community (as with a physical community) appears to be the need for a compelling purpose to exist. The most dramatic example of a community with a compelling purpose to exist is, of course, the organ transplant recipients' newsgroup. Other examples, while less dramatic from a human needs perspective, serve to illustrate the same point. In the MIT case, the compelling purpose was getting to know fellow students, while in the IRC poker case, it was the establishment of a forum to play with like-minded players. In fact the two examples where there was no clear and compelling purpose to exist are highlighted in the case of Boeing's virtual team and the case of the European Internet security specialists. In both those instances, the objectives of the teams were laudable, but no compelling purpose was evident for why these teams needed to exist in the first place.

SOMETHING NEW, SOMETHING OLD

Many chapters in the book highlight the fact that traditional processes do not always transfer to the virtual world. In other words, new structures may require new processes. Galvin and Ahuja describe the extra effort required to socialize new members in virtual teams while Niederman and Rollier point out how traditional teaching methods will not transfer to a virtual university. Others, including Mark (Chapter 5) and Venkataraman (Chapter 7) illustrate how adaptation and communication in virtual teams can be hampered by a lack of social cues. Thus, new processes and approaches are needed to operate in this new environment. The IRC poker players adapted acronyms to combat the terseness of their environment, while the Boeing teams needed a tighter agenda and limits on multitasking to thrive in their virtual environment.

Despite changes needed in response to the new structures imposed by the virtual environment, one universal theme lingered: the need for socialization. It appears that socialization in virtual teams and communities is just as important as it is in the physical world. Galvin and Ahuja examine in depth the process of new member socialization in virtual groups. Despite technological limitations, new members attempt and find ways of seeking information and socialization cues while established members find ways of providing them. Mark also discusses how members of virtual teams, to succeed, must focus on socialization in addition to getting the job done. Echoing these sentiments, Gattiker et al. view social capital as a productive resource that helps the creation of value, just as physical and human capital do. From students using an electronic bulletin board to communicate with their peers, to patients using a newsgroup to deal with personal trauma and social isolation, the need for connectedness runs as deep in the virtual world as it does in the physical world.

SIMPLICITY SUCCEEDS

Much of what we read in the press about technology is about amazing new developments, with new technologies that do complicated things. But the lesson from the chapters in this book is how much can be accomplished with very *simple* technologies. In fact, a message that reverberates throughout the book is that simplicity not only succeeds but may very well be a necessary condition for success.

In case after case presented in this book, the message is clear: the MIT students chose Yahoo!'s message board over other more sophisticated options available; the online poker players chose IRC, a precursor to modern-day chat rooms; Boeing chose audio- and computer-conferencing over the more complicated medium of videoconferencing; the organ transplant recipients chose a relatively basic newsgroup forum; the social service agencies chose simple hyperlinks to build relationships; and members of the academic-industry consortium chose e-mail over a variety of other newer media. The common themes among all the technologies chosen are their simplicity and universal accessibility.

The simple technologies listed above achieved some measure of sustained use in the cases described in this book. Was this sustained use possible despite the simplicity of these technologies or *because* of it? It seems clear that ease-of-use and easy availability of simple technologies make them more attractive to a wider range of users. In instance after repeated instance, users chose to rely on simpler rather than more sophisticated technologies. Users also learned to adapt the medium to meet their needs, as in the case of the IRC poker players' use of shorthand messages. Thus, simple technologies have a potentially rich nature, particularly as people use and become familiar with them over time.

GAINS AND LOSSES
OF THE TRANSFORMATION

The chapters in this book remind us that the transformation of our physical world to a virtual world has meant noticeable gains but also losses, and those losses are typically less often discussed. As we might have suspected, technology fills some gaps at the same time that it creates new ones. For instance, tele-democracy is viewed from two different perspectives: Igbaria and colleagues argue that it has the potential to increase communication between citizens and policy makers, but Petersen presents a counterpoint that such increased communication, while deemed "good," does not guarantee action. Oravec also presents competing views of online recreation; it does offer benefits—including stress relief and the ability to work in simulated worlds—but not without associated perils such as cyber-slacking. Thus, the technologies underlying the transformation to our virtual world may be viewed as a double-edged sword, at least in some instances.

One unmitigated gain of virtualization that a number of authors have pointed out is the idea of a world without borders. Undoubtedly, the technology brings people and places together and provides flexibility for an increasingly diverse and distributed environment for work and play. As Igbaria et al. point out, such phenomena as tele-work and tele-medicine allow for a large variety of people from a large number of places to participate. In Chapter 10, Petersen tells the delightful story of a bishop who was banished to a far corner of the world, only to "come back" from that banishment by establishing his virtual presence on the Web. This incident reinforces the notion that our virtual world is a global one and, in some compelling cases, a borderless one.

Yet, the same technology that unites the world also divides it. Petersen and others have pointed out the digital divide that separates the haves from the have-nots. This divide—spanning geographic, ethnic and socio-economic lines—is expected to increase and has the potential to create a more divided world if not addressed aggressively by policy makers.

The discussion of gains from technology makes us ask: just what is the nature of benefits afforded by this technology? When we think of advancements in information and communication technology, we typically think either of "more," e.g., more storage capacity, more memory, or of "faster," e.g., faster processing speed. These are quantitative improvements in technology, and our focus on such improvements is exemplified by our decades-long fascination with Moore's Law. Moore's Law addresses the speed and capacity of computers, but more and faster do not automatically translate to better. That is, quantitative improvements do not always become qualitative improvements. For instance, Petersen shows how easy it can be for citizens to communicate *more* with their elected representatives. But, that increased quantity of communication did not necessarily translate directly to action by the representatives.

FINAL THOUGHTS

Not surprisingly, many of the chapters suggest that the transformation to a virtual world brings with it new possibilities and new challenges. Some of the possibilities are discussed earlier; here we address a few of the challenges. A commonly cited challenge on the path to a virtual world is technical competence. While this challenge remains daunting, there are others as well: the challenge of building trust among unseen participants, highlighted in the Boeing case; the challenges of maintaining commitment among members of virtual teams seen in the EICAR case; and the challenge of training users, to name a few. Thus there is much more than technical competency that we all have to learn in the virtual world—role competence, manners and other social conventions, leadership, and interpersonal skills are equally important. Since the path to our virtual world is an uncharted one, new challenges are likely to emerge. Petersen, for instance, points out the challenges of maintaining privacy and protecting individual rights in an increasingly digital world.

In *Our Virtual World* we have showcased a broad spectrum of perspectives about the new media that are transforming the way we work, play and live. As we move from a mostly physical world to a predominantly virtual one, the way we have always done things—from selling goods to teaching children; from voting in elections to ordering stamps; from paying our bills to playing games; from how we work to where we work—will change, often dramatically. As we simultaneously engineer and absorb these changes, our institutions and society will also change, sometimes for the better but occasionally for the worse. What remain are our fundamental human beliefs and values, and the recognition that we all have a role to play in designing and creating our virtual world. While technological change may be inevitable, the shape and character of the technology are molded by the humans who develop and use it for work, play, and life. We hope this book has given the reader some insight into how that process emerges and evolves in our virtual world.

About the Authors

Manju K. Ahuja (mahuja@garnet.acns.fsu.edu) is an Assistant Professor of MIS at Florida State University. She obtained her Ph.D. in MIS from the University of Pittsburgh. She has published in journals such as *Organization Science, Communications of the ACM, Decision Support Systems,* and the *Journal of Computer-Mediated Communications.* She taught at Pennsylvania State University and University of Pittsburgh before joining Florida State University in 1996. Prior to starting a Ph.D. program, Dr. Ahuja worked as a systems analyst designing on-line database systems for several years. Her current projects include Knowledge Integration and the Structural Evolution of a Virtual Group, Media Choices in Virtual Teams, Effects of Dispositions to Trust and Distrust on Cooperation in Project Teams, Effects of Distance in Virtual Teams, Role of Network-based Coordination Mechanisms in Organizational Design, Information Technology and the Gender Factor, The Effects of Mentoring and Work-family Conflict on IT Workers' Careers, The Effect of Gender on Communication Styles in Virtual Communities, and Effects of Task Environment on Intention to Explore Technology.

Kristoffer Bohmann (kris@iprod.auc.dk) is a Ph.D. student at the Department of Production, Aalborg University. He received his Master of Public Administration (1997) and Degree in Commerce (1998) from Aalborg University. For two years he has been working with management consulting companies in Northern Jutland. His current research interest is the usability of commercial websites.

Laku Chidambaram (laku1@aol.com) is an Associate Professor of Information Systems at the University of Oklahoma's Michael F. Price College of Business. Prior to this, he held faculty appointments at Indiana University and the University of Hawaii. Professor Chidambaram has a Ph.D. in information systems and international business from Indiana University and an MBA from the University of Georgia. He has taught a variety of information systems courses and has received several awards for teaching excellence. His primary area of research deals with the application of information technology to support distributed group work in organizations. His work has been published in such journals such as *MIS Quarterly, Journal of MIS* and the *Journal of Organizational Computing and Electronic Commerce*. He is the editor-in-chief of a multi-disciplinary journal—the *e-Service Journal*—which combines both private sector and public sector perspectives regarding electronic services and thus bridges e-Business and e-Government. Dr. Chidambaram has served as a business consultant and lectured in several countries including Germany, the Netherlands, Norway, Singapore and the United States.

Nils Olaya Fonstad (howdy@mit.edu) is currently a doctoral student in Information Technologies at MIT's Sloan School of Management. For his dissertation, he is exploring how groups improvise in the workplace, focusing on the role of technology in their improvisations. His other research has focused on on-line, multiparty consensus-building, the role of technology in negotiation pedagogy, and on-line communities.

John E. Galvin (johngalvin@mail-me.com) is an assistant professor in the Kelley School of Business at Indiana University – Indianapolis. His areas of interest include technologies used to support group work and interactions, the impacts of technology implementation on individual behaviors, and new organization forms enabled through IT. Dr. Galvin has an MBA from Emory University and earned his Ph.D. at Florida State University in information systems. He has spent 30 years in the computing industry managing a variety of software development and corporate sponsored projects before embarking on a career in academia.

Diana Burley Gant (dbgant@indiana.edu) has a Ph.D. from Carnegie Mellon and is an Assistant Professor of Information Systems at the Kelley School of Business, Indiana University. Gant is particularly interested in the role that information technology plays in managing relationships both within and between organizations. She has published research on a variety of topics, including the impact of portable telephony on work groups, and the impact of information technologies on disaster response. As an applied researcher, she has both worked and consulted with organizations such as Bell Atlantic Mobile, the Pittsburgh Public Schools, and the American Red Cross.

Urs E. Gattiker (WebUrbs@WebUrb.dk) is the Obel Family Foundation Professor of Technology and Innovation Management in the Faculty of Engineering and Science at Aalborg University. Before entering academia he worked in Switzerland, South Africa, and the United States. He is an advisory board member of Bankinvest IT Venture, Denmark's largest venture fund and serves on several boards including Quizz People and Vupti.com. He received his undergraduate education in Switzerland and his Ph.D. in Management and Organization from Claremont University, in the United States in 1985. His research interests include entrepreneurship, technology management and innovation, information management, and gender issues. He has published extensively on these topics in a variety of journals and written and edited several books on these topics.

Paul Gray (Paul.Gray@cgu.edu) is Professor and Founding Chair of the Department of Information Science at Claremont Graduate University. He specializes in decision support systems and in data warehousing. He worked for 18 years in research and development organizations, including nine years at SRI International. Before coming to CGU in 1983, he was a professor at Stanford University, the Georgia Institute of Technology, the University of Southern California, and Southern Methodist University. He is the first editor of the *Communications of AIS* and a fellow of the Association for Information Systems. He was president of the Institute of Management Sciences for 1992-93, and was formerly president-elect, vice president and secretary of the Institute. He is on the editorial board of several journals. He is the author of over 115 journal articles and author/editor of 12 books, most recently *Decision Support in the Data Warehouse* (with H.J. Watson). He received his Ph.D. in Operations Research from Stanford University.

Magid Igbaria (Magid.Igbaria@cgu.edu) is a Professor of Information Science at the Claremont Graduate University and at the Faculty of Management, Graduate School of Business, Tel Aviv University. Formerly, he was a Visiting Professor of Decision Sciences at the University of Hawaii in Manoa, and a Professor of MIS, College of Business and Administration, at Drexel University. He has published articles in *Communications of the ACM, Computers & Operations Research, Decision Sciences, Decision Support Systems, Information & Management, Information Systems Research, Journal of Management Information Systems, Omega, Journal of Strategic Information Systems, MIS Quarterly*, among others. His current research interests focus on electronic commerce, virtual workplace, computer technology acceptance, information and computer economics management of IS, IS personnel, and international IS. He serves in the editorial board of numerous journals. He is the co-author of the book, *The Virtual Workplace*.

Marios Koufaris (mkoufari@stern.nyu.edu) is a Ph.D. Candidate in Information Systems at the Stern School of Business of New York University. He received a B.Sc. in Operations and Information Management from the Wharton School of Business and a B.A. in Psychology from the College of Arts and Sciences, both at the University of Pennsylvania. His research interests include electronic commerce and specifically consumer behavior in web-based commerce, socio-psychological factors in IS, and hypermedia design. As of September 2000 he joined the Zicklin School of Business, Baruch College in New York City as an Assistant Professor in Computer Information Systems.

Gloria Mark (gmark@ics.uci.edu) is an assistant professor in the Information and Computer Science Department, at the University of California, Irvine. She is very active in the field of Computer Supported Cooperative Work, and her main research interests are in virtual collocation technologies, and the methodology of design and usability evaluation of collaborative technologies. Previously she has researched virtually collocated teams while at the German National Research Center for Information Technology (GMD), and at The Boeing Company.

Fred Niederman (niederfa@slu.edu) is the Shaughnessy Endowed Associate Professor of MIS at Saint Louis University. He holds a B.A. degree from the University of California, Santa Barbara and both MBA and PhD degrees from the University of Minnesota. He has previous publications in *MIS Quarterly, Decision Sciences, Strategic Information Systems,* and *DATA BASE.* His primary research areas are information systems personnel, global information systems, decision support systems, and group decision support systems. He is currently serving as the chairman of the ACM Special Interest Group on Computer Personnel Research and as an associate editor of the *Journal of Global Information Management.*

Lorne Olfman (Lorne.Olfman@cgu.edu) is Dean of the School of Information Science and Professor of Information Science at Claremont Graduate University (CGU). He came to Claremont in 1987 after graduating with a PhD in Business (Management Information Systems) from Indiana University. Olfman's research interests involve software learning and use, impact of computer based systems on organizational memory, and in the design and adoption of systems used for group work. Olfman's publications in journals (including *MIS Quarterly*, *Journal of MIS*, and *Communications of the ACM*) and conference proceedings (including the *International Conference on Information Systems* and the *Hawaii International Conference on System Sciences*) span these three research areas.

Jo Ann Oravec (oravecj@uwwvax.uww.edu) received her MBA, MA, MS and PhD degrees from UW-Madison. She taught public policy at Baruch College of the City University of New York and also taught management and computer science at UW-Madison. She served as chair of the Privacy Council of the State of Wisconsin, the nation's first state-level council focusing on information technology and privacy issues. She has written several books and dozens of articles on computers and society topics; she has also developed software and worked for public television. She is now on the faculty of the College of Business and Economics at the University of Wisconsin-Whitewater (Whitewater, WI 53190, USA).

Wanda J. Orlikowski (wanda@mit.edu) is the Eaton-Peabody Chair of Communication Sciences at the Massachusetts Institute of Technology and an Associate Professor of Information Technologies and Organization Studies at the MIT Sloan School of Management. Her primary research interests focus on the dynamic interaction between organizations and information technology, with particular emphasis on organizing structures, cultures, and work practices. She is currently exploring the organizational and technological aspects of working virtually, and with JoAnne Yates examining the role and use of electronic communities. She serves on a number of editorial review boards and is currently a Senior Editor for *Organization Science*.

Stefano Perlusz (perlusz@iprod.auc.dk) is a Ph.D. student at the Department of Production, Aalborg University. He graduated in Economics at the Università di Pavia, Italy, and received his Master in Technical Analysis at the Scuola di Finanza in Milano. Before starting his doctoral studies he has been working at the Joint Research Centre for the European Commission. His research interests include: the impact of security and safety on the uptake of electronic commerce from customers' perspective, and the recognition of system dependability scheme as relevant explanatory framework for understanding Internet users' behaviors.

Jennifer Petersen (jennifer.petersen@activeink.net) has an MA in journalism from the University of Texas at Austin, where her studies focused on the ways in which the media are used as venues for both social replication and dissemination of ideology and for social critique and transformation. Her thesis research focused on attempts to use personal web sites as alternative media. She is currently working for an educational software company, developing web content for teenagers.

Bruce Rollier (rolliers@home.com) is an associate professor of MIS at the University of Baltimore. He holds a B.S. from Oklahoma State University, an MBA from Northwestern University, and a Ph.D. from New York University. His research interests include strategic information systems, human information processing, systems design, and the applications of technology to education.

Conrad Shayo (cshayo@cactus.csusb.edu) is an Associate Professor of Information Science at California State University San Bernardino. He holds a Doctor of Philosophy Degree and a Master of Science Degree in Information Science from the Claremont Graduate University, formerly Claremont Graduate School. He also holds an MBA in Management Science from the University of Nairobi, Kenya; and a Bachelor of Commerce Degree in Finance from the University of Dar-Es-Salaam, Tanzania. His research interests are in the areas of IT assimilation, end-user computing, organizational memory, information strategy, and "virtual societies". His most recent publications can be found in the *Information Systems Journal, Journal of End User Computing,* and the *Encyclopedia of Library Sciences and Information Technology.*

Christian Mørck Sørensen (Christian@WebUrb.dk) received his Master in Engineering Management (2000) from Aalborg University. His interests include decision making in electronic environments, and an understanding of how human risk and trust processes develop on the Internet. He is also working with security and safety issues related to the Internet.

Ramesh Venkataraman (venkat@indiana.edu) is an Assistant Professor of Information Systems in the Department of Accounting and Information Systems, Kelley School of Business at Indiana University. His areas of expertise are in database modeling and design, systems design and development, heterogeneous databases and groupware systems. His papers have been published in *ACM Transactions on Information Systems, IEEE Expert,*

Information Systems, Journal of Systems and Software and other journals. He received his Ph.D. in Business Administration (MIS) from the University of Arizona.

JoAnne Yates (jyates@mit.edu) the Sloan Distinguished Professor of Management at MIT's Sloan School of Management, examines communication and information as they shape and are shaped by technologies and organizational policies and practices over time. Her book *Control through Communication* looks at the evolution of communication systems in firms historically. She and Wanda Orlikowski have collaborated on several studies of electronic communication in contemporary organizations, with papers published in *AMR, ASQ, Organization Science*, and various conference proceedings. She is 2000/2001 Division Chair of the Organizational Communication and Information Systems Division of the Academy of Management.

Ilze Zigurs (zigurs@colorado.edu) is an Associate Professor of Information Systems at the University of Colorado, Boulder, where she teaches courses in systems analysis and design, as well as doctoral seminars in e-business and conceptual foundations of information systems. Her Ph.D. is from the University of Minnesota. Her research focuses on the intersection of information technology with collaborative work in an increasingly virtual world. She has published in such journals as the *MIS Quarterly, Journal of Management Information Systems, Journal of Organizational Computing and Electronic Commerce*, and *Data Base for Advances in Information Systems*. She currently serves as senior editor for *MIS Quarterly*, senior editor for *e-Service Journal*, and department editor for *IEEE Transactions on Engineering Management*. Ilze has also been active for many years in the executive committee of the Organizational Communication and Information Systems Division of the Academy of Management.

Index

NEW from Idea Group Publishing